THE UNKNOWN BASEBALL PLAYER

Marvin P. Ferguson

PARKER PUBLISHING

Copyright © 2006 by Marvin P. Ferguson

Library of Congress Control Number: 2006900428

ISBN-10: 1-882286-01-4
ISBN-13: 978-1-882286-01-0

Published June 2006. First Edition

Parker Publishing
P.O. Box 65
Island Lake, Illinois 60042-0065

Printed in the United States of America

THE UNKNOWN BASEBALL PLAYER

ONE

Goose bumps ran down Orville's spine watching Pete Rose walk out of the Cincinnati dugout swinging a couple of bats. He felt honored being a member of a major league baseball team. "I never thought the day would come when I would be playing with such baseball greats like Pete Rose and Johnny Bench."

The crowd went wild watching Pete at the plate. Seats rumbled. Fans cheered.

"C'mon Pete! Show 'em your stuff!" The old man with a potbelly, struggled to keep a cigar in his mouth.

During all the excitement a lady, carrying a couple of hot dogs, spilled her soda on a man wearing a blue plaid shirt while struggling to get back to her seat.

Everywhere baseball fans stayed glued to their TV sets, listening to the play-by-play action. "And here we are in the bottom of the ninth inning. Cubs 3. Redlegs 3. A pitcher's duel right up to the end."

Once his feet were firmly planted in the large chalk square,

1

the man with arms like Popeye flexed his muscles, took a couple of warm up swings, and stared at the pitcher.

Kenny Holtzman, the Cub left-hander, leaned forward to shake off some signs from his catcher. Once satisfied, he brought his hands together at his chest, kicked his right leg up high into the air, and delivered a stinging fastball.

As the ball traveled very fast toward the plate, Pete swung viciously. "Strike!" The ump shouted, motioning with his arm. The loud thud sound in the catcher's glove left no doubt that he missed the ball completely. Boos voiced the fans disapproval.

Momentarily, Pete stepped out of the batter's box to get a sign from the first base coach. Like a rain dance on an Indian reservation, he clapped his hands, tapped one knee, and rubbed his cheek repeatedly. Once he was satisfied, Pete stepped back into the box.

As Kenny was about to deliver the next pitch, Randy Huntley called time. Standing, he flipped off his mask and jogged out to the mound. Soon Ernie Banks, along with other members of the infield joined them.

Meetings on the pitcher's mound were frequent. Perhaps Randy saw something he didn't like. The manager may have tipped him off from the dugout. Sometimes it's merely a ploy for time.

Again Pete stepped out of the batter's box, and took several more warm-up swings." C'mon you guys! Let's go! I wanna get this over with."

With his hands placed firmly on his waist, chest sticking out, and legs braced, the ump stared at the mound. Then, after glancing at his watch, he slowly walked out to issue a warning. "C'mon boys! Move it!" Without waiting for a response, he wheeled around and returned to the plate with a mean look on his face.

"Yeah ump!" Leo, the Cub manager shouted peeking out of the huddle. Undisturbed, arched backs remained in the circle. Finally, the group scattered back to their positions around the infield. Kenny delivered another stinging fastball. The ball nipped the corner of the plate as Pete watched it sail by.

On a 0-2 count, another arched slow ball traveled toward the plate. Pete twitched his fingers and gestured to swing. The ball hugged the outside edge of the plate. Silence filled the park. Fans were at awe until they heard the ump shout ball, while placing his hands together behind his back.

The next pitch sailed under his knuckles and evened up the count at 2-2.

Another fastball connected with his bat and sailed deep into the right field corner. Running hard, Hickman followed it into the seats for some lucky fan. Boos echoed throughout River Front Stadium. After dusting off the plate, the ump threw out a new ball.

Pete sliced the next pitch into the seats behind the visitors' dugout. Fans scrambled to get it. Unfortunately, most of them returned to their seats empty handed with bruised knuckles and hurt pride.

Now, to protect the plate, Pete swung at every pitch. One ball rolled high up the screen behind him. A fastball missed fair play only by inches near first base. A slow curve ball bounced off the Cincinnati dugout. Quick reflexes prevented the third base coach from losing his head.

Again, Pete stepped out of the batter's box. Stretching, he looked at the first base coach.

After fouling off several more pitches, Kenny looked worried. Circling the mound, he wiped the sweat off his forehead. Then, following an abbreviated windup, he delivered another pitch. The ball sailed from the edge of the mound. Midway it straightened itself out and fluttered over the plate. Pete watched it sail by. Again, silence filled the park. "Ball!" The ump shouted. "Full count, 3-2!" And the fans cheered.

Pete continued to connect with the ball. Another lucky fan scrambled for a souvenir. Randy crashed into the net behind him, chasing a cheap popup. A blooper landed on the chalk line.

Kenny circled the mound several more times while tossing the ball into the web of his glove. Beneath a hot sun, a mild breeze whipped in his face. Taking a deep breath to ingest fresh air into his lungs made him feel more relaxed.

On a tired slow ball, Pete swung viciously. Then, after tossing his bat a side, with arms swinging and chest held high, he hustled toward first base. And like a gasoline can suddenly ignited, the Redleg dugout came alive. Soon the entire bench was empty as everyone stood on the apron watching a fly ball sail into the outfield.

Quickly, Jim Hickman flipped his sun visor down to shield his eyes from the sun. Running hard, he refused to lose sight of the ball. However, playing close to right-center, thinking Pete might not pull the ball to the corner, now the tall right fielder struggled to get to it.

"It dropped into the corner!" Sounds from the radio screamed into baseball fans ears everywhere. "After one bounce, Hickman wheeled and fired the ball toward the infield."

As he saw the ball coming toward him, Pete dove toward the bag. A cloud of dust irrupted leaving the fans spellbound. When the dust finally settled, the husky ballplayer called time, and stepped off the bag to brush off his uniform. The fans got excited, and once again cheers echoed throughout River Front Stadium.

Back in the dugout the whole team was ecstatic. Bumping shoulders. Clapping hands. Verbalizing obscenities. The excitement never ended.

"OK! All right!" The coach voiced his approval while quickly getting off the bench, and weaving his way through the other players toward the other end of the dugout.

Dave Bristol, the Redleg manager sat stoic, staring out at the field, when the coach hunched over him to get a better look at the roster tacked on the wall.

"Whom I gona send out?" The Robert Mitchum like voice mumbled to himself while scratching his beard. Slowly, his eyes rolled down the page following his finger. Occasionally, he'd stop long enough to glance at the row of players, now settled back on the bench.

The names were familiar and drew lots of memories from spring training: Lee May, Billy Tolan, Woody Woodward, and more. "Don't know what'd we do without 'em." The thoughts raced through his mind.

They sat with their arms folded across their chest. A couple guys couldn't stop talking. Another was so preoccupied chewing tobacco it was doubtful if his mind was ever really in the game.

As he continued to scan the bench, and carefully match each player with the name listed above his finger, he noticed an unfamiliar face. "Hey Boy! C'mere!"

Half way down the row Orville sat, chewing bubble gum while watching the Cubs reposition themselves on the field. As he remained totally absorbed in the game for the moment, Johnny Bench nudged his arm. "Hey buddy! The coach is talkin' to ya."

"Hey Boy! Get over here! I wanna talk to ya!" In the midst of a tight ballgame which added to the frustration, the coach didn't like to be kept waiting.

After another nudge, finally Orville slowly got up and walked to the end of the dugout. "Yes sir! Ya wanted to see me?"

"Yeah! Who are ya? I don't recognize your name on my list?" He pointed to the roster.

"Yes sir! Or-Or-Orville Hodge, sir!" He shouted, hoping to be heard above all the noise from the fans in the ballpark, standing at attention, like a soldier before a drill sergeant.

"Relax! This isn't the army."

"Yes sir!" Orville respected the coach.

"When did ya get here?"

"Yesterday, sir!"

"How did ya get here? Never mind. Don't answer that. Just go sit down with the rest of those guys over there." He pointed to a place still vacant on the bench next to Johnny Bench.

The coach remained puzzled. A tie game by the ninth inning has already sent many players to the shower. Now, it was slim pickings.

"Ladies and gentlemen. The next batter is Tommy Halms." A loud voice blared out over the PA system throughout River Front Stadium.

After swinging a couple of bats, Tommy tossed one aside as he stepped into the batter's box. Then, while keeping his eye on the ball that Kenny manipulated behind his left knee, in a batting stance, he anxiously waited for the next pitch while Pete took a big lead off first base.

TWO

Breakfast was served. And now flight attendants stayed busy collecting food trays while the big silver bird flew high above the clouds.

"Yuck! These eggs tasted horrible. Flat. No flavor. My mother could've done a better job. At least the coffee wasn't that bad. In fact, next time that gal comes around get me another cup."

"Excuse me Boy, but I have a few words for that man." Orville was wedged between a grumpy old man on his left sitting by the window, and a sweet lady on his right.

"Yes ma'am."

"Sir! You should be ashamed of yourself. Hasn't your mother ever taught you anything about manners? I thought the eggs were delicious myself. In fact I wish I could have some more. And the bacon, orange juice, along with the hash browns." The slender lady in a blue cotton dress with white butterflies leaned forward as she lectured. All Orville could do was roll his eyes in disbelief and listen.

"Ladies and gentlemen, this is your captain speaking. We ask that you fasten your seat belts. We are experiencing some turbulence. When the light above your seat goes out, you may loosen your seat belt and get up and walk around. Thank you for your cooperation." The ride felt bumpy like a speedboat turning around and going over its own waves.

Later, as the calm resumed, the flight attendants slowly walked down the isles in one last attempt to keep the passengers comfortable.

"May I get you another pillow, Sir?" An elderly gentleman struggled to get comfortable in his seat. And when she returned after weaving between two children running down the isle, he was fast asleep. It was a long flight from Los Angeles by way of Chicago traveling east.

The five-foot blonde, wearing a navy blue suit with a silver wing pin on her lapel, displayed a consoling affect on all the passengers. Faces quickly lit up when they saw her coming. Just her presence alone settled tattered nerves.

Down a couple rows of seats a teenager couldn't stop laughing. A brown ponytail bobbed behind a blushing face while her eyes stayed glued to a movie on the screen. Totally absorbed in the story, Sally was shocked when her friend suddenly pulled the plug on her earphones.

Moving along, the flight attendant noticed Orville's glass was empty while he gazed at a sports magazine. "Would ya like another soda, Sir?" The Boy chuckled and felt relieved that someone actually addressed him as Sir. Maybe the Boy stuff was gone forever.

"Hey! Watch what you're doin'. I'm tryin' to count these stitches." The sweet little old lady didn't like Jean, the flight attendant, brushing her knitting needle when she walked by with another Coke for Orville.

The food carts were stashed away and the isles at last clear. Flight attendants walked the path for one last check on all the passengers. While some people looked anxious for the trip to end others remained content.

"Ladies and gentlemen. This is your captain speaking. In just a few minutes we will be landing at Lunkin Municipal Airport. The weather in Cincinnati is sunny and clear. The temperature is seventy-six degrees with a mild breeze. There's lots to see in Cincinnati, so enjoy your visit. We hope you had a pleasant flight, and thank you for flying United."

When the fasten your seat belt sign lit up, the people cheered and breathed a sigh of relief. "At last a long trip is about over," thought a young lady whose toddler finally fell asleep.

Outside, white clouds below gradually crept up on the airplane. Soon the aircraft was completely engulfed in a thick white opaque maze. Before long the clouds were above them and distancing themselves from the plane as the earth drew closer below. Finally, a vast landscape disappeared when buildings, homes, and moving vehicles came into view.

Slowly the landing gear began to peek out. There were four big wheels under each wing and two more under the nose of the plane. As the markers on the runway quickly went by, suddenly each wheel started to spin. And passengers looked in awe out the windows when the loud engines roared and carried them to a nearby ramp parked at gate number thirty-three.

When the green sign went out, the commotion of unbuckled seat belts got over two hundred people to stand up. "Let 'em go," Orville thought. "Rome was not built in a day. I'm in no hurry."

People rushed through the terminal. "They passed me up in bunches. Some gave me a dirty look. Like the anxious driver behind a slow car on the open road."

Slowly Orville walked toward the luggage carousal. And when all the people arrived, a long wait began. There was nothing on the track. A strange motorized sound kept the path moving. But still nothing was there. It felt like eternity to a tired traveler. Finally, a parade of celebrities began to appear. Every size, shape, and color imaginable of luggage came out.

"Where did all this stuff come from? Expensive Samsonite, Tourister, and more." Orville mumbled, while gawking eyes drew closer to the carousal to read the tags. To the rich it all looked the same. When Orville's suitcase crawled toward him he quickly snatched it from the track without hesitating. It was a small brown box with lots of nicks, tattered leather handle, a broken clasp, and reinforced with a strap. Surely, it was something nobody would be proud to have in his or her collection.

Orville looked over the many bobbing heads searching for an exit sign. The six-footer had at least one advantage over the airport crowd. "Sometimes I feel like Abe Lincoln back in Illinois." People scattered everywhere in and out of shops, around magazine racks, and along with Orville walking toward an exit door.

Outside the terminal Orville signaled for a taxi. Immediately the next in a long line raced toward the arrival entrance. In a split second a bald short man wearing a white T-shirt was out of his cab, rushing around to the other side, and assisting the young man into the back seat, luggage and all.

After sounding his horn the bright yellow taxicab with the checkered trim was moving away from the curb and weaving through all the other cars toward the highway. "Where to, Mister?"

"River Front Stadium, Sir. Home of the Redlegs. Do ya know where that's at, Sir?" Butterflies churned in a nervous stomach. The Boy wasn't use to riding in a taxicab. It was his first trip to the Big City.

"Ha! Ha! Ha! Do ya think I'm stupid? Do I know where it's at?" The driver mumbled in his Italian accent, chuckling as he flipped the flag down on his meter. "Yes, Mister! Everybody in this town knows where River Front Stadium is."

"OK!"

"Are ya new in these here parts, Boy?" The man was eager to talk. Driving a cab could get boring.

"Yeah! You could say that."

"I thought so. Ya don't look like the usual kind of guy traveling in these here parts."

"Maybe not." Orville paused long enough to glance at the surroundings. There were lots of cars on the highway and tall buildings in the distance. People everywhere. "How long will it take us to get there, Sir?"

Orville shifted his eyes to look around inside the cab. A partition separated him from the seat up front. On the dashboard under a light was a picture of the driver next to a four-digit number. And the sound of a meter kept ticking as the numbers in a small window kept flipping intermittently while the cost of Orville's ride increased.

The yellow cab crawled along like a herd of turtles in the midst of bumper-to-bumper traffic. Impatient drivers sounded their horn while other people shouted obscenities. "Get a horse old timer!" A limousine driver rolled down his window and made a fist to display his muscles like a wrestler in a ring before cheering fans.

"Get off the road!" A teenager threw an apple at them as his hot rod speeded by.

The wheels squeaked on Hilda's blue Chevy when she abruptly cut into the right lane, thus allowing her to pass the little yellow bubble. And when Andy turned his head to look at the speeding vehicle, he noticed four stoic elderly schoolteachers enjoying the ride.

Up ahead the little taxicab, along with other cars, exited the super highway. After turning left at the end of the ramp, they cruised along on commercial streets at thirty miles per hour. Surely, there was more than enough time to observe every store and pedestrian along the way. And Andy loved to entertain his passenger with lots of nonsense chatter.

"I get stuck at more intersections than I care to remember. If I had my way there would be no more red lights or other traffic signals," Andy said, murdering the King's English with his Italian accent. The thought is ironic, especially since Andy likes to take his time. After all, his livelihood depended on how long the meter box ticks, thus increasing the numbers while the flag is down.

"Don't make much difference to me. Where I come from we take our good old sweet time." Orville obliged the driver by politely responding to all the small talk.

"Hey buddy! Over there!" Andy pointed over the steering wheel of his cab, while still waiting for the traffic light to change. "If ya ever want some good pizza, Boy, go to Mario's. Ma mouth waters just thinkin' 'bout it. They have the best deep dish in town. Sausage. Melted cheese. Onions. Mushrooms. You name it. It's yours for thee askin'. Everybody goes to Mario's Pizza."

"I wonder who pays him." Orville chuckled, shifting his eyes from Andy to staring out the window.

Finally, the light changed to green and the little taxi was off and running again. As the engine spluttered and gasped for air, the driver gave her more gas and soon she was purring like a kitten.

"And if it's Chinese ya want, let me tell ya 'bout . . .Buffalo Bill's makes the best Bar–BQ Beef. . .Chopped Salad or Chicken. . . ." Andy always got so involved in the conversation that he couldn't stop talking.

Orville rolled his eyes and looked at his watch. "Will I ever get there?" The ride felt like eternity. Finally, after rounding another corner he breathes a sigh of relief when he saw the big sign that read: River Front Stadium, home of the Cincinnati Redlegs.

Dodging heavy traffic, the yellow cab crossed over a couple of lanes and cut into another row of cars. Honk! Honk! "Hey Mister! Who da ya think you are? What's the big idea? Try that again and I'll run ya over." An angry driver slammed on his brakes to avoid a near collision. Ignoring the green Chevy, Andy wheeled his cab over close to the curb and suddenly stopped.

"What'll I owe ya, Mister?"

"Andy. Just call me Andy, Boy. Everybody call's me Andy."

He grimaced when he stretched to lift the white flag on his meter. "That'll be three dollars and fifty cents please."

Orville lifted his butt off the back seat allowing him to force his hand into his pocket for some money. "There ya are, Sir. And thank you for the ride."

Outside, the Boy from Indiana paused to gaze at the huge structure. Goose bumps ran down his spine, as he couldn't take his eyes off the big sign: River Front Stadium.

Slowly, with a suitcase in his hand he walked over to the far gate passing several ticket stands along the way. Since there was no baseball game scheduled, the big sidewalk remained empty accept for a couple of pigeons searching for some crumbs. Reluctantly, feeling nervous, Orville entered the building and walked toward the iron stairwell that led to a catwalk over head.

"Hey Boy! Where ya goin'?" A heavyset man with a double chin in a white shirt and blue pants huffed and puffed running after Orville.

"Upstairs! Lookin' for the boss." The young enthusiastic baseball player barely got one foot up on the first step before he was interrupted.

"You can't go up there. No visitors allowed. Besides, there's no game today." The man remained adamant. "Hey fellow! What's your name, anyway?"

"Hodge! Orville Hodge!"

"Are you new in town? Never saw ya before in my life." Puzzled, the man kept a safe distance from the Boy.

"Yeah! You could say that." Orville grinned as he took a couple more steps up the stairwell.

Silence followed. The building attendant stared at the ground, pondering many thoughts that raced through his mind. Finally, his face lit up like a light bulb as he looked at Orville, now at the top of the stairs. "Hey! Are you that new guy that's joinin' the team?"

"Yep! You could say that." The boy gave short answers, hesitating, not sure what new guy he was talking about.

"Ha! Ha! Ha!" The old timer laughed. "Well why didn't ya say so? Go ahead. You'll find the boss at the last door on the catwalk."

Proudly, Orville walked down the steel path holding his head up high. Occasionally, he paused to look at the people below him. Concessionaires stayed busy stuffing soda pop bottles in ice. Over a hot grill hot dogs sizzled before being packed in a cozy bun, wrapped in foil, and placed in a warmer to be eaten by hungry baseball fans later. Finally, he stood by a dark wood mahogany door that appeared out of place to the surrounding steel frame supporting thousands of seats.

As the tall lengthy figure raised his fist to knock, he heard loud voices on the other side of the door. Not pleasant thoughts shared with one another, but more like an argument.

The plumb lady in a red dress and curly blond hair sat at her desk mumbling. "Can't make much money if we don't draw a crowd." Her eyes rolled across the pages of her bankbook.

"Ya can say that again, ma'am." The old age man, wearing a detective hat like Dick Tracy the cartoon character, manipulating a cigar between two fingers, always responded sarcastically regardless of the subject matter being discussed.

"But how do we get more fans? More enthusiastic excited baseball fans?" The lady in red continued to mumble oblivious to those around her.

"How many times do I gotta tell ya? Play good ball! Baseball! Lots of hits! Runs! Win games!" After taking another whiff from his cigar, the man repositioned his head to get a better look at the baseball field, peeking through the shades on the window.

"Ya need good ball players to do that."

"Ha! Ha! Ha! What else is new?" The man chuckled while choking on his cigar. "Doesn't everybody want good ball players ma'am?'

"Hey! Stop the arguing you two." Bud got up off the couch and placed his thumbs in the sleeves of his vest. "I been tryin' to tell ya, I've been lookin' around lately."

"Oh?" Suddenly the pair questioned Bud's intrusion into the conversion.

"Last month—"

Suddenly, a knock on the door again caught them off guard. "Whose there? Go away! We don't want any!" The man flicked the ashes off the end of his cigar into an ashtray. In a dimly lit room no one ever noticed all the ashes on the plush carpet.

"Sir! My name is—!" A weak voice uttered behind the door.

"Get outta here!" Soon a loud voice started to mellow. "Probably some young kid sellin' somethin'."

"Boss! I'm tryin' to tell ya." Bud said, looking at the old man.

"I'm the boss. I've owned this Club for many years. My poppa always said—." The lady in red stood up and boldly interrupted.

"Let 'em in boss. Sorry Peggy. No offense. The old man reminds me of your father."

As the door opened, a tall thin figure entered the room and stood in front of the boss. His eyes bulged staring at the big desk. "Hi! I'm Orville."

"Who?" Peggy looked surprised. Puzzled. The name didn't ring a bell. Nothing registered in her mind as she struggled to recall the name.

"I gotta here this one." The grumpy old man mumbled while dusting the window shade with some smoke, like a dragon spitting fire out of his mouth on his enemy.

"Who are you?" The lady in red, who everybody called Peggy, waved her arm motioning for the fat man near the window to be quiet and not interrupt.

13

"If I may get a word in here edgewise you guys, I'll explain."

"Oh! You know something we don't know, Bud." Peggy shifted her position around behind her desk to stare directly at the man dressed in a faded blue pin strip suit, straw hat, and seated on the arm of an old stuffed chair.

"We need hitters if we're gona win ball games, Ma." He always addressed her as Ma. "Yes! We need lots of hits. Runs. The things that get baseball fans excited."

"So?" The lady wheeled her chair around while the man near the window drew closer to her.

"Yes! Let me tell ya what I found out." Bud stood up, placed one hand in his pocket, and braced his legs. "What I did. By the way old man, come over here and get comfortable in this chair." He motioned with his free hand.

"Whatta ya talkin' about, Bud? Ya sound as if you're out to save the world." The old man chuckled after taking another puff on his cigar while leaning against Peggy's desk. "As if you alone can do it and no body else."

"Now hold on, Sir." Bud motioned, pointing all four fingers on one hand at the grumpy old man who was standing across the room.

"Be quiet!" Peggy shouted. "Let Bud talk. I wanna hear what he has to say."

"Thank you, ma'am." Bud looked at the kid. "Don't mind us, Boy. We do this all the time."

Peggy remained calm sitting behind her desk, while the grumpy old man got comfortable in a stuffed armchair.

It was a bright sunny day in Chicago. There wasn't a cloud in the sky when Bud happened to be passing through on business. "I knew it would be a long week, so I decided to go to a few ball games at Wrigley Field to break up the boredom."

Day one. Bud got comfortable in the box seats section along the first base foul line. No one in the crowd recognized him, an agent for the Cincinnati Redlegs.

"Hey hot dogs! Red hots! Get your hot dogs here!" A vendor wearing a baseball cap, smothered with souvenir buttons of various sport teams, struggled carrying a big silver box strapped over his shoulder down the isle.

14

"Hey! Over here!" Bud signaled, waving a ten-dollar bill in his hand. Shortly thereafter, two dogs traveled down a row of fans, before the man was gone selling more hot dogs to other people.

"Thank you, partner." Bud nodded, when the fan sitting next to him handed him two prized possessions wrapped in white paper.

"Pepsi! Ice-cold Pepsi! Get your ice-cold Pepsi here!" Like the girl all dressed up carrying a tray of d'oeuvres around at a party, another vender drew the attention of thirsty baseball fans. Now Bud's menu was complete.

"As I got comfortable in my seat my eyes rolled across the field watching the Cubs warm up during batting practice. Today they played the St. Louis Cardinals. Cheers had every seat in the park vibrating when the Chicago Cubs came out of the dugout.

"Each player strategically positioned himself on the field. A couple of guys sat near the foul line and did some stretching exercises. Another group of players jogged back and forth along the back left field wall. A ball traveled quickly around the infield from third to first, to shortstop to home plate, to second to first, and back to third again in a game of hot potato before repeating itself.

"On the pitcher's mound a tall right hander delivered several fast balls to a batter standing on the third base foul line, whom placed them perfectly into left, center, and right field intermittently.

"But what struck my attention most is when they changed batter's. After swallowing my last bite of a delicious hot dog, I noticed something different and quickly sat up straight in my chair."

A six-foot thin player in a loose fitting baseball uniform slowly walked up to the plate, swinging a bat. "I thought my turn to bat would never come," he mumbled. "A sarcastic tone expressed discontent for keeping the bench warm during most of the regular season.

"Hit one, Boy!" The husky Cub utility batter tapped the new comer on the rump when he walked passed him. "Show 'em how it's done."

Orville braced himself in the batter's box getting ready for the first pitch. No sweat. There was nothing to lose. After all, it was only batting practice.

The first pitch sailed toward the plate. Swing! And the ball sailed into left field. Perfectly placed, Billy Williams caught it without moving an inch.

Several more balls traveled toward home plate. And after putting some wood on each one of them, they sailed into center, right, and left field respectively. It was just routine and nothing out of the ordinary.

But then Orville momentarily stepped out of the batter's box. After holding his bat high over his head with both hands and stretching toward the sky, he resumed his position back in the batter's box.

The next ball hit the left field wall, catching Billy Williams off guard. He raced toward the warning track, and stretched on a dive, attempting to catch it. However, after missing it completely, he quickly got back on his feet, chased after it, and threw it back to the infield.

Another ball hit the center field wall. Don Young caught it on the rebound, wheeled around and threw it toward second base.

The ball never saw the wall in right field. Instead several fans scrambled for a souvenir. And every ball thereafter cleared the ballpark.

"I never saw a ball hit that many times leave the ballpark before with such consistency." Bud mumbled to Peggy and the grumpy old man while munching on some popcorn.

"Wait just a minute!" Leo Durocher, the Cub manager, shouted while racing out of the dugout. "Keep 'em in the Park! Ya here me? This isn't a game! Only batting practice!" After motioning with his hands, he wheeled around and trotted back to the dugout.

The Boy didn't know his own strength. He had a very intense power of concentration. Every ball sailed out of the ballpark. The fans watched in awe. Spellbound. Silence ruled the day.

"Every day the same thing. Where did this kid come from? I wondered. We need good ball players like this. Guys that can hit the ball. I gotta talk to the Club manager about this.

Peggy and the grumpy old man dropped their jaws, listening in awe as Bud revealed his experience.

"And so folks. Here he is. Meet Orville Hodge."

THREE

Orville felt upbeat when he entered the Clubhouse. The locker room echoed the usual chitchat. Locker doors slammed shut. Tempers flared. No body was embarrassed walking around in skin. Procrastinators in the shower were urged to speed it up.

Against the water spraying on broad shoulders in the shower, a fellow teammate complained. "Man! Does my shoulder ache.!"

"I always said George, man's arms weren't made for pitching."

"Just cause you ain't a pitcher Lee—."

"Yeah, but my body's achin' too. I can't say it's a piece a cake playin' other positions either."

"The guy with the ice . . .packin' my arm like a piece of meat in a meat packin' house. Yep! The rub down after the game . . .and does it ever hurt walkin' off the field."

"Ha! Ha! Ha!" Woody laughed, walking by flipping a towel over his shoulder. "There ya go complaining again." The other guys paid no attention to him.

"Wow! This hot water really feels good on my back."

Down a row of lockers other players stayed busy suiting up.

Humped over, Alex struggled reaching to tie his shoe. Number twenty-eight twisted and turned in front of a mirror buttoning his shirt. Only the vain would spend so much time staring at his profile.

"That old lady spilled some soda all over me when I reached for a foul ball." The right fielder mumbled while adjusting his belt.

"Ha!"

"Or misjudging the ball in centerfield." A deep southern voice said from the other side of the lockers.

"Ha!"

"What about the ball hitting my knee?"

"What about it?"

"The ump called it a strike. My knee wasn't over the plate. No where near it."

"Ha!" All the guys in the room shouted.

"Hey! Do ya hear what I'm sayin'?" Jerry asked, standing near another row of lockers.

"Yeah! I hear ya." Ted bobbed his head above the lockers.

"What ya lookin' at?"

"Over there—."

"Ya keep staring. What ya staring at?"

"Over there at the Abe Lincoln figure. Skeleton like. Tall. Thin. White as a ghost."

"Can't take my eyes off him." Another player joined in the conversation. "Just thinkin' makes me wonder how he ever got here. He doesn't look like the usual type of baseball player."

Orville drew a lot of attention standing catatonic in his shorts. Soon everybody was staring at him. Cold piercing eyes made him feel more like a freak in the sideshow of a circus, rather than a professional league baseball player.

Nervously, Orville lathered up in the shower and allowed the water to splash off his chest. And so goes the story of his life. Introvert. Didn't bond well with other people. "Relax! Loosen up! Don't be so serious." His friends always found it hard to warm up to him. Throughout his life he had many acquaintances, but few real friends. Yet he longed to be a part of the group.

Curiosity drew the staring crowd closer. Slowly, the spokesman for the bunch nudged his way up to the shower. "Hey Boy!"

The sound of several sprays spitting out water forced him to repeat himself louder than before. "Hey Boy!"

Startled, Orville turned off the shower and wheeled around to face them.

"Thank you, Boy! At least a dozen eyes stared at the new-comer up and down, making him feel like a piece of meat being inspected on an assembly line.

"Yeah!" Shivering with goose bumps all over his body resembled a chicken without any feathers.

"Where'd ya come from, Boy? Ya look like something straight outta the woods. A misfit like ya doesn't fit in. Are ya one of us? A Redleg?" Without hesitating the fearless spokes person recited a long list of negatives.

"You can't judge a book by its cover." Orville remembered his mother always telling him that. So he learned to let negative comments roll off his back.

"I'm a ball player, Sir!" The rookie shouted back like a private responding to an army sergeant during a drill.

"Yeah. Yeah. Yeah. Yeah. I know." The teammate nodded his head while motioning with his hands. "But can ya play ball? He paused. "Ya here me?" Doubts started to race through his mind along with a cynical laugh from the other guys.

"You bet! Baseball! I'm ready to play." His voice quivered. "No body's gona walk all over me."

Puzzled, the guys returned to their lockers and finished getting dressed for today's game.

"Hopeless." One guy muttered. "Utterly hopeless. Don't see how he ever got here."

Following a nice hot shower, Orville paraded with the rest of the team through the tunnel to the dugout. Even though he felt apprehensive about his teammates, still he proudly wore the Cincinnati Redleg uniform: White jersey's, big numbers on the back of his shirt, and a red baseball cap. "It feels great to be a professional league baseball player." And he didn't shy away from wearing a silly grin from one ear to the other.

It was his first day with the ball club. And again, a chill trickled down his spine listening to the fans when the team race out on the field for batting practice.

The guys wasted no time taking their positions. After making a fist and pounding his glove, one guy anticipated a fastball sailing toward him. While waiting, another player padded the ground with his foot around second base, thus breaking up some lumps of dirt into fine sand. Two other players standing near the foul line, folded their arms and chatted while watching fly balls sail into the outfield.

Like a game of hot potato, a ball quickly sailed around the infield. They made it look easy. From the third base foul line, a batter hit fly balls into the outfield. Placing them perfectly into left, center, and right field, other guys caught them.

Meanwhile, back in the bullpen a right-hander was warming up for today's game. Sailing toward a catcher in full gear with one knee firmly placed on the ground, Orville heard a crackling sound each time the ball landed in his glove.

Batting practice was important to the entire team. Each player spent endless hours in the locker room listening to the coach. "Loosen up those muscles, boys. Conditioning is our middle name." They can still see the diagrams on the blackboard, and the squeaking chalk that drove everybody crazy.

Orville saw lots of people in the ballpark that day. "They came to watch us play ball. It felt good. Especially when I think of the route I took to get here. It wasn't easy. I suppose there's a vain streak in all of us."

The fans were happy. Smiles. Lots of chatter echoed throughout the park. People stuffed their mouth's full of hot dogs while trying to talk at the same time, not to mention gulping down ice-cold soda pop. They stayed busy with a pencil in hand writing down today's roster.

"Ladies and gentlemen! Young and old! All baseball fans! The announcer's tone blared out of loud speakers scattered throughout River Front Stadium. Immediately, the fans cheered looking forward to an exciting baseball game.

"OK! Get your scorecards ready! Here's today's line-up for the Chicago Cubs." Boos filled the ballpark. "For the Chicago Cubs: Beckert . . .Kissinger . . .Santo . . .Banks." More boos followed after each name was given.

"Now for the Cincinnati Redlegs!" Immediately the fans

cheered after hearing each name. Often the announcer had to pause till quiet resumed. "Leading off and playing third base, Tony Perez . . .right field . . .Pete Rose . . .Lee May . . .Johnny Bench." Again Orville felt proud sitting in the dugout listening to the rundown. "Someday, just someday, I may have a chance to be in the starting line-up."

The guys quickly took their places on the field during batting practice. Orville felt stupid, like a fifth wheel, until one of the coach's tossed him a glove. ""Here! Let's play some catch."

"Sure coach! Sounds great!" Again Orville remembered his mother always telling him to be polite and do what he was told. So he followed the coach over to the third base foul line.

"You new here?"

"Yep! First day in uniform."

"I thought so. These guys follow a routine during batting practice. Don't think you've been a part of that." The man with the handlebar mustache showed concern. Orville liked someone taking an interest in him. It felt good.

The ball sailed through the air and very methodically established a pace of its own. It went back and forth to each player. Nothing fancy. It was a simple game of catch, and offered them a chance to loosen up their muscles before the game.

Orville liked throwing the ball and felt like he was in his second heaven. He watched it sail through the air and heard a crackling sound when it landed in his glove after each catch. It was fun. He could do it all day.

But just as he was getting more comfortable, the coach waved stop and walked toward him, with his own glove tucked under his arm. "Let's go. Time to run." He didn't wait for a reply. Instead, he kept right on walking. Orville had no choice but to follow and skip along, struggling to keep up with him.

The same activity continued. No body traded places. Quickly, Orville and the coach weaved through a maze of players on the first base foul line. Sitting on his butt, one guy stretched to reach his toes. Another, standing with his legs firmly braced, twisted his trunk. A greeting party met them near the right field wall. Orville felt perplexed. "What's up coach?'

"Boys meet ah,ah,ah . . ." A pair of evil eyes stared at Orville.

"What'd ya say your name is?"

"Or, Or, Orville, coach. Orville Hodge!" A nervous voice replied.

"Yeah! Meet Orville Hodge!"

"Howdy!"

Orville nodded.

"Howdy, Boy!"

Grinning, Orville gestured by jerking his head.

"Hey! Aren't you the guy we . . .yeah . . .the shower . . .back in the locker room."

"Never mind. There's no time for small talk. You and you! Get over here!" He pointed to the chalk line. "I want ya to run with Orville. Run to center field. Stop! Wheel around and run back. Do it again and again and again." The coach clapped his hands. "Do it several times."

"Yes Sir, coach. Anything you say." The guys stared at the tall thin figure, moving their eyes up and down this strange creature, casting doubts on his ability to run. "Hey Boy! Can ya keep up with me?" The guys laughed.

"Yep!" Orville hated being harassed. It followed him around everywhere he went. Again he got ready to defend himself.

All four of them lined up. On the count of three they took off. Halfway down the path Orville lost sight of them. When he wheeled around to return to the foul line, he saw them struggling to catch up with him. At the finish line it was a long time before they all got there, and another waiting game.

"Again!" The coach shouted, clapping his hands.

Without hesitating, Orville wheeled around, held his chest up high and took off. On the third time around his legs started to ache. Racing toward the finish line, he hoped the coach wouldn't ask them to do it again.

Meanwhile his buddies were huffing and puffing as they walked back toward home plate. Orville felt relaxed.

Hey wise guy!" A sarcastic voice shouted from the dugout. "Quit showin' off."

"I wasn't . . ."

"Like blankity-blank you weren't." The guy walking along side him interrupted. "We're supposed to be a team and do it together.

Remember?"

"I—I—I."

"No excuses. We've seen your kind before."

"It seems like you're darned if you do and darned if you don't." Orville remained puzzled and discouraged. "If I can't perform I'm criticized. And if I out-perform them they don't like that either. Good grief! What is a guy suppose to do? I can't win. And they don't like the put down when the shoe is on the other foot."

"Grab a bat Orville! Gotta hit a couple."

The Boy from the backwoods walked with confidence toward the dugout holding his head up high. As the new kid on the block, the coach continued to make him feel at home.

After firmly bracing his legs in the batter's box, Orville took a couple of warm-up swings. Then, as the ball sailed slowly toward the plate, he swung viciously but missed.

"Hey buddy!"

"I doubt if he can hit, Lee. Look at him. He's so thin. Weak. Ya probably can blow him over with one blow." Tommy sneered from second base.

"Just meet the ball." Tony motioned with his hands at third. "Ya just meet the ball!"

"Do ya think ya can hit it to us out here on the infield?"

"Don't worry about those guys out there." Jimmy gestured, looking over his shoulder.

"Ya might put us all to sleep, but just try to meet the ball."

They laughed at him. They thought he was too weak and immature to be there, a part of a major league baseball team. "But I'll show them. I'll make them eat those words. I did it before and I'll do it again." Orville was bound and determined to fulfill a life long dream.

On the next pitch he sent the ball over the left field wall. The outfielder didn't even attempt to chase it. Instead, he just stood there with his hands on his waist and stared. Another pitch easily sailed out of the park over centerfield. Several more balls left the park consecutively. Finally, feeling angry, manager Bristol raced out of the dugout to have a chat with him. "What are ya doin', Orville?"

"Hitting the ball, Sir."

"Who told ya to do that?" The manager puckered his lips as they nearly rubbed noses.

"Those guys out there." The innocent Boy stared at his accusers while pointing to the infield.

"Just hit fly balls to the outfield. All fields. Let 'em catch 'em. Ya got all that?"

"Yep!"

"Good! Let's go!"

The guys chuckled while returning to their positions.

Back in the batter's box, Orville let up on his swing and hit fly balls in all directions. The fans watched in awe. His bat connected with every ball. There was nothing unusual about that. His fellow teammates did it all the time. But to constantly send them out of the ballpark was amazing. For the moment fans forgot about sipping soda and eating hot dogs. Scorecards fell out of their laps. A star was born.

FOUR

Pete watched Kenny manipulate the ball in his hand hidden behind his leg. As he remained hutched over, he stared at Randy, squatting behind home plate, giving several signs with his fingers between his legs. Finally, the left-hander brought his hands together, kicked his right leg up high into the air, and delivered the next pitch. On the throw, Pete took off for second base.

Tommy swung and missed while the fans booed. "Strike!" The umpire shouted, cocking his right arm, giving the strike sign.

Randy wasted no time picking the ball out of his glove, and stepping forward on the throw to second base. The ball traveled high. Beckert, the second baseman, stretched his arm to catch it. Pete quickly dove toward the bag when a hand carrying the ball plunged into a cloud of dust. Meanwhile, the fans were silent. Spellbound. They watched in awe. And when the dust cleared, Pete's hand was resting on the bag with Beckert's on top of his holding the ball.

The second base umpire looked puzzled. With his arms folded

and his chin resting on one hand, he pondered the situation. Finally, he motioned for the other umpires to join him for a friendly chat.

Meanwhile the fans anxiously waited and waited and waited. For the moment it felt like a challenge in an NFL football game. The crowd never saw the likes of this before.

Following moments of silence, the umpires split up as each resumed his original position at first, third, and home plate. As all eyes stayed glued to second base, the small man in the black suit braced his legs and spread his hands, thus, giving the safe sign. And immediately all the Redleg fans went crazy with cheers.

However, Leo Durocher, the Cub manager wasn't satisfied. Immediately, he raced out of the dugout toward second base. "Ump are ya crazy? You couldn't see the ball! From where I was sitting, I saw it perfectly. From the dugout, a sliver of clearance between the ground and the dust showed he was definitely out."

They stuck out their chest. Noses rubbed. Jaws rapidly moved up and down dispelling angry feelings. Disagreements echoed around the baseball diamond. Boos mixed with cheers came from the fans. And when it was all over, Leo reluctantly trotted back to the dugout. Safe. The decision stands.

After getting a sign from the first base coach, Tommy stepped back into the batter's box and took a couple more warm-up swings. When a fastball quickly sailed toward the plate, he twitched his fingers just before getting ready to hit the ball. However, at the last minute he decided to hold up as the ball curved slightly away from the plate.

Again the fans got quiet. Silence ruled the day at River Front Stadium. Eyes stared at the home plate ump while other people checked their scorecards. Even all the venders paused and waited for the moment.

Finally, the umpire placed his hands together behind his back and turned to his right. "Ball one!" Before he could finish giving the sign the crowd voiced their approval. Cub fans couldn't be heard above all the cheers.

Back in the batter's box, Tommy let the next pitch go by. "Ball two!" And still another ball flickered as it got near the plate. "Ball three!" The fans got ecstatic, anticipating another runner on first base.

On the next pitch Pete took off for third. Halfway down the path, he stopped, wheeled around and hustled back to second. But Randy Huntley didn't second-guess anybody. On his knees from home plate, he fired the ball to third. Ron Santo quickly caught it, and with the ball tucked safely in the web of his glove, he forced Pete back to second. The fans reacted with mixed feelings. Boos displayed dissatisfaction when he didn't make it to third. On the other hand, cheers approved that he got back to second safely.

Now it was time to protect the plate. The next pitch connected with the fat part of Tommy's bat and sailed into the seats above the third base dugout. "Strike two!" The ump again cocked his arm to give the sign. "Full count! Ball three, strike two!"

Momentarily, he stepped out of the batter's box to regain his composure. He already knew what the first base coach wanted. After a big stretch Tommy was back in the box. Carefully he stared at the ball. All other sounds and activities were oblivious to him. The ball got top priority.

As the ball left the pitcher's mound, Tommy knew he was in control. He lined several balls down the third base line. Ron Santo, the third baseman, dove for a couple of them and missed them completely. Billy Williams also raced toward the wall along the foul line, only to watch them sail into the seats for some lucky fan.

The situation grew tense when the fans got anxious. Seats rumbled. Soon everybody was chanting at the same time. "Hit! Hit! Hit! We wanna hit!"

To heighten the drama, Kenny Holtzman the Cub left-hander, stepped off the rubber and circled the mound while scanning the outfield. The waiting game intensified Tommy's nerves.

The next pitch left Kenny's hand spinning like a top and sailing toward the outside of the plate. Again Tommy twitched his fingers, anticipating to swing his bat when the ball got near him. Still, he wasn't sure whether to hit it or let it go by. Ball four meant another runner. A strike and there's one out in the bottom of the ninth. Finally, with all his might, he swung viciously. The last thing he remembered was hearing a sound when the ball connected with his bat, and he found himself racing toward first base.

The fans were on their feet. Pete Rose was already rounding third and on his way home with the winning run. Billy Williams, the Cub left fielder, never took his eye off the ball. Running hard, he leaped at the last moment in foul territory by the left field corner. With his arm stretched out, and his hand above the guardrail, the ball landed in the web of his glove. And while the fans voiced their disapproval, Pete returned to second.

"Hello fans, back in TV land! And here we are in the bottom of the ninth with a tie game. Cubs three. Redlegs three.

"Folks! The excitement here is just out of this world. With Pete Rose standing safely at second after a steal, Tommy Halms hit one that I thought went into orbit. Even the fans thought so. However, at the last minute, Billy Williams leaped up high into the air to make a spectacular catch. It just might safe this game and send us into extra innings.

"So baseball fans, stay tune to this TV station for more play-by-play action."

Meanwhile, the Redleg team sat stoic with their arms folded on the bench in the dugout. Flat affect. All the guys looked serious. Emotionless.

Orville could take it no longer, so he jumped up off the bench and moseyed on down to the drinking fountain. Once his thirst was satisfied, he returned to his designated spot on the bench.

As he got more comfortable and folded his arms, he watched the game like everybody else until his mind began to wander: "Wow! I never thought I'd be playing on a team with so many baseball greats." Just then a fly ball sailed toward the dugout. "Duck!" A loud voice abruptly interrupted the Boy's thoughts. And quickly, the ball hit the wall on the back of the dugout before rolling out on the field.

Ernie Banks, home run hitter. Ron Santo playing third base. Don Kissinger scooping up speeding fastballs at short. Even Pete Rose. The thoughts raced through Orville's mind till he felt another interruption with a bump on his shoulder.

"What'd ya think of that last play?"

"Oh! You mean the fly ball to the left field corner?"

"Yeah! Do ya think he was out?"

"Well sure! Of course!" Orville chuckled, raising his shoulders and feeling confident to answer easy questions. "Billy caught the ball. The batter was out. No doubt about it. Not that it made me happy."

"Yeah! I agree!" Pause. "Say! I'm Johnny Bench. Who are you?"

Immediately goose bumps engulfed Orville's body. The Boy from Indiana got a bad case of the shakes. Nervous. He froze in his tracks. He was speechless. "Or—Or—Orville. Orville Hodge."

"Pleased to meet ya, Orville. How long have ya been here?"

"Not very long."

"You new to the team?"

"Yeah. Ya can say that. Just got here a couple days ago."

"What position do ya play?" The Redleg catcher showed a genuine interest in the new comer.

"Don't know yet . . .I mean the manager hasn't made up his mind yet."

"Are ya a pitcher?" Johnny was ready to give the Boy some helpful tips, looking at things from behind the plate.

"Nope!" Orville was glad that he was asking all the questions. With butterflies starting to churn in his stomach, he doubted if he could strum up a conversation for the moment.

"Anyway! Welcome to the team." A cordial handshake sealed their friendship.

"Likewise!"

"Is this your first time in the majors?"

"Nope!"

"Where ya comin' from?" What other team have ya played with?"

"That one over there. The Chicago Cubs." He pointed to the dugout across the diamond, while they both remained engrossed in a lengthy conversation.

FIVE

A lightly lit tunnel led to the left field corner of Wrigley Field, where on the other side of a door was the Cub bullpen and a path leading to the dugout. The sound of spikes on a metal floor mat clicked like cadence to the beat of a drum in a parade. A grumpy voice mumbling against a pair of jaws chewing gum disturbed delicate ears.

Four husky ball players fully dressed in Cub uniforms slowly walked out toward the field. Behind them struggling, a bat boy dragged a bag full of bats, baseballs, and gloves.

The guts of the ball club, along with one rookie, gathered to strategize some important plays for future games. "How do we look, Bob?"

"Not good, Leo. Ya wanna know where we're at?"

"Yeah! Give it to me straight. The full scoop."

"Ya know I wouldn't put ya on, boss. I always shoot straight from the hip."

"Yeah! Yeah! Yeah! Yeah! Skip the bull—. Just give me the facts."

"OK! Lookin' at my notes, it looks like—"

Meanwhile, outside beneath a clear blue sky the sun shined down on an empty ballpark. All thirty-four thousand seats were empty. There wasn't a soul stirring in the whole place, not even a church mouse.

The meeting continued as the four huddled near the third base coach's box. Ideas flowed from one brain to another. Tempers flared. Arguments were unavoidable. But in the end, they all will remain friends. Modifications in planning often made for a better baseball game, and a winning team.

Through it all, Orville patiently stood by with his arms folded and legs braced listening. "Sometimes I don't know why they asked me to be here. After joining the team just a few days ago, I hardly know what they expect from me. Now I'm here, as if I've been a part of the team for many years."

While listening to all the chatter, Orville's eyes started to wander around the park. From the grandstands to the broadcaster's booth, to the scoreboard perched high above the bleachers in centerfield, the Boy from nowhere began to reflect on earlier thoughts about Wrigley Field and the Chicago Cubs.

The Hodges lived on a farm in Cedar Lane, Indiana throughout most of Orville's early life. Hard work, toiling in the fields, or caring for the animals comprised a good part of the day, while the ladies stayed busy in the kitchen.

Following dinner it was time for some relaxation before hitting the sack for some sleep and preparation for another day. That meant reading the newspaper or indulging in some chitchat to get caught up on the latest gossip. To break the boredom, often they'd all sit around and listen to the radio.

On a small stand near an armchair stood a cathedral shaped brown radio with many knobs. A dim light behind some numbers displayed the station everybody was listening to. "I recall how Uncle John got mad when only a couple of 'em came in loud and clear. There was enough static to choke ten horses, the saying often went. Needless to say, we couldn't always listen to our favorite program. However, the baseball station never gave us any trouble. And the ladies learned to reluctantly accept the men's wishes in the house.

"Many nights we listened to the Chicago Cubs at Wrigley Field over WGN radio from Chicago. As the men sat on the edge of their seat, grossly involved in the game, the ladies occasionally lent a passive ear while knitting or glancing through a magazine. Silence. No one uttered a sound during the game."

"Hello baseball fans! This is Jack Quinland along with Lou Boudreau, bringing you Cub's baseball over WGN radio." Orville heard it many times through the years. Jack always had a way to make a baseball game come alive. Even though the fans weren't actually there, it felt as if they were right there watching every move.

The Hodge family along with a few Uncles all sat stoically in the living room around the radio. For the moment the noise box ruled the day.

"Hello fans! Now batting, number—, Hank Aaron." Milwaukee Brave fans suddenly came alive. Boos from the opposition soon blended in, leaving much uncertainty and a mixture of boos and cheers throughout the ballpark.

"All right!" Uncle John shouted, clapping his hands and stomping his foot.

"Who ya rooting for, Unck? I thought you were a Cub fan."

"Ya know I'm a Cub fan through and through. That is when they're winning. Ya knew that Lizzie. But right now I know who the winning team is. The Braves always give the north-siders a hard time."

"Ha!" Uncle Dan interrupted, sarcastically. "Just goes to show where your loyalty is."

"Swing, and a miss! Strike one! Even Hank agreed when he heard the ball land in the catcher's mitt. Lou, he was aiming for the seats when he swung that bat."

"That's right, Jack! After looking into the dugout, the first base coach gave the hit sign. A good move to put the fans on the edge of their seat."

"Thatta way, Hank!" Uncle Dan never shied away from letting his feelings be known. "Two more like that and we're outta trouble."

"He ain't gonna do that again." Differences of opinion always preceded an argument. The Indiana farmers were a stubborn bunch.

"Hey you guys! Stop it! It's only a game." Aunt Martha interjected to cool hot tempers.

"That's it!" Jack muttered when the bat connected with the ball. "No doubt about it! It's gone! Everybody here is on their feet watching it clear the right field wall."

"All right!" Cousin Al chimed in when everybody in the room stood up to stretch their legs and applaud the hitter. Then he rushed into the kitchen for a bowl of potato chips. Mama Hodge followed him back into the living room with an ice-cold pitcher of lemonade.

Another time Cub fans were on the edge of their seat's listening to Don Cardwell taking the Cubs through nine innings of no hit baseball. "That day all my Uncles were in agreement for a Cub victory."

"OK fans! Here we are in the top of the ninth." Jack was at his best giving all the play-by-play action.

"The right-hander brought his hands together and kicked his left leg up high into the air before throwing the ball. A stinging fastball nipped the outside corner of the plate. The ump put his hands together behind his back and shouted ball one. Boos echoed throughout Wrigley Field."

"C'mon, Cardwell! Strikes man! Strikes! Let's get this game over with."

"Be cool, John! It's comin'." Uncle Dan padded him on the shoulder after sipping some lemonade.

"Another pitch, fans. Again ball two! What's happenin' Lou? Has he lost his touch?"

"Cardwell might be gettin' tired, Jack. Perhaps Sammy, the Cub catcher, should get out to the mound and try to settle him down."

"That's exactly what he's doin'. With time called, we'll take a short station break—."

"Skip the commercials Jack." The Uncles muttered. "Get us back to the game. We're here to listen to a ball game."

Several more pitches left the pitcher's mound. "Ball three, strike two!" The ump motioned the sign and shouted the count. The batter fouled many of them off keeping the fans spellbound.

Finally he swung and sent the ball into left field.

Immediately, the fans were on their feet following the ball. Quickly, Walt raced toward the wall. While leaping he stretched his arm. And when the ball landed in the web of his glove, the fans were ecstatic. Shortly thereafter, everybody was racing out on the field.

"I knew he'd do it."

"Oh fiddle-faddle, Mike. You're just sayin' that to make us think you know everything there is to know 'bout baseball."

"Nope, Millie! I heard it with my own ears. Right here in this here room with everybody else."

Baseball was a passion to these hard working farmers. Every chance they got they huddled around the radio. If one neighbor didn't have one, they'd all get-to-gether at another neighbor's house. The brown box provided cheap relaxing entertainment.

"I remember the time when everybody was mesmerized when Richie—of the Philadelphia Phillies stepped up to the plate." Orville sat on the floor looking up at their faces. "They were captivated on how the lead-off man manipulated every pitch."

The ball sailed quickly toward the plate. "Strike!" the ump shouted, cocking his right arm giving the sign.

Another ball crossed the plate. Swing! "Strike two!"

Several more balls sailed toward the plate. Richie connected with each one of them and sent them into the seats for some lucky fan. "Protection! Gotta protect the plate." The thoughts raced through his mind.

With a keen eye the star player let the next three pitches go by. The fans watched in awe. Spellbound. Silence filled the park. Then, on a full count, he fouled off a couple more balls, before looking at ball four. After tossing his bat aside he trotted down the line toward first base to a standing ovation.

"Yep! They were good times, sittin' and listenin' to the radio." Orville remembered.

"As I looked around and stared at the empty seats, I recalled my first day at Wrigley Field. Uncle Milton surprised the living day lights out of me at a time when nobody ever left the farm. Wow! That was a long time ago.

"People were everywhere. I never saw so many people together in one place." The sidewalk was packed with people rushing to the gate. Everybody was thinkin' baseball. All ages—men, women, boys, and girls were there to cheer on their favorite team.

Boys stood on orange crates shouting while holding up a newspaper. "Extra! Extra! Tribune here!" Not too far away other boys held up a Chicago Sun Times or Chicago Daily News.

Inside the ball park a batter hit fly balls into all directions. He placed them perfectly into right, center, and left field. "I was intrigued watching so many balls fly into a fielder's glove. He made it look so easy."

No game was complete without a hot dog and some soda pop. " Nice and cozy in a bun, smothered with ketchup, mustard, relish, and onions, I could eat 'em all day. But Uncle Milt said no. I pouted and went back to watching the game."

Memories. Lots of memories raced through Orville's mind standing there, next to some grumpy old men muttering on the foul line in an empty park.

Not too long ago a group of boys started to play ball on a corner lot in their neighborhood. Dressed like the Little Rascals in the TV series, in overalls, sport skirts, and gym shoes, baseball was their passion. Eventually they left behind the splintered bats and tattered baseballs to develop a baseball team in Lincoln park with the help of a retired janitor they called 'Pop". Finally, they played the Chicago Cubs.

Wrigley Field was packed. "My friends told me lots of things about it." The Cub's took a big lead in the early innings. In the eighth it was tied, and in a pitcher's dual to the end, eventually the Boys won. The crowd was ecstatic.

They called themselves the Boys on the Gold Coast, from a neighborhood that bared its name on the near north side of Chicago. It was a time when organized youth baseball was nonexistent.

Meanwhile, back in the huddle by third base, ideas continued to get kicked around. "Our bullpen's doin' all right. It could be better, but I think we'll get by."

"Great! That's what I wanna hear, Bob." Leo always thought ahead, so he jumped to the next thing on the agenda. "How we doin' on the bases?"

"We need to pick it up a bit, Leo. Maybe these guys should eat more Wheaties." Everybody laughed.

"Very funny, Billy. Look! I've got more important things on my mind."

"As my mind continued to drift into a different world, I suddenly felt a nudge on my arm."

"Hey, Orville! Get over here! I wanna see how ya run."

Orville was startled back into a world of reality. "Sure Leo! I'm comin'!"

"Billy! Whose a fast runner on our team?"

"I think it's—."

"Good! Go get 'em."

"Yes, Sir!"

"Quick! Like a bunny! I don't have time to waste here all day." The manager clapped his hands.

When Billy returned Leo was giving Orville some last minute instructions. "Don't waste time. Stay alert. Keep those legs movin'! Watch—."

"Here I am boss." Billy interrupted, huffing and puffing almost out of breath.

"Whose this?" Leo stopped in the middle of his sentence and turned around with a mean look on his face. Needless to say he didn't like being interrupted.

"This is Bert."

"Bert? Bert who?"

"Just came up from the minors last week. He's a utility outfielder. The running coach says he's the fastest guy we got on the team right now."

"Great! That's what I like to hear." Leo paused momentarily before motioning with his arm. "Get over here with Orville. I wanna see ya run."

Quickly the boys lined up near home plate. On the count of three Bob blew his whistle and they took off. After rounding second and half way to third, Bert finally touched the second base bag.

"Stop!" Leo shouted, waving his arm. "Get over here! Let's try it again!"

"I didn't think the new comer had it in him."

"Yeah! You're right Bob. I won't stand to have this tall thin creature make a fool out of one of our own—somebody already a part of the Cub organization."

Again they lined up near the plate. Bob raised his arm, counted to three, blew his whistle, and they were off. As Orville touched third base, Bert struggled getting to second."

"Stop!" Again Leo waved his arm. "That's it! Forget it! I've seen enough!" Anger started to take control of his mood. "I don't like to be out done!"

As they started to walk toward the dugout, suddenly they stopped. "Wait just a minute guys. I wanna see him hit."

"Oh?"

"Yeah! I don't know this guy. Gotta figure out how I will use him."

"The front office says he can hit, Leo."

"Yeah! Well seein' is believin'."

"OK, boss. Anything you say."

"Get me a pitcher out here, Billy. Then you get in left field. And while your at it, get me a couple more outfielders." He shouted from third base as Billy already entered the dimly lit tunnel.

"He doesn't look like he can hit much to me either, Leo." Bob always agreed with the headman regardless of the circumstances. "Look at 'em. Tall. Thin. Why I bet I can blow him over with one breath."

Orville stepped into the batter's box swinging a couple of bats and ready for the first pitch.

As if the ball had a pair of eyes, it left his bat and sailed toward the seats beyond the left field wall. More pitches and more balls into the empty seats. Not one ever touched the field.

"Stop!" Again Leo waved his arms as he stomped out toward the plate. "Never mind! I've seen enough."

Like following behind a drill sergeant in the army, they followed Leo toward the tunnel mumbling. "Hmm!"

"What's his name?"

"Orville!"

"Orville who?"

"Orville Hodge!"

"Who?"

"Ya know what I said!"

"Never heard of 'em!"
"Either have I!"
"Thought he couldn't hit!"
"That's what you think!"
"We'll see!"
"An unknown baseball player on our team!"
"Our team?"
"That's what I said!"

SIX

"Slowly I spun around in someone's fingers. Upside down. Right side up. Shifting back and forth. The world was in constant motion.

"When everything looked still, I felt two fingers grip the temples on my face and begin to squeeze like a vice holding a piece of wood. As the pressure increased I fell back slightly, only to be supported by a third finger that helped hold me in place.

"A breeze whipped in my face when I traveled over his shoulder toward his chest, where I was met by a baseball glove.

"Now I felt nice and cozy tucked away in the web of a pitcher's glove. Secure. Safe. It was the best place to be for the moment. Then, some fingers started to move me around again. Soon I was staring at the tough leather pressing against my face.

"Before long I was plucked out of my favorite spot and flipped back over this guy's shoulder. The wind shifted on my face when his arm reversed itself, thus bringing me forward again and back over that same shoulder. Finally, I was let loose, out of a pair of clause, and sailing on my own toward another baseball glove up ahead.

"I closed my eyes and twitched, knowing I was about to be trapped in a padded catcher's mitt, when suddenly, out of nowhere, I was hit by a piece of wood and sent into a different direction. So goes the life of a baseball."

The ball sailed toward the Cub dugout. Nothing stood in its way. It was a sharp hit that could take a player's head off.

This was a young man's game. A time all baseball players must stay alert less they encounter a serious injury. "Keep your eye on the ball. I heard it over and over again in the Clubhouse many times." One player remembered. "Don't allow yourself to be distracted."

The big right-hander quickly tossed his bat aside and started to race down the first base line. Staring only at the coach, who was jumping up and down while waving his arm, he picked up speed, thus hoping to beat out a cheap hit.

"Duck!" Tony screamed, as the ball traveled straight toward the guys. "No time to think! Duck!" The team crier cupped his hands close to his mouth as he quickly lowered his body into the pit.

Like a bunch of ants piled on a piece of cheese, everybody hit the floor. Continuing to sail undisturbed the ball hit the wall of the dugout before bouncing off the concrete apron and rolling back out on the field.

Slowly the more fortunate players got up, brushed off their jerseys, and returned to the bench. Moans from the wounded at the bottom of the pile limped into the Clubhouse.

"I didn't wanna move. Besides the scraps and bruises on my knuckles, my back ached. For the moment the pain didn't wanna leave me."

"Hey buddy! Let's go! Ya gotta get up. This game must go on." Two husky ball players walked toward Orville.

"All I could remember is a big shove. Then I was on the floor under the entire Cub team. I guess I just didn't move fast enough for these guys."

"OK, Al! You grab one arm and I'll get the other."

"Right on, Dale!"

"Before I could regroup my thoughts and get back into the game, I felt a pressure under my armpits as I was lifted up and placed back on the bench. Nobody stayed around any longer to soothe my wounds. To feel sorry for myself was out of the question."

"Thatta boy, Orville. Hang in there!" A fellow teammate tapped him on the knee as he passed by in the dugout.

It didn't take long for the other guys to lick their wounds, regroup, and get back into the ball game. A nod from the first base coach signaled for play to resume.

Frustrated, the Pittsburgh Pirate batter slowly wheeled around first base and trotted back to home plate.

It was Orville's first day in a Cub uniform. Having never been formerly introduced to the other guys, it wasn't long before he felt out of place.

Everybody on the team knew what they were suppose to be doing in the dugout except Orville. As a new comer, he knew nothing about The Shuffle, a pet name used to confuse their opponent's.

"Hey! That's my place. Don't sit there!" Number twenty-eight quickly moved toward a vacant spot on the bench. Before he realized where he was, Orville twisted and turned in search for another spot in the dugout.

Two other players stood up and placed their foot on the apron in front of the dugout. "Here's my chance." So the tall Boy from Indiana walked over to sit down. However, as he did so, all the guys on the bench scooted over on their butts to fill the vacancy. Through the early innings, Orville stood around, feeling like a fifth wheel, and more of a hindrance to the team than help.

As the game progressed, all the guys moved about like in a game of musical chairs. Intermittently different guys would either stand up, relocate on the bench, or spit on the ground. Orville remained puzzled. "Perhaps the object of a good joke." He mused.

"Bet your wonderin' what's going on around here." The deep voice with a southern brawl caught him off guard.

"Yeah! Lots of things goin' on here, not to mention out there on the field. I haven't been able to follow any of the game thus far."

"Maybe your not suppose to."

Orville felt tense and almost froze in his tracks. He didn't know how to respond to the voice.

"Relax kid! I'm Bob—, one of the coaches."

Suddenly Orville felt relieved. "Some one's finally takin' an interest in me."

"Look Boy! There's a reason why their doin' all that movin' around."

"Oh?" Orville was stumped and couldn't imagine what the coach would say next.

"Ya see those guys out there?" Bob pointed to the visitor's dugout.

"Ya mean the Pittsburgh—?"

"Yeah!" The coach rudely interrupted. " In the game of baseball we gotta tell our fielders and hitters how to play."

"Hah?"

"I mean tell 'em where to position themselves in the field or hit the next pitch or let it go by."

"Oh!" Orville grinned, thinking he now knew everything that was taking place.

"But! We can't let them know what we're thinkin'."

"So!" Again Orville looked puzzled.

"That's why the movin' around. Our boys have an assignment. Sammy, this is what you do—, Billy do this—, Bobby—, and so on and so forth." The coach tried to put Orville at ease.

"But how do they know what they're saying? I mean the message their giving." Orville was curious.

The coach chuckled. "Doesn't matter! They don't have to know. Just do what the boss says."

"Boss?"

"Yeah! You know! Leo! The manager!"

"Oh yeah!" The Boy grinned. "I know who he is."

"You betcha! And ya better do what your told or else your outta here." The coach looked at him straight in the eye.

"So how do I fit into all this?" Orville was reluctant to ask, fearing that the expectations of The Shuffle were suppose to be assumed.

"C'mere Boy! Here's what your suppose to do." Bob walked him over to the drinking fountain and pulled some notes on an index card out of his hip pocket.

"Da ya think these other guys care?" Orville started to have doubts about fitting in with all the other boys in the Club.

The coach nodded. "These boys already know where you be-long." Grinning. "The problem is you have to figure it out."

"OK boss! I mean coach! Shoot! Let's here it." The new comer started to feel more confident.

"Move around the bench. I don't care where. Anywhere you can find a place."

"But what if those guys push me out?"

"They won't! Just don't get too comfortable in one spot."

"Do you mean even if I just sit down for a second, if another spot opens up, move?"

Now ya got it, Boy!" The coach slapped Orville on his back. I knew ya'd catch on!"

"That's not hard to figure out."

"But that's not all. Ya gotta do other things."

"Oh?"

"Yep! Move around! Occasionally walk up and down the dugout. Scratch your right ear. Maybe your left. Stand up and im-mediately sit down again in the same place on the bench. Tie your shoe. There are lots of things you can do, Boy. Lots of things."

"I got it coach."

"But remember one thing." The coach pointed while motion-ing with his hand.

"What's that?"

"Don't do the same thing too many times in a row. Mix 'em up."

"Why?"

"Because if all your opponents see is you walking the path over and over again, they'll connect that to the batter, runner, or fielder. And for sure we don't want that to happen."

"Is it sort of like connecting the dots, coach?"

"Yeah! You could say that."

"Don't repeat!"

"Ya gotta repeat, Boy. Just not in a way that gives away all our moves."

"Right! I got it, coach."

It didn't take long for Orville to blend in with the boys. The Cub uniforms were a look-a-like. Only the numbers on the back of their jerseys distinguished them from each other. And, in the dugout they all looked like little pegs moving about on a checkerboard.

"And so here I sit warming the bench and watching the game, while my passion to play ball lingers. Sometimes I wish I were still back with the Boys on the Gold Coast."

SEVEN

"Hello baseball fans. Jack Quiland along with Lou Boudreau over WGN-radio—.

"Billy Williams quickly returned the ball to the infield. Don Kessinger, the Cub shortstop, wheeled and fired the ball to first base. Ernie Banks wasted no time throwing it across the diamond to third. Ron Santo side armed it to Beckert, standing close to the runner on second, and finally returned it to Kenny Holtzman, who was standing on the infield grass near the pitcher's mound. Now, with all their muscles loosened up, play resumed. "

Pete Rose stood on the bag motionless. Fans cheered, edging him on to steal third. The third base coach nodded his head and paced in the box, but the star player did nothing. For the moment the take sign wasn't on.

"Ladies and gentlemen, now batting number—, Lee May!" A loud voice blared over the PA system before lots of cheering fans and a standing ovation. The fans loved their Redlegs.

After swinging a couple of bats, Lee tossed one aside and

stepped into the batter's box. A couple more warm-up swings and he was ready for the first pitch. Likewise, Randy held up his mitt as a target while the ump leaned forward and looked over his shoulder, staring at the plate.

Kenny braced his legs with one foot on the rubber. Then, after bringing his hands together at his chest, he quickly turned his head to eye the runner behind him, before completing his wind-up and throwing the ball.

The excitement mounded as the fans followed the ball sailing through the air toward the plate. "It looks good!" The old timer mumbled to the misses sitting next to him, whom couldn't care less what he was saying. "Straight down the middle. If he knows what's good for him, he'd put some wood on it and end this game once and for all."

"I heard ya old man. I'm with ya. It's a good pitch." The fan on the other side of him interrupted.

"You're darn right. By the way my name's Barney." The old timer extended his hand.

"I'm Herald. Pleased to meet ya."

"Likewise I'm sure. The lady on my left over here couldn't care less 'bout a baseball game. Say's she goes with me just to keep me happy. Yeah! I'm glad someone understands what I'm talkin' 'bout, Harold."

"Yeah, well my partner over here has me walkin' all over the park."

"Oh?"

"Yeah! First it's popcorn! Then hot dogs. Now she's thirsty. I don't get much chance to watch the game."

"Sounds like what a lot of fans are goin' through, Herald." The old timers chuckled.

"So what's happening, Barney?"

"Pete's over there on second. Lee May is the batter—. Watch that pitch—." Just like a couple of old buddies, a mutual friendship developed at the ballpark, and they talked and talked and talked. People sitting close to them had doubts about just how much of their minds were in the game.

Lee kept his eye on the ball, twitched his fingers as he choked up on his bat, gesturing to swing. However, after deciding at the

46

last moment to let it go by, Randy quickly picked it out of his glove and fired the ball to Glen, racing toward second.

As the ball left the mound, Pete took off for third. Half way down the line, the coach held up his hands. Thus, the husky runner put on the brakes, as he slid on the ground. Quickly without another thought, he reversed his direction, as he scampered to his feet and raced back to second. The fans went ballistic with mixed emotions.

Meanwhile, the ball traveled toward second long before Glen Beckert ever got there. Then, out of nowhere as if timed perfectly, a glove reached out and caught the ball as it went over the bag. Quickly the second baseman lowered his arm to touch the base. Nobody else was on it till a couple of fingers circumvented the leather and burrowed its fingernails into the ground. "Safe!" The ump shouted the call so loud people heard it all over the ballpark without the aide of a microphone.

Leo Durocher wasted no time racing out of the dugout. Already Beckert and Kessinger were out there arguing with the ump when he arrived. Finally, Bob—, the coach pushed the threesome away, fearing an ejection from the game. Cheers changed to boos from the fans when the guys resumed their original positions on the field as the skipper returned to the dugout.

"To all you out there in radio land this, by no stretch of the imagination, is an exciting game. We wish you all could be—."

"That's right, Jack. A very close play. Certainly some head's up running by Pete Rose to avoid the tag."

"Thanks Lou. To all you fans just joining us, it's 3—3 in the bottom of the ninth. One out and a man at second."

Lee stood outside the batter's box and took a couple of warm-up swings. Then, after scanning the outfield, he stepped back into the batter's box. Remembering what the coach always said, he kept his eye on the ball. Meanwhile, Kenny did his best to make it difficult by manipulating the ball between his fingers hidden behind his left knee.

Squatting behind the plate, Randy Huntley displayed three fingers, then two, then four, and finally three again. From the mound, Kenny leaned forward and stared at the sign language, shaking his head either agreeing with or disapproving it. In the midst of all the noise in the ballpark, the fans weren't aware of the dialogue-taking place behind home plate.

"How's your mother, Lee?"

"Hah?"

"Is she still sick?"

"Don't know, Randy."

"Maybe feeling better these days?"

"Hah, Randy?"

"Your feet don't look good. Have ya been takin' care of 'em lately? Maybe ya oughta see a doctor, hah?"

"Hah?" Lee didn't want to chat. Full concentration was absolutely necessary to the batter.

"Did ya remember to get groceries on the way home?" Randy did his best to keep up with the nonsense chatter, hoping to throw the Redleg batter off guard.

"Wear clean socks everyday?"

"Yep!"

"What's wrong with your arm?"

"Hah?"

"Looks swollen. Did ya injure it swinging that bat? Maybe ya shouldn't be batting." The nonsense chatter was endless.

Once Kenny got the right sign, he went into an abbreviated windup and threw the ball. "Ball!" The ump gave the sign while the fans cheered.

Another pitch sailed near the plate. "Ball!" Again the ump put his hands together behind his back and turned to his right before a happy crowd of baseball fans.

The next pitch sailed straight toward the plate. Surely a strike until it veered to the inside of the plate. "Ball three!" The fans anxiously sat on the edge of their seats. "Ball three, strike one!" Mixed emotions echoed throughout the park while Lee stood like a statue in the batter's box.

There was nothing on the next pitch. No spin. No flutter. No arch in its path toward home plate. Just a slow moving junk ball that Lee connected with, thus bringing every baseball fan in the park to their feet. Eyes rolled following it into the seats behind the visitors' dugout. "Foul ball! Strike two! Full count!" Lee trotted passed the dugout where he was handed another bat.

Without wasting any time, Kenny quickly delivered another pitch that sent the batter racing toward first. "Ball four! Take your base!" The ump pointed to the bag.

Meanwhile, back in the dugout, a row of Redleg players bumped elbows with each other until it reached the last guy sitting next to Orville on the bench. "Grab a bat, Boy! Get on deck! Dave wants you to bat next!"

"Hah?"

"Dave!"

"Who?"

"The manager! That's who! Remember?"

"Oh yeah!"

"By the way, Boy!" Alex grabbed Orville's arm when he stood up. "What farm system did ya come through?"

"Hah?"

"Farm system!" Alex shouted above all the noise from the fans.

"Didn't!"

"What'd you say?" Alex looked puzzled.

"Got my start with the Boys on the Gold Coast!"

"Who?"

"Boys on the Gold Coast!" To be heard above the ballpark noise, now both players shouted.

"Who are they?" Alex was curious.

"Not much time to talk 'bout it now! Maybe later!"

"Good! OK!"

Orville walked up the steps of the Redleg dugout swinging a couple of bats. Shortly thereafter, he knelt in the batter's circle.

"Ladies and gentlemen! In the batter's circle, number—, Orville Hodge!" The familiar voice blared through the PA system. "Now batting! On your scorecard—!"

The fans were stun. No cheers. No boos. They watched in awe.

EIGHT

The cars were backed up on Rose Hill Road for as far back as the eye could see. Crawling along like a herd of turtles, it felt like the trip would take forever. Some folks doubted ever getting there. Even worse was the car that came to a sudden halt when the driver realized the traffic jam ahead.

Hoping to beat the crowd, a tall thin man parked his car by Todd's farm and started walking. "It wasn't much fun on a hot sunny day in ankle high, unlaced boots, but who felt like waiting around?"

Albert took big steps quickly moving at a great distance. The average person took three steps for every one of his. The ice-cold Boy Scout canteen felt good dangling against his leg, while the sweat drops rolled down his cheeks beneath a red and white bandanna underneath a hot sun. With his sleeves rolled up, he anxiously walked along, chewing gum, and passing up the long line of cars, entertaining thoughts in another world.

The folks living close to the forest preserves chose to walk, breathe fresh air, and enjoy the sunshine. From a distance the foot traffic looked like a long line of migrate workers or refugees desperate to leave a village behind. Thus, the crowd grew in numbers, congested the roadside, and made walking difficult.

"Where are all those folks goin'?" Roger asked, staring through his binoculars out the living room window of his farmhouse.

"Beats me, honey." Sophie sat in her stuffed armchair, more concerned about her knitting than what was going on outside. "Folks say there's somethin' goin' on down at the forest preserves."

"Well I'll be darn." Roger moved his binoculars back and forth to get a better look. "Gotta be somethin' good for all those folks to be goin' there."

Back on the road a scratched up bike without fenders and rusty handlebars cruised between the car line-up. And, keeping pace with the rising temperatures under a hot sun, drivers' tempers began to flare.

"Hey! Who ya think ya are, peddling that thing around here? This road's for cars, not you!" The angry driver rolled down his window and made a fist while sticking his arm out the window, ready to punch him.

"Harry!" Grace said, padding his knee during the long wait. "Don't be so hard on the kid."

"Poor guy! Huh! Scumbag! That's all he is."

"Harry!"

"Look at 'em! Moving along while we all sit here!"

As the crowd continued to grow cognitive skills suffered. Thought processes got blur. People were easily provoked. Angry feelings irrupted. Soon the conversations didn't make any sense at all.

The would-be hobo didn't pay much attention to the drivers either. In black tattered loose fitting pants and torn shoes, he cruised between cars. Scratching his beard and pushing the long strands of hair out of his face, he focused on getting to the forest preserves on time. For once in his life he had an advantage over driving a car.

Up ahead, closer to the front of the line, Dorothy sounded her horn. "C'mon!" The heavyset lady stuffed behind the steering wheel of her Dodge, shouted. "I had no idea it'd take this long."

In another car three ladies giggled, responding to a joke about Brother Andrew. Even the driver, Mrs. Crawford, adjusted her plumb body to look at the girls in the back seat. As the laughs got louder, no one heard Peggy mumbling over the sound of a horn in the car.

The ladies were all members of The Needle and Thread Sewing Circle, a club that met weekly in one of the member's home. Fellowship and giving to a local charity kept them busy and glued together. Several times each year they put their projects down and attended a social event. They were all senior citizens with a few widows in the bunch. Today they rushed to the forest preserves with three more cars full of giggling women following behind them.

The rock wobbled as it rolled along over the rough sandy-pebbled roadside. And when it stopped, with one swift kick by a tennis shoe, it rolled a few more feet in front of them.

"Johnny! Will you listen to me?" Patty, the short gal with the freckles dotting her face wearing pigtails, screamed. She talked about the last day of school and he wasn't listening. Instead, he focused on that rock while walking with the junior high class toward the forest preserves.

"When ya gona cut your hair, Patty?" A pretty blue-eyed brunette wearing bangs and a ponytail walked alongside her.

"Never, Linda!" Patty didn't like the comment and got angry. "My mother will never let me cut my hair. That's why I wear these stupid braids. Haven't ya noticed?"

"Well yeah, silly. I just thought it might be cooler to have short hair during the summer."

"Just because your hair is short, my mom doesn't think that everybody looks good with short hair. I've tried to tell her."

"Maybe my mom should say somethin' to her." Linda interrupted, in an attempt to calm her mood.

"Nooo! Thanks anyway." Patty motioned with her hands while tossing her head back and forth. "It's already been done. Let's just say I've tried and tried and tried, but to no avail. That's it! End of conversation."

"OK, Patty. I just wanted to—"

"No! That's it! End of subject! I don't wanna talk about it any-more."

"OK! I'm sorry." Linda was always use to having her own way. Changing her own hairstyle a couple of times a year was never a problem with her.

"Let's talk 'bout somethin' else."

"Is your mom still tryin' to lose weight?" Linda was always curious to know what other people were doing.

"Nope. Don't think so."

"Is she still fat?"

Patty turned around and stared at Linda. "Not any fatter than that lady pinched behind the steering wheel in that car over there." She pouted while pointing to one of the cars in the line up.

"Gee! That's too bad. She's such a nice lady too. It's a shame she has to carry so much weight around."

"She tried, but after a while just gave up tryin' to diet. I sup-pose it wasn't worth it to her. Ya know what I mean? It takes a lot of work to try and lose some weight."

"Well I wouldn't if I were her," Linda said, flipping her right hand up. "My mother's not exactly on the thin side either. I don't know what it is 'bout women. This body thing is always an issue. Ya know what I mean?"

"Yeah." After some more girlish chitchat, they focused on something else. "Hey Billy!" Billy was walking several feet ahead of the girls with Frankie, and paid no attention to them.

"See that tree over there?" Billy pointed.

"Yep! Frankie always felt stupid when they started talking about all the trees along the road.

"It's a big old Oak tree. Ya can tell by the shape of its leaves."

"I thought it was a Maple."

"No stupid. That's a Maple over there. Look at the way the leaves are shaped." Billy was a nerd. His nose was always in books. Trees fascinated him the most, and whenever he was out walking, he'd name off all the trees. His personality was his weakness.

Not too far behind the kids, Myrtle struggled with her picnic basket. "Brad! Get over here! It'd be nice if ya gave your mother a hand once in a while."

"Yes mom." The six-foot high school basketball player reluctantly grabbed it from her arm.

The basket was loaded with goodies for the Burns family. There were several packages of hot dogs for a hot grill. Potato chips and a large bowl of potato salad, mom hoped wouldn't spoil in the summer heat. There were paper plates, napkins, and plastic silverware to compliment the event.

Behind mama Burns was Elaine and Tommy, the youngest of the Burns clan, struggling with an ice chest full of sodas, along with some ketchup, mustard, and relish for the wieners.

Everybody was going to the forest preserves. There were more people than the entire Cedar Lane population attending this event. They must've come from the surrounding towns. News traveled fast. People have been talking about the big day for months.

A police officer directed traffic at the corner of route Thirty-Three and Rose Hill Road. Up ahead beyond Rose Hill Road, it stayed clear for miles. A driver could gas her up to fifty miles per hour. However, turning left the cars crawled like a herd of turtles.

A black Studebaker pulled up to the corner of the intersection and the driver rolled down his window. "What's goin' on here, officer?" Like many other drivers, it didn't take him long to get angry in the summer heat. "Why all these cars? Can't they get into the forest preserves? Is there a problem?"

Bending over to get a better look at the driver, the man in the blue uniform with well-creased pants and sparkling badge replied. "More cars than expected Sir. We had to re-route some of 'em so everyone will have a place to park."

The driver's anger started to escalate. "This is ridiculous. I've been baking out here for hours. There must be a better way. Wouldn't ya think so, officer?"

"Sorry Sir." The officer wearing badge number 2314 tipped his hat. "We're doin' the best we can."

Wheeling around, the policeman resumed his position at the center of the intersection. In a white shirt, blue uniform, and shining black shoes, he looked like a military soldier ready for inspection. Raising one hand, he signaled with the other for the inner lane to turn left. Then, while backing up, he motioned for the other lane to do likewise. Slowly, the cars moved cautiously along route Thirty-Three.

The big sign just to the right of the entrance read SHERWOOD FOREST. In smaller print underneath it read: A place for friends and family to gather for fun. View nature at its best and enjoy the outdoors.

Inside the forest preserves another officer continued to direct the traffic. Earlier the parking lot filled up quickly. Now, all the remaining cars lined up on the grass. The township provided red and white Willet buses to transport the overflow from other nearby lots.

Angry folks grabbed their lawn chairs and began the long walk. Through a path camouflaged by trees they paraded on winding curves, over creeks and running brooks, occasionally crossing the path of a squirrel or deer while birds flew above, till they approached a sidewalk. Now, distancing themselves from the trees and wild life, they knew the open fields weren't too far away.

Up ahead a police car was parked on the sidewalk. Leaning against the front right fender an officer stood with folded arms, smiling, watching the crowd go by.

Beyond him, not too far away, was a white Chevrolet sedan parked parallel to the police car, sparkling in the sun as if it just came off the assembly line or out of a car wash. Engraved on the front door was the ABC-TV logo. Further down the path curious folks saw a TV van.

Next to the van a generator on the back of a white truck with a huge fan nearly blew the folks away. Fed by a gasoline engine, it provided the necessary electricity to broadcast today's event. Long cables scattered across the landscape tightly secured to nozzles on the side of the vehicle, sent an electric current into a long RV without windows parked alongside.

The RV unit was the guts of the broadcasting team. Inside, a technician sat in front of many TV monitors, carefully manipulating a series of knobs on a panel. With a keen eye, he decided which angle shots would be eventually seen by millions of TV viewers. Meanwhile, on top of the van, a satellite dish rotated transmitting signals throughout the country.

"Fantastic!" A spectator mumbled, joining the crowd, pushing their way through to peek inside the truck. There was something intriguing about television equipment. A human change of police officers kept the curious at a distance.

From the RV was some coaxial cable, strung along the ground that met camera number one perched on a platform near the field. And, seated comfortably behind it, a technician manipulated three lenses zooming in on all the action.

"Mom! What's that?" A boy pointed to a black and white screen. Desperately, he tried to pull away from her so that he could get a better look.

A camera on a tripod with three different lenses, rotated very methodically, bringing into view different angles determined by a cameraman. And the children continued to gather around it, gawking at the spectacle.

From all the cameras circulated around the playing field, another technician back in the RV viewed several monitors. First there was a batter at close range. Then, another screen showed a picture of all the players on the field. Finally, following a fly ball, one monitor displayed an outfielder running very fast trying to catch it. A speaker in one corner of the room broadcast baseball fans cheering.

Behind home plate a mini-cam perched on a man's shoulder, aimed his lens at an announcer holding up a microphone, while asking the fans some questions.

"Where ya from, Sir?"

"Milwaukee." A man replied, with a potbelly in a white shirt and suspender's holding up his baggy pants.

"Milwaukee! Well great! We're glad ya came! By the way, where's that? Milwaukee, California?"

"Nope!" The man chuckled. "Milwaukee, Wisconsin."

"Good! Nice to see ya here. What brings ya to Indiana?"

"When I saw the Boys from the Gold Coast play the Chicago Cubs last year at Wrigley Field, I wanted to see them for myself."

"So here ya are!" The announcer continued to move the microphone back and forth between the fans and himself as he spoke.

"Yep!"

"Well good!" Soon he started walking along the first base foul line while the Boys warmed up in the background during batting practice. A TV camera followed him while another technician not too far behind assisted, holding an electrical chord.

"Hi lady! Why are you here?"

"I'm a baseball fan from way back. I always went crazy when my mom turned on the game. Now I'm different. I like baseball myself, and ever since I heard about the Boys playing the Chicago Cubs, I followed them around wherever they went."

"Well good!" The TV man held the microphone up close to his mouth, wearing a Paul Winshall style tattered hat.

Like a major event, the folks continued to gather on the field. There were thousands of them. The police had their hands full keeping people at a distance without designated markers on the field.

Meanwhile, the roving reporter continued to chat with all the fans along the foul line, as the momentum increased. Screaming. Laughing. Waving hands. It was hard for them to control themselves. And everybody wanted to be in front of the camera.

"My name is Jerry. I wanna be a baseball player someday just like those guys out there." Playing baseball like the Boys from the Gold Coast, and eventually be in the major league captured the hearts of all the kids.

"My dad says they're a bunch of good guys."

"We like baseball," Susie said, giggling to her friends while shrugging her shoulders. "I like Bill, the catcher. He's my kind of guy. He's got big muscles. Wow!" And the girls couldn't stop giggling.

"I like Stringbean." A brunette grinned from one ear to the other, blushing with blue eyes.

"Sir, I'm here from Carbondale, Illinois. What Pop did for those Boys should never be forgotten. Thank goodness for baseball."

After interviewing many fans, he walked away from the foul line, again with a TV camera on his trail along with a circle of friends, still talking to millions of TV viewers. "So ladies and gentlemen, we're here today, at Sherwood Forest, watching the Boys from the Gold Coast warmin' up for a game to be played later this week. Rest assured, we'll bring you all the play-by-play action. It was a great day in baseball history when Pop, a retired janitor, took it upon himself, to develop a baseball team against all the odds. Did ya ever think they'd be playin' the Cubs? That's what I said. . . And so . . ."

Along both foul lines police officers in navy blue uniforms and sparkling badges braced themselves to prevent the fans from running out on the field. Over two hundred policemen, many from other nearby towns, assisted with the traffic flow at Sherwood Forest. No thoughts of money, only baseball filled peoples minds.

Bill Sherick, in full gear, rested one knee on the plate. Then, first a curve ball, followed by a junk ball pitch, and finally a fastball, sailed into his mitt. The loud thud sound as it landed in his glove captured the hearts of many fans. Placing both knees on the ground, he quickly returned the ball back to the pitcher's mound with cheers in the background.

"Thatta way, Bill!" Pop, the coach, mumbled from the bench clapping his hands.

Next Larry, the team's power hitter stepped up to the plate. He loved to bat. Hitting the ball energized him. One mighty swing and the ball would be sailing into the bushes every time.

Without hesitation, Stringbean quickly brought his hands together at his chest. As they looked at the tall wiry figure, the fans entertained doubts as to whether the ball will ever reach the plate. However, after completing an abbreviated windup, and releasing the ball, the loud thud sound in the catcher's glove, convinced them otherwise, and all fears quickly vanished.

Larry hit several routine ground balls on the infield grass. At third, short, and second, the Boys scooped them up, judged their distance, and fired the ball across the diamond to first.

After awhile, hitting baseballs to the infield got boring, so Larry put something extra on each swing. Thus, fast rolling ground balls soon took funny hop's, causing the infielders to fumble easy plays. Fans, in awe, dropped their jaw watching them roll into the outfield.

As the Boys got frustrated trying to field the ball, Larry added more salt to the wound. "Ha! Ha! Ha!" He laughed. "I did it again."

"Good Boy, Larry!" Pop shouted, cupping his hands close to his mouth. "That's the way I like to see ya hit."

From the infield to the outfield, he continued swinging viciously, thus sending high fly balls to the different fielders. After a few routine hits that were easily caught, he started hitting the ball harder, sending it further, higher, and deeper into the outfield. Several of them got lost in the sun. The fans tried to shield their eyes with their hand, but to no avail. Soon they started landing in the bushes. The fielders scrambled, like searching for gold, only to come out of the woods empty handed, looking stupid.

"Not so hard, Larry!" John shouted from the bench. "Let those guys catch 'em." During batting practice all Pop wanted was for the outfielders to get a feel of running and catching baseballs.

"Never mind, John!" Pop looked at him before walking out to the mound. After giving the signal, Darrell tossed his jacket down in the bullpen, and trotted out to join him and Stringbean. Following the usual chitchat the ball traded hands and play resumed.

Bringing his hands together at his chest, Darrell kicked his right leg up high before throwing a fastball. Several more stinging fastballs caught Larry off guard, swinging viciously and missing all of them. Soon the outfielders were bored. Eyelids got heavy. They yawned. Even the fans grew restless and started chanting. "Action! Action! Action! We want more action!"

"Let up! Gotta let 'em hit a few!" Pop repeated his intentions several times while clapping his hands, standing in front of the bench.

Though Darrell loved to challenge the hitters with his fastball, Pop's suggestion left no choice but for him to slow down. So he mixed up the pitches. Slow ball, curve, and straight nothing pitch, Larry was forced to change his hitting style. Soon the ball started to fly into different directions again, challenging the fielders, and arousing the fans.

A fan sitting in the front row above the Boy's dugout had his transistor radio blasting. "And so baseball fans, this is your old friend Buzz back here at the microphone." The chummy flattop redhead loved to gab. "This is live baseball over the American Broadcasting Network. It's the bottom of the sixth, 3-2 red-bands over the blue-caps."

Meanwhile, back on the farm Orville's mom kept busy in the kitchen making lunch. In a hot skillet, melted butter sizzled around a cheese sandwich, getting brown on both sides.

"Afternoon, Lizzie." Uncle John greeted her as he walked in from the barn.

"Gotta wash your hands before eatin'." She waved a spatula in his face warning him to never sit down for a meal without first washing his hands. Mama was the only one who had control over the crabby old man. Lizzie always had mixed feelings about standing up to Uncle John. Often she was forced to accept his condescending attitude toward Orville because he provided a roof over their head.

"Oh woman! Ya always bug me 'bout somethin'." He moaned while walking over to the sink.

Before long, Lizzie had a plate full of grilled cheese sandwiches on the table next to a hot bowl of tomato soup. After rinsing her hands and wiping them on a towel looped through the refrigerator handle, she joined them.

"Hey! Where's Orville?" Uncle John always expected everything in place when he entered the room. The sarcastic tone in his voice displayed a troubled king.

"I thought he was on his way down, John." Lizzie quickly stopped what she was doing to look around the room.

"Your brother is always late." He gave Ann an evil stare. "It's a good thing his head is connected to his shoulders." His sarcasm continued to dominate the conversation. The family froze in their tracks with fear and trembling whenever he spoke. Often they wondered if he ever really enjoyed life.

Ann remained quiet, shrugging her shoulders. She knew that children were to be seen and not heard. "Why bother talking?"

"Hi mom! Hi Unck! Orville interrupted, barging into the kitchen smiling, concealing his true feelings.

"Well it's about time." Uncle John continued to dominate the conversation as if Orville wasn't even there. "Prices goin' up all the time in the stores. Sure wish we'd get some of the money."

"Eli, down the road says farmin' ain't fun anymore."

"He should talk. Welcome to the club, Eli." Uncle John mumbled while sipping some soup. "Where are the crackers? Ya know I always like crackers with my soup."

"Old man Perkins gotta lot of sick chickens." Lizzie tried her best to humor him along, responding to his small talk while looking at the newspaper.

Uncle John loved to hear himself talk and paid no attention to her. "Somethin' always goin' wrong. If it ain't a leak in the roof, it's the tractor. If it ain't the tractor, it's electric wires in the barn or a broken window. Always somethin' to fix." Startled. "Hey wait a minute. What's that? What's that noise I hear?"

"It's the radio, John."

"Weather today will be in the 80's. Sunny. Hot. Sounds like a good day for a swim. And now . . ."

"Who turned the radio on?" Uncle John complained. "Turn it off. I want some peace and quiet around here." That's the understatement of the year coming from a man who likes to talk.

"Your niece, Ann turned it on. She probably was lookin' for some music."

Uncle John mellowed when Lizzie mentioned Ann. He was always more patient with her than with Orville. Consequently she got more freedom than her brother, to do what ever she wanted to do around the house.

"And now for sports. This is KYZ radio, 660 on your radio dial. Today, thousands of baseball fans have gathered here at Sherwood Forest to watch the Boys from the Gold Coast. It's a pregame warm up session before the big game actually takes place later this week. The police stay busy keeping the crowd back. Lots of excitement goin' on for everybody."

"Gotta go! Thanks for the lunch." Orville wiped his mouth with a napkin before excusing himself from the table.

"Wait a minute, Boy! You're not done yet!"

"Sorry Unck! Gotta go!" Nervously, he rushed upstairs to his room.

"No! You don't talk to me that way. I'm not done with ya yet!" Uncle John pushed his chair back away from the table and stood up. "Get back here this minute." He never liked being out of control. Power plays in the family were frequent.

"Let 'em go, John!" Lizzie said, compassionately. "Just this one time, let him be."

"Let him be nothing! I'm the boss 'round here. What I say goes." Leaving the table, he quickly limped up the stairs after him.

Uncle John struggled to open a locked bedroom door. It wouldn't budge. After mumbling a few cuss words under his breath, he limped back down the stairs and into the kitchen.

The thin transparent drape flopped in a breeze on the window upstairs in the tiny bedroom. Inside, no Orville. Outside, he scampered down a drain pipe, like a prisoner escaping jail for a quick get-a-way, as if his life depended upon it.

Quickly, quietly, he unlatched the padlock on the door. Then, with his eyes quickly moving back and forth searching for the enemy, he took his JC Higgins bike out of the shed. Soon, with no thought for tomorrow, he was peddling down a hill, over the creek, and on his way to Sherwood Forest, traveling as fast as the wheels on his bike could carry him.

Leaving the farm behind, he rode down the street, crossed a main intersection toward O'Leary's farm. Up a long driveway, he cut through a grassy field before entering the woods with a lot of tall trees. As a homespun kid, he knew every turn in the path. Out on the other side of the woods, he peddled on a sun-baked highway, turned sharply on Rose Hill Road, traveled a short distance, and saw the big sign that read Sherwood Forest.

Thousands of people stood around, making it nearly impossible to get close to the Boys from the Gold Coast. Riding along on the sidewalk, Orville saw a Paul Winshall style hat resting on top of a broom handle, leaning against the ABC-TV RV, and a sport jacket on a hook alongside it. That gave him an idea. First, he ditched his bike back in the woods. Then, he tiptoed up to the van and put on the jacket and hat. Luckily, tucked into the ribbon surrounding the two inch brim was a press sign in big, black, capital letters against a white background that no one was sure to miss. Next to the big white truck was a microphone on a long chord. Now, his appearance was complete.

"Hello Buzz! I had no idea you look like that up close." A red headed lady smiled, wearing jeans and a red and white plaid blouse, unbuttoned to create a large V-neck collar and broadly expose the dibble between her breast. The tall thin Boy with the southern accent in broken English appeared out of character for a well-known TV personality. Tickled to be up close to Buzz, she was anxious to be interviewed. "Where's the camera? Will people see me on TV?" She giggled.

"Ah! Yes ma'am. Camera will be comin'. Meanwhile I'd like to ask ya-you a few questions." Pretending to be a TV personality, Orville often stuttered for the right words before the interviewee.

Immediately, goose bumps went down her spine as she wiggled her behind giggling, feeling silly. "Oh Buzz! Me? You gonna ask me some questions?"

"Yep! Yes ma'am." Orville fumbled around for a note pad. Finally, he pulled a brown paper bag out of his hip pocket, smoothed out the wrinkles, and folded it to give it a more sophisticated appearance. During the interview lots of people gathered around him, gawking.

"Ask away, Buzz! I'm ready."

"Let's start with ya-your name." His poor grammar didn't go over very well for a TV commentator. "Please tell these folkspeople your name." He corrected his speech several times during the interview, hoping she wouldn't notice. Getting panicky, he searched for a pencil in the pocket of his jacket.

"Lookin' for something, Buzz?" Staring up at his face, a little boy tapped his knee.

"Thought—I thought I had a pencil. But I must've lost it." Orville's eyes nervously rolled through the crowd.

"My mom gave me this." The boy held up a white number two lead pencil decorated with circus colors wrapped around it. "She said I should sit quietly and draw pictures while she watched the Boys play baseball. Here! You can have it." With a twinkle in his eye, standing on his toes, he stretched his short arm to give it to Orville.

"Thank you, boy. What's your name?"

"Richard. My friends call me Ritchie."

"That's a nice name, boy. I mean Ritchie." Tickled to death to be talking to a TV personality, the shy little boy grinned from one ear to the other, before running away and getting lost in the crowd.

"My name is Becky, Buzz!"

"Hello Becky! Where do ya—you come from?"

"I live in Crown Point. Not too far from here."

"Well good! And why are ya here today in Sherwood Forest?"

"Like everybody else, I come to see the Boys all the folks are talkin' 'bout. I wanted to see for myself."

Orville frantically wrote down every word she said along with several other peoples comments whom he interviewed. Then, most of the folks got lost in the crowd. So Orville got up closer to the baseball diamond without a TV camera and watched the game. Gawking, with his eyes ready to pop out of his head, he saw Bill Sherick squatting behind home plate wearing shin guards, a breast protector, facemask, and a catcher's glove.

"Hey Boy! Get away! You're too close to the line." A police officer saw him sitting just a couple of feet behind Bill. The thrill of catching fastballs, while dropping to his knees, and quickly returning them to the pitcher's mound, fascinated Orville.

Watching the pitcher going through all the motions before throwing the ball also intrigued him. "Maybe I can be a pitcher some day just like him." Dreaming of grandiose thoughts was his specialty. "The pitcher leaned forward, shook off some signs, brought his hands together, kicked his leg up high into the air, and threw the ball. "Strike!" The umpire shouted. "You're out!" Then the batter threw down his bat and walked away angry. The fans cheered." It was fun to dream.

The more Orville saw, the more he liked, and there was so much to see. A ball quickly sailed around the infield. High fly balls tested the Boys skills. A pair of hands scooped up a speeding fastball at short and fired it to first, beating the runner only by inches. Cheers echoed throughout Sherwood Forest.

Ever since their debut at Wrigley Field, the Boys from the Gold Coast traveled on many goodwill tours throughout the Midwest, bringing lots of cheer and excitement to many people. Now, invited to play the Cedar Lane Wolves, it will be a day to remember.

NINE

Like being in a palace adorned with all its riches before the Queen, the room had tall ceilings with peach colored walls, fancy chandeliers, tall windows and expensive draperies. White tablecloths' on round tables with elegant flowered china and sparkling silverware dotted the floor. Red and white wines filled glasses to overflowing. Hot dinner rolls wrapped in a towel in baskets made everybody's mouth water. A delicious salad mixed with lettuce, tomatoes, cheese, and other greens was a veggie lover's delight. And on each plate were mashed potatoes smothered in gravy alongside a juicy slice of roast beef, and mixed vegetables of peas and carrots. Coming up, dessert, a rich cream cheese cake covered with a strawberry syrup. Surely, it was a meal fit for a king.

The room was filled with the rich and famous, along with the media. Every major newspaper was there like the Washington Post, New York Times, and Chicago Tribune along with others from the west coast, and they all stayed busy with a pad and pencil in hand. Every major league baseball franchise was also well represented along with some politicians from the Washington, D.C. area.

As waitresses, wearing a black dress, white laced apron, and hair piece, stayed busy serving each table, they all moved about cautiously, being careful not to trip over any of the electrical chords that stemmed from the center of the room, where a C-Span camera and operator remained perched on a small platform. A mini-cam followed another man around holding a microphone, eager to interview key personalities.

In the front of the conference room was a distinguished list of celebrities at the speaker's table. Like old friends who hadn't seen each other for many years, they talked, thus adding to the chatter that already filled the room, till the host tapped his water glass, seeking everybody's attention, hoping to introduce the celebrities.

"Ladies and gentlemen." He paused till the room got quiet. "May I please have your attention?"

With lunch coming to a conclusion, all eyes now focused on their host. One lady dapped her mouth with a napkin. Another sipped some water. Still, another stuffed her mouth with the last dinner roll that nobody else wanted. And so everybody got comfortable, ready to hear a great speaker.

"Thank you, ladies and gentlemen. My name is Ron Overly, and I'll be your host for the remainder of this meeting." Dressed in a navy blue suit with a red and blue stripped tie against a well starched white shirt, the man with the George Gobel flat top, drew the attention of his audience.

"Before introducing our special guest, I'd like you all to meet the people up here with me at this table. First, to my far left is Ms Keely Smart, president of the LSAA, Ladies Sports Association of America." The guest applauded.

"If you'd please hold your applause till the end, we'd very much appreciate it. That way we can save some time and get to our special guest, which I'm sure you're all anxious to hear."

Silence resumed throughout the room. It was so quiet that a person could hear a pin drop.

"Thank you. To Ms Smart's right is Joyce Kramer, outstanding reporter with the New York Times. To her right, and the left of our podium is Mr. Peterson, our speaker. We'll talk more about him in a moment. On the other side of me, to my far right is Jack Luker, president of the American Broadcasting Association (ABA), and to his left Jerry Saltzman, president of our Club."

Following the introductions, the guest applauded while a mini-cam scanned the room. Candid shots caught one person yawning. Another person rested her chin, cupped in her hand supported by her elbow, on the table. One lady picked up her napkin that slid off her lap. Bored faces struggled to stay awake and keep their attention on the upcoming main event.

"Ladies and gentlemen, on behalf of The National Press Club, I'd like to welcome you, invited guest. And now, our speaker, Mr. Peterson, needs no real introduction. A retired janitor turned baseball manager, overnight developed a Boys' baseball team that eventually played the Chicago Cubs at Wrigley Field. Through much resistance the team survived. The Boys love him, and like a father, started calling him 'Pop'. Never having any kids of his own, he preferred it. Now, known the world over, they do goodwill tours, bringing joy and happiness to many people, thus drawing large crowds wherever they go. I know your anxious to hear his story, so without any further ado, ladies and gentlemen, I proudly present to you, Mr. Peterson, better known as 'Pop'."

Rising to his feet, the fifty-eight year old, five feet eight inches tall man, with long black hair, some strands of gray, and a pot-belly, slid his chair back and moseyed on over to the podium to a standing ovation from everybody in the room. Applauding with tears rolling down their cheeks, others smiled while experiencing goose bumps running down their spine. Not too long ago, many recalled how out of a heart filled with love, he started something with a group of Boys at a time when organized youth baseball didn't exist.

"Thank you. Thank you." He tried to get a word in edgewise while holding up his hands. The applause wouldn't stop. Finally, after Ron moved up to the microphone and begged them to cooperate, they settled down.

"I thank you for that hardy welcome. You are all most kind. However, I'm not sure that I'm deserving of it." He paused to look at all the different faces around the room. "When I see you all dressed up in your Sunday goin' best, I'm not sure I'm in the right place." The audience laughed. "Yep. That's right. Gentlemen in pin strip suits. You ladies decked out in the prettiest dresses I've ever seen. Pinks. Blues. Lace. Nice." More laughs. Everybody enjoyed a good laugh once in awhile. "I had to do some diggin' myself, in my closet back home, lookin' for a suit to wear to this occasion. Finally, the misses found this old tattered brown and white sport jacket. She insisted that I buy these blue slacks. Pretty good, a? Especially since most of my clothes were hand-me-downs to begin with." More laughs irrupted from the crowd.

"I've often heard it said that it's not what you know, but who you know, that makes you successful. Think about that one for a moment. Except for all the professionals like medical doctors, lawyers, teachers, and preachers, to mention only a few, our colleges and universities really promote the idea that a person's credentials aren't complete until he or she has a college degree. Ya never hear them say anything 'bout who ya know as paramount to success. Yet, though a person's credentials may be impressive, without getting someone to like you, you can wait till the cows come home before they get the big break." Immediately a mixture of moans and groans along with some cheers from the guests filled the room.

"But what is success? Financial security? Home? Lots of new clothes? No pun intended." The guests chuckled. "All the food you can eat? Oh yes, I almost forgot. A new car? Lots of new cars parked in your driveway?

"Or is the key to success the silver spoon theory? Do ya know what I mean? You're already part of a wealthy family." The audience looked puzzled. Some questioned his comments. "Yes. That's right. Doesn't money buy everything? Or, you already have a celebrity status. Think about it. You may be a nobody, but your father is President of the United States. I think with those credentials, you'll be well received just about anywhere you go for the rest of your life.

"There's a myth in our society. Have a silver spoon in your mouth and you're quickly on your way up the social ladder. Or, with celebrity status, there's no turnin' back. Your on your way to the stars." The crowd chuckled. "Doesn't it all sound nice?"

Scanning the audience with his eyes, Pop wanted to set the record straight. "Not everybody was lucky enough to claim celebrity status for themselves before they made it big. A good example of this is the former mix master salesman who energized the fast food industry by selling hamburgers. Or the chicken king whose secret recipe became popular all over the world. Or the horseless carriage, developed in a backwoods garage that eventually set the pace for our modern day automobile. Lots of things came from common folks with humble beginnings just like you and me.

"So what ever happened to the average guy? Where are they? I heard a friend of mine once say; "God must've found favor with the average guy because He made so many of them." The audience grinned, but remained silent. "When I think about it, I agree. And that's what the Boys from the Gold Coast are all about, average people like you and me."

After taking a deep breath and a sip of water while continuing to scan the room with his eyes, Pop resumed his presentation before all the Club members. "Without boring you all to death, and you've been a good audience so far, and I thank you for that, I wanna give you a brief run down of just who these Boys are.

"Darrell McDaniel. Nothing special about him. He was the average kid on the block who loved to throw his tennis ball against the garage wall in his backyard. It was a ten-foot high wall that joined a four story building on one side and a coach house on the other.

"When his chores were done, he often frequented his favorite spot in the backyard, and threw his ball against the garage wall to his heart's content. Anxiously, while throwing the ball, he dreamed that he was a star baseball player. There wasn't anything he couldn't do. Strike out pitcher, the fans cheered every time he threw a strike. Easily he fielded ground balls to the shortstop, and threw out the runners. Pop-ups were easy outs. It was fun to dream.

"I wish I could tell ya more about Darrell folks. However, time would not permit me to do so." Pop looked at his watch.

"Bill Sherick was a superb catcher with an attitude problem. He was tough, spoiled, and very stubborn. Often it was hard to get through to him and offer some practical advice. Experience was his best teacher.

"The car coughed and sputtered when he turned the ignition on and gave her some more gas before she got quiet and started purring like a kitten. The noise aroused a spectator upstairs who stuck her head out the bedroom window. Hey Bill! Where ya goin'?

"As the big white Cadillac backed out of the driveway, Bill motioned with his hand that he was going to meet the Boys on the Gold Coast. Then he said to his mother that he was going to play ball with them. His loud voice echoed throughout the neighborhood.

"In time with a lot of hard work, patience, and some practical guidelines, Bill Sherick became our team catcher, and a good one at that. Even though it was hard to warm-up to him, eventually he was well liked by all the Boys.

"Mike Foster, our shortstop, has a great pair of hands. Coming from the south, his parents struggled up here. However, willing to persevere, Mike joined our team, and eventually the whole family got more comfortable. Hurray for Mike! Three cheers for Mike." The audience applauded.

"Larry, who loved to hit the long ball, got Mr. Lucas mad by hitting baseballs on the green canopy of his store, across the street from the school. Finally, he got so angry one day that he had the Boys kicked out of the schoolyard.

"Poor, rich, tall, and short, they were a great bunch of guys. The schoolyard was a melting pod that brought all that talent together, and a baseball team was formed." Pop took a deep breath and paused momentarily to regain his thoughts. "I can still recall the day I saw them in the schoolyard, and other events that led up to organizing a Boys baseball team."

Coffee cups clashed with saucers as people sipped their favorite beverage so that they could get re-energized. The waitresses stayed busy placing coffee pots on every table. And jaws slowly munched on desserts while Pop continued his presentation.

Back home, the sound of the dial tone was heard as Larry put his finger into the slot, started to dial the number, and mumbled to himself. "Lincoln nine, six, eight, nine, oh. L as in lady . . ."

The dial quickly returned to its original position.

"I as in iron . . ."

Again the dial returned to its original position.

"Nine . . ."

He almost lost it when his finger got stuck in the slot, allowing the dial to reverse itself and go back around. Finally, six, eight, nine, oh, and his dialing was complete. Then, anxiously he waited for the phone to ring. "Ah, at last it's ringing."

On the other end of the line it rang three times before a grumpy voice of a lady in her late thirties answered it. "Hello!"

"Hello, Mrs. McDaniel?"

"Yes, speaking."

"Mrs. McDaniel. Hi I'm Larry. Is Darrell there?"

"Yes." She answered short and abrupt before placing the receiver down. "Darrell!" No response. "Darrell, are ya there?" Again there was no response until she called a third time, cupping her hands close to her mouth.

"Yeah! Whatta ya want?"

"Telephone!"

While waiting, Larry heard the rustling of somebody moving about before a screen door opened and slammed shut. Then, more footsteps that kept getting louder and louder till somebody lifted the receiver. Heavy breathing followed as if somebody had been running the hundred-yard dash and was out of breath.

"Hello!"

"Darrell, old buddy! How ya doin'?"

"Great! Whose this?"

"Larry, old buddy!"

"Oh yeah! Ya sound different over the telephone. Whatta ya want?"

"Wonderin' what your doin' today. I'm bored. Thought maybe we could get together with a few other guys down at the schoolyard and hit a few."

"Yeah! Sounds good to me!" After taking a deep breath. "Gotta get outta here anyway. My old lady's driven me crazy."

"Great! I'll call Greg. You …"

It wasn't long before a group of teenage Boys gathered at the schoolyard. With school out for the summer, it was a favorite hangout for all the kids.

By a wrought-iron fence, chest high, some girls played catch tossing a pink rubber ball around, while other kids played some games. Maggie chased Michael in a game of tag, while another fellow shot baskets through a hoop. A tennis ball kept rebounding off the school wall into a baseball glove. To a song, a girl jumped rope while her friends spun it faster and faster. Other kids joked around and watched all the activities. There was so much to do at the schoolyard.

The school was located on a corner lot with the yard at one end and facing a series of apartment buildings across the street. An adjoining street was lined with little shops that were the furthest point from the school wall. There was a tailor shop, grocery store, shoemaker, and drugstore. Each shop had its dark green canopy down that day to provide a shield against the hot sun.

At the far end of the schoolyard, a group of Boys played baseball. Actually they were having fun at batting practice and fielding.

"C'mon Larry!" Darrell got impatient, standing on the pitcher's mound with his hands firmly placed on his waist.

"Be cool man! Gotta get the right bat!" Larry handled five different bats neatly lined up on the ground, being fussy, selecting just the right one in size and weight. Finally, he chose a Louieville Slugger. A bat so big it looked like something Fred Flintstone the TV cartoon character used to club a bear in the woods.

Standing near a makeshift cardboard base, while taking a couple of warm-up swings, Larry was ready to play ball. "OK Darrell! Let's see the ball!" And when a fastball went sailing toward him, he swung, sending it high into the sky over second base.

"I got it! Back off you guys." Tony's eyes were almost in his forehead leaving only the white showing, as he stared up at the ball, while pounding his glove. And so baseball practice just began.

Larry stood in the batter's box swinging his bat while Darrell pitched to him. He was a strong boy and placed the ball perfectly into every field.

"C'mon Darrell!" Larry took a couple more warm-up swings. "Pitch the ball."

Then Darrell went into an abbreviated windup and threw the ball. As it traveled toward the plate, Larry lined a deep fly ball into left field. The fielder kept his eye on the ball, trotted forward a couple of feet, positioned himself, and caught the ball. Quickly, he threw it to the cutoff man at short, who wheeled around and threw it back to Darrell on the mound.

Batting was Larry's favorite position. As Darrell pitched, Larry sent them sailing through the air into the outfield. And, after catching them the outfielder returned them to the infield.

Then, Larry slowed up on his swing and started hitting ground balls to the infield. Repeatedly, he hit the ball to Tony at second base, whom scooped them up like an old pro and threw to Greg covering first base. Occasionally the ball took a funny bounce off his bat and popped up high into the air before landing in a glove at third.

Time went by quickly and before long the Boys completed two hours of practice. Now, they wanted to have some fun. So Larry walked up to the plate with a bat taking a couple of warm-up swings. Then, he stood very still, like a statue in the batter's box, concentrating very hard on every pitch.

Meanwhile, Darrell wiped the sweat off his forehead and looked around before stepping back on the mound. Then, after going into the usual windup, he threw several pitches.

On the first pitch, Larry lined a sharp hit grounder through the infield out into left field. The catcher positioned himself on the plate when he flipped off his facemask to catch the next ball that sailed high into the air. After several more swings, Larry settled down and started hitting ground balls and fly balls more consistently.

Larry liked to hit deep fly balls to the outfield. He loved to challenge the fielders, send them deep, and pin them against the fence. Several balls sailed out of reach of any fielder. Soon they started to land on the green canopy of the little shops across the street.

Mr. Lucas, owner of the general store, got angry and came stomping out waving a broomstick. "I told you guys not to do that again!"

Some of the Boys tried to apologize, but he wouldn't listen. Instead, he went back into his store and called the police. Moments later a squad car rolled up to the schoolyard. Two police officers got out of their car and approached the Boys, who had resumed play. When they saw them coming they quickly scattered.

All eyes at The National press Club remained glued on Pop. It was so quiet that not even a church mouse could be heard stirring if there were one there. Only the sound of a cup placed back on a saucer was heard occasionally after a visitor sipped some coffee.

"I was standing near the fence, Pop continued, resting my forearms on the crossbar between the spokes, watching the Boys when the police arrived. Yeah, they scattered like a bunch of scared rabbits in all directions. Later, when I was completing my routine walk, I stumbled across them by Esther's School Store. Naturally, with my curiosity up, I stopped to chat. The usual moans and groans went around the circle. "Yep! We're just a bunch of bad Boys." Greg chewed his bottom lip while staring at the ground.

"No one understands us." Tony concurred.

"Isn't that great! Here we are with nothin' to do, but play baseball, mind our own business, get into trouble, and can't do anything right." Bud summarized their feelings. Soon the chatter escalated till everybody was talking at the same time. A disturbing noise echoed throughout the neighborhood. Then, silence when they saw Pop coming.

"Hey guys! How ya all doin'?" Pop asked, smiling.

Silence followed. They didn't know what to say. Finally, avoiding direct eye contact with Pop, one of them hesitantly replied in a sarcastic tone. "Oh we're just fine."

"I saw a cop car at the schoolyard today. Before I could turn around and see what happened, you guys scattered like a bunch of wild bumblebees."

"Pop. Old man Lucas is on our case again. He doesn't like Larry hitting baseballs on his canopy. So he caused a big stink. Now we can't play baseball in the schoolyard anymore." Tony finally got up enough courage to tell the whole story.

After more conversation Pop suggested that they meet the next day. Sure enough, they all showed up at Esther's with a sack lunch, got into Pop's Ford wagon, and took off.

Still glued on the guest speaker at The Press Club, Pop continued to share the history of the Boys baseball team while maintaining good eye contact with his audience.

"And so, that was the beginning of the Boys on the Gold Coast. We worked hard. We learned new techniques. Improved on old ones. And, I must say, through lots of sweat and tears, it was fun.

"But that's not all. Sorry to say, we did meet with some resistance. Not everybody was happy with what we were doing."

The Press members stayed spellbound, and listened very intensely to what Pop was saying. A grievance was filed in the local community and the twelve-member committee of the Parent Neighborhood Association (PNA), met at the local school to decide its fate. All members were present.

Mrs. Dawson, chairwoman, presided at the meeting. Soon Mr. Webb, the vice chairman joined her, and Mrs. Clark, secretary, on the platform of the small meeting room. Quickly she tapped the podium with her gavel.

"Ladies and gentlemen! We very much appreciate your coming here today to deal with this very important matter." Mrs. Dawson, in her shaky high pitch voice and serious look on her face, immediately caught their attention.

Everyone stared at the lady standing behind the podium. For the moment no one knew about the agenda. All they knew was that they received a personal telephone call from Mrs. Clark, an important meeting had been called, and it was necessary that they attend. The sad facial expressions denoted the apprehensive feelings of each member present.

After the roll call, the room was completely silent. Occasionally the sound of paper shuffling was heard as Mrs. Clark took notes at the meeting.

"All people are present and accounted for." Mrs. Dawson acknowledged the results of the attendance when the secretary handed her a piece of paper. "We shall now proceed to here the minutes from our last meeting."

Almost instantly, as if without warning, the room filled with a lot of commotion. Everybody shuffled their chairs around and started talking simultaneously.

A few minutes later the room was quiet once again. And, following some friendly suggestions from some of the members, they decided to skip with the reading of the minutes.

So, very carefully, Mrs. Dawson put on her wire-rim glasses, looked around the room at all the familiar faces, and started to speak. "Mr. Lucas has brought it to my attention that the Boys baseball team has been hitting their baseballs on the green canopy that hangs over his storefront window. He goes on to say, as I glance at his letter, that he warned the Boys several times to stop, but they didn't. Therefore, he asked that in the best interest of the community, the Boys baseball team be discontinued and not allowed to play any more ball."

The members had mixed feelings. Some folks were outraged. Other people concurred that they should be banned from the neighborhood. One lady refused to let her boy play anymore ball with all those rascals. Soon all the ladies started to voice their disapproval to this outrageous act by mumbling among themselves.

Other complaints followed as Mrs. Dawson continued to read the grievances. There was too much noise in the neighborhood. The Boys weren't returning home for dinner on time. And, some of the Boys pestered their mom for a new baseball glove. The lists were endless.

As the meeting continued, more people entered the room eager to hear Pop, who was invited to attend by the PNA members. Angry feelings toward him escalated. It was easy to point a finger at someone else. Finally, the vote, and in the end when the folks gave it more thought, after allowing their temper's to cool, the Boys won an uphill battle. The next day newspaper headlines read: BOYS BASEBALL TEAM CONTINUES; ANGRY MOB LOSES; POP GETS VICTORY.

An arousing applause followed with a standing ovation by all the Press Club members. Some voiced their feelings while others backed them up with opinions of their own. Meanwhile, Pop watched as his eyes welled up with tears. Briefly, he smiled, hoping to cover up his emotions. And when silence resumed, he continued his presentation.

"We didn't have youth baseball teams in the community in those days. So, naturally our get-to-gather was very important to each one of us.

"The Boys were no different than you and me. They were the average kid on the block. Not afraid to get dirty or play with splintered bats and tattered baseballs. Corner lots were their home. A broken fence separated them from an alley. Cardboard from an old box served as bases. No fancy uniforms.

"They were a great bunch of guys. They were special. I wish I could take every one of the boys and girls in the neighborhood, and put them on the team. I loved them all. But that wasn't possible.

"Mark, Tom, Greg, Jack, and the list goes on. We met in Lincoln Park, located in Chicago, Illinois, on the edge of the Gold Coast. Everyday we did our best to develop the team. Beneath a hot sun, sweating in T-shirts, jeans, and tennis shoes, they played. Reluctantly sometimes, while like a piece of cake at other times, they learned techniques in batting and ball handling. Tempers flared even though they remained the best of friends. It was always a welcome sight to sit under a shade tree, sip ice-cold soda and swap jokes, and other stories. Looking back on it now, it was lots of fun.

"I remember Tony at second. Frustrated, he learned to stay alert in this fast moving game and concentrate. With lots of practice he perfected the skill of judging his distance on the throw to first.

"Then there was Mike. As a minority from the south, it took a lot of convincing to gain his trust. In the beginning he was very cynical toward all of us, and the world as well. However, in time, we developed a good relationship and a good shortstop for the team. Whatta proud day it was when he joined our team.

"And Darrell, our pitcher." Pop chuckled. "He got discouraged easily when everybody was hitting his pitches. But when we started to fine tune his technique." Again Pop chuckled. "The other guys were baffled when they couldn't hit his pitches anymore.

"I never forgot Bill. He was born into a wealthy family. He had everything his heart could ever ask for. He was always use to being the center of attention. He could do nothing wrong." Chuckling. "But that was about to change. You see! In time we brought our catcher down to earth to be with the rest of us.

"Larry continued to be our power at the plate. Our opponents backed up to the wall with fear and trembling when they saw him come to bat." The Press Club members chuckled with Pop, imagining the scare he must've given the other team.

"We needed back up pitchers. Stringbean, looked like the wind could blow him over. But he surprised us all." The audience laughed. "Did he ever? And John was our ace right-hander. Yes! We never went into a game empty handed.

"A bunch of guys from the neighborhood having fun playing baseball. Nothing else.

"As time went by, there was another change. We began to notice the people watching us." Pop smiled when he noticed he had the full attention of the Press Club members. "We didn't think anything of it at first. After all, who were we? Nobody special. However, after awhile the crowd grew. Soon the sidewalks were packed with viewers. Nobody could pass. It even spilled over into the street.

"I recall one day, a police officer approaching me inquiring 'bout what's goin' on there. I shrugged my shoulders claiming innocence. We weren't doin' anything wrong. Just havin' some fun playin' baseball. And when the officer took a good look around while taking off his hat to scratch the top of his head, he walked away, shaking his head, mumbling to himself. "Well see that it doesn't happen again." And whatever that meant beats me. I didn't know what he was talkin' 'bout.

"Needless to say the crowd kept growing. All we were doin' was playin' ball and here's all these people gatherin' around to watch us. Soon, it was necessary for the police to be present just to keep law and order. Meanwhile, we just went 'bout our business."

That brought all the Press Club members to their feet applauding. Pop wasn't use to all this attention when he stepped away from the podium, allowing them to express their feelings. Finally, five minutes later it was quiet once again.

"Thank you, ladies and gentlemen. You are so kind. I can assure you that I'm not deserving of it.

"Anyway, word quickly spread about the Boys baseball team. And soon everybody read about them in their local newspaper." Pop chuckled with disbelief. "Surely, they were the talk of the town.

"Then, one day I received a telephone call from a friendly stranger. His name was Charles Matthews. The kids called him Chuck. He was the baseball coach at Harper High, and invited us to play his team."

Pop took another big breath and paused to regain his thoughts. "Yes! I can still remember the day. It was an exciting day for all of us. Lots of people attended the event. It became a nuisance to the neighborhood."

Immediately, everybody in the Club laughed. Pop tried to get a word in edgewise, but they wouldn't let him. Soon more cheers and another standing ovation followed.

"But that's not all. Shortly thereafter when I took ill, our assistant coach, Mr. Carlson, a successful insurance man, received a very interesting letter at his office. It read as follows:

Dear Mr. Carlson:

It's always nice to learn about what's happening in our neighborhoods, and across this great land of ours for our youth and baseball.

Recently I learned about your Boy's baseball team, and the impact they are having in our city. Their love for the game, and desire to play have drawn attention to many parents whose sons would likewise desire to become a part of this fine sport. And who knows, perhaps these Boys will develop into fine professional players themselves.

On my desk are many letters, requesting how other neighborhoods may get started, and have a team of their own. But many lack money and know-how experience.

We would like to assist you in your endeavor promoting youth baseball, by offering your Boys the chance to play the Chicago Cubs in a benefit game, with all proceeds going to the Youth baseball Association of America.

The story of your team can never be accurately told. And we would appreciate hearing from you.

Respectively yours,
The General Manager.

"Whoopee!" Mr. Carlson shouted, jumping out of his chair. His jubilation carried into the other room and soon had Debbie,

Bud, and Andy, in his office.

"What happened, Mr. Carlson?" Bud spoke on behalf of all the curious office staff. He inquired if he was all right, thinking the floor might have just dropped out from under him. Or perhaps he suffered a stroke.

"All right!" He showed them the letter as he tried to maintain his composure. "Wait till the Boys see this. The Chicago Cubs have just invited them to play at Wrigley Field."

"Next the entire office gave a rousing cheer for the Boys after congratulating our assistant coach. Immediately thereafter, he left the office to tell the Boys.

"When the Boys heard the news, they all went crazy. In the days ahead they sharpened their baseball skills like never before. They started a newspaper drive to earn money for some baseball shoes. The local sewing circle made them uniforms. And, when the big day finally arrived, it was the happiest day in their life.

"They're good Boys. All they needed was a chance, I thought. We had lots of fun. Practicing together we got to know each other real well. We shared our joys and sorrows. We became a close knit family in the midst of a big city."

For the first time in his life, Pop started to break down. Tears started to roll down his cheeks and over his whiskers. For the moment, he paused and reflected, staring at the floor. He tried to shield his true emotions with a grin.

After taking a deep breath and regaining his composure, he continued his speech. "But it didn't end there. From then on our popularity grew. Everywhere we went, the people followed us in large numbers. They didn't want all that notoriety, just a chance to play ball and have some fun."

Finally, Press Club members were let loose to voice their approval uninterrupted, and they did. Out of a heart filled with appreciation, they stood and applauded for a long time. Looking around the room, smiling faces filled with tears told the whole story.

Not use to so much attention, Pop sat quietly with his hands folded on the table. Again a smile attempted to cover up his true feelings as his eyes welled up with tears while goose bumps ran down his spine.

Ron Overly, the Press Club host, returned to the microphone. "Thank you very much ladies and gentlemen for a kind welcome to our guest. It was our pleasure to have Pop as our special guest here today. I must tell you, he refused our first invitation. It took several more and a little persuading to get him here. But we're deeply grateful that that day has finally come."

The speaker looked at Pop for the moment while he continued to speak. "Now Pop, if you would stand by me, we'd like to give our audience an opportunity to ask a few questions."

Immediately, several people stood up and started talking at the same time. When Pop acknowledged the lady in a blue plaid dress, everybody else sat down while the microphone perched on a long rod zoomed overhead toward her. "Yes, go ahead ma'am."

"My name is Bonnie Kane of the Boston Journal, Pop. We'd like to know what are your plans now since the Boys have made it big?"

"We're not a professional baseball team. Nor have we created a league."

"I realize that, Sir. But you have to admit, you do attract a large audience everywhere you go."

"For the moment we'll continue to do what we have been doin'. Play baseball. Perhaps, make some goodwill tours."

Next the microphone swung around to the other side of the room, as all heads and eyes turned to follow it to the next person asking a question.

"I'm Joe Frantz of the Milwaukee Star. "How much do you pay the Boys now that they are celebrities?"

"Not one cent." The audience responded with a laugh, gesturing that money to these guys was a big joke. "None of us get any money. You gotta remember our intention is strictly recreational."

More people anxiously rose to their feet. Patiently, with Ron's assistance, they went down the line, allowing everybody the same opportunity to be heard.

"Yes. I see the lady in the back of the room."

Several people wheeled around in their chair, thinking it was them.

"That's right." Pop pointed his finger. "You in the yellow blouse with the white trim."

"Hi! I'm from the LA Monitor. How long are you going to continue to play ball? Is it difficult to keep up with this pace? And, have you considered ever replacing any of the Boys as they get older and go their separate ways?"

Everywhere in the room, people with a pencil in one hand and a pad of paper in the other were quickly writing down the comments as if there were no tomorrow. Occasionally, they'd look up at Pop before their eyes were back in their notes.

Concluding the Q and A time, Ron gave some closing comments. "Mr. Peterson, or Pop, again we'd like to thank you for coming, and as a token of our appreciation, we're giving a thousand dollars to the charity of your choice. Also, we'd like you to have this life time membership certificate to The National Press Club, and last but not least …" Everybody laughed, interrupting Ron's presentation, anticipating his next comment. "This coffee mug with The National Press Club logo on it."

"Thank you." Pop shook his hand with a humble look on his face. He felt the Boys deserved the credit a lot more than he did.

"And one final question. Can I have a ticket to your next game?"

More laughs followed before many people huddled around Pop at the speaker's table to chat.

TEN

It was very quiet in the early morning hours. High above, a dark clear sky filled with stars hovered over the landscape. No signs of life could be seen anywhere. Not even a bird chirping about in search of insects. Then, suddenly out of nowhere an orange flash darted through the trees and bushes.

Faster and faster the wheels spun down a path, as a breeze wiped in a Boy's face. "No time to waste. I must get there on time. Hurry! Hurry! Hurry!" The thoughts raced through Orville's mind.

A mile down the road, near a blue frame house, he parked his bike against the shed. Then, quickly and quietly, he lifted a tall ladder up over his shoulder and carried it around to the other side of the house. With both hands firmly griping it, he placed it near the window. Finally, he started to climb when he noticed the bright lights of a vehicle coming down the road. Startled and wasting no time, he quickly descended and hid behind some bushes.

After catching his breath, and slowly peeking above the bushes, he saw Martin, the milkman. Slowly, the little truck backed up the driveway and stopped near the house. Then, a man in a white uniform walked up to the back door, exchanged two empty bottles for a couple of full ones, and returned to his truck. "I should've known he'd be up this early." Lots of thoughts started to race through Orville's mind.

Standing up, Orville cautiously looked around before resuming his position on the ladder. When he reached the top of the ladder, he leaned against it to maintain his balance and nudged the window up until it was wide open, before climbing inside the house.

Like a sack of potatoes under a blanket in one corner of the room came a loud sound of somebody snoring. Only the ticking sound of a clock on the bedside table competed with the person in the bed.

Rushing over on his tiptoes, Orville vigorously shook the sack till the boy rolled over and sat up. Startled, he rubbed his eyes and stared momentarily, as if he was just hit by a truck. "Ah! What? Whose here? Whatta ya want?"

"Louie! It's me! Orville!" The Boy whispered.

"Yeah! What time is it? Whatta ya want?"

"Shhh! Not so loud. Don't wanna wake the whole house up."

"Yeah man." Louie took a deep breath, rubbed his eyes again, and stretched while raising his arms toward the ceiling to gain his composure and realize where he was. "Sure! Whatta ya want?"

"I want ya to do me a favor." Orville continued to whisper, leaning over close to Louie's ear.

"Yeah! Sure! What is it?"

"I gotta get over to Sherwood Forest today. Unck must not know this, but I want ya to help me by sweeping out the cow stalls this morning. Must be done before Unck gets up. Like now."

Soon, they were scampering down the ladder. Then each boy grabbed an end and carried it over to the side of the shed. And while Louie moseyed on over to the farm, Orville was off, like a flash, into the woods.

He knew the trails perfectly. All the short cuts through town were at his command. Peddling faster than his legs would allow him to go, with a wobbling front wheel, and a rear wheel anxious to spin faster than the other one, Orville's bike almost toppled winding down a path. After crossing the highway, he picked up speed. Even the squirrels and other fury creatures of the forest couldn't keep up with him. Down a steep embankment, up a knoll, around a turn, nothing stood in his way till his bike lost control going over a root peeking out of the ground from a big old Oak tree. Bang! Over went the bike leaving Orville laying flat on the ground, staring up at the sky as the stars began to disappear before a beautiful sunrise in the east.

Meanwhile, back on the farm, grumpy old Unck anxiously waited for Orville at the breakfast table. "Where is that Boy, ma? I'm nearly done with my breakfast and haven't seen high or tail of 'em yet."

"Probably tending to his own business like ya always say Unck." Lizzie snickered.

"Oh hush, woman! If I wanted your opinion, I'd have asked for it." Feeling frustrated and angry, he pushed himself away from the table, stood up, and limped toward the door.

Getting use to the idle chatter, Lizzie just turned around and went about her usual household chores, minding her own business.

Outside, Unck continued to mumble to himself as he walked over to the barn. "I always say a little work does a Boy good. Nothin' wrong with that. Makes a man out of 'em. Now where is he?"

Inside the barn Unck grabbed a lantern off a nail by a stall post. Raising the glass shield he adjusted the wick while lighting a match before igniting it. Then, slowly he moseyed on down the lanes searching for his lost prodigal. Pausing at several stalls, he noticed that they were neatly swept out. "Hmm! Best job I've ever seen done. Couldn't have done a better job myself." Satisfied that the job was done, though still no sign of Orville, he returned to the house.

Meanwhile, very slowly, Orville got back up on his feet and brushed the dirt off his overalls, while the pain radiated through his leg. Leaning against that Oak tree, his number one enemy for the moment, he took a couple deep breaths before hopping over to pick up his bike. Torn between the thought of hurrying and the bruises on an aching body, very slowly, he resumed peddling down a familiar path.

In Sherwood Forest, even at the break of dawn, a large crowd had gathered. Gradually, gently nudging his way past all the on-lookers, Orville approached a police officer standing by his patrol car. "Are ya with the rest of 'em, Laddie?" His Irish accent left no secret to where he was from.

"Yes Sir! Officer! I heard the Boys were lookin' for new ball players." Orville tried to remain firm even though he felt nervous.

"Come with me, Laddie." The officer led him over to meet another officer, while the Boy limped along with his bike.

"Patrick! This Lad needs to be with all the others. Can ya be so kind and get him over yonder?"

"Why sure, Dudley! Will be no problem at tall." Patrick used the same familiar accent. "You take the Boy's bike and put it with all the others, while I take him up yonder." Looking at the Boy. "C'mon Laddie! Get in me car and we'll be off."

Orville never rode in a police car before. From the back seat it felt strange looking through the metal grid separating him from the driver up front. And, with bulging eyes, he stared at all the buttons on the dashboard.

"Calling car number twenty-three! Car twenty-three over!" The dispatcher's voice blared from the car radio.

"Car twenty-three here! What's up Dot? Go!"

"State your location! Over!"

"Ya know where I'm at, Dot! Sherwood Forest! What's up? Over!"

"The crowd is getting restless! It's difficult holding them back! Should I get more help or let 'em through? Over!"

"Nooo! Dot!" Patrick needed more time to think about the situation. "Pop says nobody is to get near him and the Boys during tryouts." Pausing. "Tell ya what! Get more help! More cars! More Officers! Over!"

"Roger, Patrick! You're a charm." She chuckled. "Over and out!"

Looking through the car window, Orville saw the red beacon light reflecting off the trees as they rode through the crowd. Soon, curious faces huddled around them anxious to see who was sitting in the back seat. "Never felt this way before." Lots of thoughts raced through his mind. "Is this the way all celebrities are treated?"

Away from the main parking lot, the car hung to the right. Officer Patrick chose a strange, convoluted path deep into the forest and opening up on the other side close to a grassy field. Tall trees overshadowed the winding curves. Moving slowly at fifteen miles per hour, it felt like car number twenty-three would never get there. Finally, a smaller crowd appeared hugging a makeshift foul line.

On the field a line-up extended as far as the eye could see comprising of at least a hundred or so anxious young people eager to play ball. Word of mouth spread quickly throughout the town about the team seeking additional players. No body wanted to be left out.

Tall, short, heavy set, and thin, they all came from different backgrounds. Long serious faces displayed nervous feelings. Thoughts of mixed emotions had them doubting their own abilities to play ball. In overall's, white T-shirt or plaid sport shirt, cap, ankle high boot's or gym shoes, chewing a bottom lip or mumbling to themselves, slowly the lined moved up. And so the long wait began.

At a small table near a bench by the first base foul line, Pop sat looking over a long list of names on his clipboard. Anybody interested in trying out for the team had to pre-register by putting his name, address, and phone number on a three by five index card. Later they were collected from baskets located at strategic spots throughout town like Ma & Pa Gas, Lucinda's Bakery, First National Bank of Cedar Lane, and Jerry's Grocery. Needless to say, next to his pencil on the table were many stacks of cards. "Again, I'm surprised at the number of folks wanting to play ball." Pop raised his eyebrows and scratched his head with the eraser on the end of his number two lead pencil, while pondering what to do with all these people.

Ben, James, Wally, Joe, and so on, each gave his name before taken out to the field. The test was simple. It was a game of catch with one of the Boys. Ideally anybody who could throw a ball eighty miles an hour down the length of a football field might be chosen. However, Pop didn't want to be too hard on a bunch of deserving startups, so he resorted to a simple game of ball handling as well.

Next, could they catch a ball? Tony Martinello, the team second baseman, took them through several catching drills. Grounders took funny hop's rolling over the grass. High fly balls did a funny dance while caught in the wind. Just when a fellow thought he was under it, it swerved away from him at the last minute. How embarrassing to miss an easy catch. And sharp throws to a player nearly knocked him off his feet.

Finally batting. Each boy was given a bat and told to stand by a cardboard base. Darrell McDaniel pitched easy slow moving balls with nothing on them, like in the old days when the Boys just started playing ball back at the schoolyard. Meeting the ball was all the coach expected of them. Nothing too hard or too easy about that. Perfection would come later to would-be players.

"Next player." Pop motioned, with a clipboard in his hand.

"Fudgie, Sir!"

"Hah?" Puzzled. Pop stared at the boy while dropping his jaw and scratching the top of his head. He thought the kid was kidding.

"Fudgie, Mr. Peterson." The boy repeated himself in a more serious tone.

"Boy! You can call me Pop. Everybody else does. Now what's your real name?"

"Don't know, Sir. I just know everybody calls me Fudgie."

"Why?"

"Don't know that either, Sir."

"And don't call me Sir! Just Pop! OK?" The coach got angry, as his questioning speeded up for the moment.

"Yes Sir! I mean, Pop!"

"Good! Now let's get on with it! So ya wanna be a baseball player, right?"

"Yes Sir! I mean Pop!"

The Boys on the Gold Coast eyed him from head to toe, like an army sergeant inspecting his troops. "Ya look a little bit on the heavy side, Fudgie."

"Yeah! Guest I like to eat, Sir! I mean Pop!"

"Ya think ya can handle a baseball?"

"Yeah! Sir! Pop!"

"What's your favorite position?"

"Catch! Do ya think anybody could get by me, Sir? I mean Pop." The boy was nervous and couldn't always keep his thoughts straight in his head.

"Any other position, Fudgie?"

"I like to bat, Sir! Pop!"

Pop looked around for one of his players. "Just a moment, Fudgie!" After cupping his hands over his eyes to shield them from the sun. "Hey, Larry!"

Larry was busy cleaning off some baseball bats with a rag on the sidelines when he heard his name being called. While resting with one knee on the ground, he replied. "Yeah, Pop!"

"C'mere! I want ya to do somethin' for me …"

Before long Larry was pitching to Fudgie who stood a good distance away from him. Not afraid to meet the ball, he swung at every pitch sending the ball deep into the bushes. Later, the guys would search for them, like a golfer trying to pick golf balls out of a pond. Even Pop, who viewed him from the sideline, was surprised that this tub of lard was so good with a bat.

There was no question in Pop's mind that Fudgie; just by his size alone could protect the plate. But can he catch? That was the big question.

Now Larry loved to hit the ball and challenge the fielders. However, several times that day, he had to be reminded to cool it. Simple taps to the outfield were all that was necessary. Though not very agile on his feet, Fudgie did make some good catches.

"That's it, Larry! He's done!" Pop shouted. "I've seen all I wanna see!"

As Fudgie slowly left the field walking by Pop, where the long line didn't appear to be getting any shorter, he looked worried.

"Thanks for comin' out, Fudgie." Without second-guessing him, even though he remained courteous to all the boys, Pop concealed his true feelings. "You'll be notified in a few days in the mail 'bout our decision."

"Yes Sir. I mean Pop." The boy looked sad, staring at the ground. "Oh Sir!"

"Yes, Fudgie!"

"Can I ask you a question?"

"Sure can. Anything ya wanna know. Ask away." Pop always took the time to treat people with respect. Every individual was an important person to him.

"Does my weight hurt my chances? I mean do I really have a chance?"

"Of course not son! Everybody here is treated the same. Your chances are as good as the next guy."

Those comments made him feel real good. So, he walked away smiling with lots of confidence. Pop's reputation as a fair coach just struck home.

"Oh, one more thing, boy!"

Suddenly, a smiling face turned sad when he stopped in his tracks and looked at Pop.

"Ya might think 'bout changin' your name. Instead of Fudgie, if ya join our team, we might call ya Tiny." And they both laughed.

The line continued to move slowly with no end in sight. Tired and anxious boys who had been standing a long time, patiently waited for their turn. Watching the other boys on the field trying out, soon started to cast doubts in their own mind. Fumbling. Falling in a foxhole while chasing a ball. Catching a few good fly balls. Struggling to get it back to the infield. All kinds of ideas left them with mixed feelings.

"Next!" Pop shouted, above all the chatter, putting his clipboard down. "State your name, please!"

"Orville Hodge!" The Boy shouted, while standing at attention with his hands at his side. "Orville Hodge! Mr. Pop!"

"Just Pop. Skip the mister stuff, Boy." The coach smiled.

"Yes Pop!" The Boy looked serious.

"And relax. This isn't the army. And stop shouting."

"Yes Pop!" He shouted again before breaking the attention stance. "I'm sorry Pop." Then he lowered his voice. "I have to talk above a lot of machinery back home ...ya know what I mean?"

"Yep! Think I do." Pop stared at Orville from head to toe. "So ya wanna play baseball, do ya?"

"Yep!" The Boy answered with confidence.

Pop chuckled. "Hey Stringbean! Come over here!"

The tall lean pitcher who could easily be missed depending on which angle you're looking at, quickly put his baseball down and trotted over to join them.

"You called, Pop?"

"Yeah! Look at this, a fellow that looks just like you."

"Maybe it's just the loose fitting overalls, Pop."

"I don't think so."

"Sir." Orville interrupted. "Is their somethin' wrong with my looks, Sir?"

Pop was caught off guard. "Oh no! Nothing wrong. It's just that ya look so thin like Stringbean here. I had my doubts 'bout him too at one time. Didn't think he'd amount to much." He chuckled with the thought. "Wow! Was I ever wrong. He turned out to be a mighty fine baseball player."

The clumsy six-foot Boy in ankle high half laced shoes, followed Stringbean out to the field. After giving him some brief instructions, Pop watched Orville struggle to catch several fly balls. Nothing spectacular, he raced in to trap several sharp hit liners in the web of his glove, only to fumble most of them, while catching a few. He even struggled tripping over his own feet. People along the sideline laughed, and that didn't make things look any easier.

"C'mon, Orville!" Stringbean shouted, cupping his hands close to his mouth from the bench. "Keep your eye on the ball! You can do it! I know ya can!"

But the harder he tried, the clumsier he got. Soon his nerves got the best of him. However, something inside him told him to just keep on going.

"OK, Orville! Let's try somethin' else! How 'bout fieldin' some ground balls? Yeah! Never mind. Don't answer that one." Stringbean looked at Larry. "Hey buddy! How 'bout helping an old pal out?"

"Like what, Stringbean?"

"How 'bout hittin' a few grounders to my friend Orville?"

After feeling hesitate, Larry changed his mind when he realized how much he loved to hit the ball. "Yeah! Sure! Why not?"

"Good!" Then, after locating Jerry, he cupped his hands close to his mouth and shouted. "Hey Jerry! Do me a favor. How 'bout catching a few from my friend Orville?"

Once Orville positioned himself on the edge of the outfield grass, he nodded that he was ready. Next, a series of ground balls rolled toward him. Stooping close to the ground with his long legs was hard. Often several balls went straight through his legs into the outfield. Though he gave it his best, the basketball physique just didn't make things look any easier. Even Jerry, who rolled his eyes while staring at the sky, got bored. However, for every ball that Jerry caught, Pop noticed something unique.

"Time!" Pop called, walking out to chat with Stringbean, and signaling for Orville to join them. After a brief discussion Pop returned to his chair by the table. Then Stringbean tossed Orville a ball, which he threw to Jerry. Another ball tossed, and another ball fired to first. Still another ball and another and another. Every ball sailed across the diamond with superb accuracy. Slow balls floating through the air soon sailed faster. Halfway through this exercise, Jerry called time to check the padding in his glove, as every ball started to sting his hand.

"Bravo! Bravo! Bravo!" Pop cheered. "Now, let's see how ya handle a bat."

The ball arched, traveling toward the cardboard plate. Curving, Orville didn't get out of the way in time when it bumped his shoulder. "Ouch!"

Another ball, much slower than before, sailed toward the plate, where Orville swung his bat and met the ball, thus sending it into shallow left field. More slow balls, and without much effort behind each swing, he tapped them lightly toward the shortstop. Then, with a little more gusto, the ball started sailing toward shallow left field again. Keeping his eye on each pitch, he met the ball perfectly every time, thus sending them into various spots in the outfield. It was hard to believe that the tall lengthy figure, like Stringbean, had any muscle behind each swing at all, but he did.

"Swing harder!" Tom shouted, cupping his hands close to his mouth from the third base foul line.

Soon, Orville was swinging harder at every pitch, thus sending them deep near the trees. Like so many other boys, there was nothing unusual about sending them into the trees. However, when the boys heard a sound like a golf ball dropping into a pond, it raised lots of eyebrows and doubts. Upon discovering, it turned out that his baseballs were sailing high above a cluster of trees and landing in the water hole on the other side.

"Fantastic!" Pop muttered. "Clumsy as an ox, this farm Boy is, but he can sure hit." Everybody standing around Pop agreed.

"Next! Whose next?" Pop asked.

"Me, Sir." A soft quiet voice replied.

"Me who? Please state your name."

"Nellie. I mean Nell, Sir."

"Nell?"

"I'm sorry Sir. Nel-Nel-Nel-Nelson."

"Nelson who?"

"Nelson Swa-Swa-Swa …"

"Oh never mind! Names aren't that important to me anyway." Pop searched for his name on his clipboard.

"Yes Sir!"

"And forget the Sir stuff, OK?' Pop rolled his eyes off the clipboard to get a better look at Nelson. "I just got finished telling the other guy that." The coach motioned toward the crowd with his pencil.

"OK!" Nelson tried his best to oblige Pop.

"So ya wanna play ball do ya?" Pop questioned him while leaning back in his chair.

"Yes!"

"Can ya look me straight in the eye when ya talk?'

"Yes." To accommodate his nerves, Nelson repeatedly looked over Pop's shoulder.

"And why are ya wearing that hat? Most of the other guys here aren't wearing a hat. Besides, it's too hot to wear a hat."

"What's wrong with it? It's my favorite Cub hat. I've had it for years."

"Nothin' wrong with it. It's just a little large for your head. Are you sure it's the right size?"

Knowing that he was trying to hide something, Nelson got angry when Pop kept staring at him. "Because, Mr. Pop! I can wear it if I want to."

"And that jacket. Why ya wearin' that jacket on a day like

today?" The temperature was already in the 70's on a sunny day beneath a clear blue sky.

"I chill easy. Didn't wanna catch a cold." Pop's interrogating started to put Nelson more on the defensive.

"And those gloves." Chuckling. "Why are ya wearin' those gloves?"

"What difference does it make, Sirrr?" Now it was Nelson's turn to stared at Pop.

"No difference at all." Pop avoided direct eye contact with him, as he started to feel warm around the neck.

"If ya don't mind my saying so, you sure ask a lot of questions. Do you do this with all the guys?" Nelson had baseball on his mind and didn't feel like playing school.

"Oh never mind! Here! Use this!" He tossed Nelson a baseball glove. "Get out there on the grass. Over there next to the pitcher's mound. Let's see what ya can do."

When Nelson put the glove on and walked away, Pop stared at him as if he was in a trance for the moment entertaining thoughts far away in another world. "Hey! Whatta staring at, Pop?" Even Don, one of the team members noticed a difference in the expression on Pop's face.

"Nothing much. Just wondering." Pop mumbled as he shifted his eyes to stare at the ground.

"Nothing? I don't believe ya. What ya thinking 'bout?" Don's curiosity was aroused.

"Nothing much."

"C'mon Pop! You can tell me!" Don pleaded. "Remember me? The team? We've been through a lot together. All of us."

"Look at him. Look at the way Nelson walks. Not weird. Not strange."

"Oh?"

"Yeah! Just different."

"Uh?" Don looked puzzled. "Whatta ya mean different?"

"She! I mean he walks like a girl."

Don laughed. "Oh come on, Pop! Now I've heard everything. Don't be silly. Like a girl?"

"Yeah! Remember the movie Jentel? Where Barbara Streisand impersonates a man because she wanted to be a Rabbi, and there were no female rabbi's in the Rabbi school?"

Wrinkling his eyebrows, puckering his lips, and scratching his head, Don had to give that one some more thought. "Yep! I think I can vaguely remember the movie."

"Well that's what I'm thinking about." As he continued to think about it, the more sure he was about Nelson's feminine mannerisms.

From the first base foul line, Jerry threw several grounders to Nelson, who scooped them up, took a couple of steps forward each time, wobbled his hips, and threw to Bill at first base. Nothing uneventful about it. A few high fly balls followed. Staring up at the sky, while prancing his feet to position himself, he caught every one of them. Then, using his shoulder muscles to assist him, he threw the ball after each catch back to Bill. Again there was nothing unusual about his fielding.

"Saw enough!" Pop shouted. "Take first! Wanna see how ya play the bag!"

The medium height, five feet four inch blond, always kept his foot on the bag and stretched to catch the ball. Maybe a couple more inches in height would help him stretch for some close plays. However, he was quick and his speed made up the difference.

Meanwhile, Larry watched this little throwing-catching exercise from home plate. "Hey Tom! Do me a favor. Get out there and pitch a couple to me. I wanna have some fun."

"Uh?" Puzzled, Tom trotted over to chat.

"Yeah! I wanna see just how tough this Nelson guy really is. So I want ya to pitch to me. After I hit the ball, I'm gonna race down the line." Chuckling. "Believe me. Nelson will never know what hit 'em."

"Are you crazy?"

"No man!" Larry motioned with his big muscular arms like Pop Eye The Sailor Man. "Just wanna have a little fun."

"Well I don't know, Larry." Doubts started to raced through Tom's mind.

"Oh come on. No body's gonna get hurt."

After some convincing, Tom grabbed his glove, ball, and walked out to the pitcher's mound. Not use to pitching, he doubted if he could make a decent throw to the plate. But it didn't matter.

Larry swung viciously at the first pitch, and raced down the base line like a mean bull ready to attack its enemy.

Continuing to field throws from the shortstop, Nelson saw out of the corner of his eye the monster coming. Suddenly, Larry wasn't running anymore, but diving toward the bag, like a linebacker in the NFL charging the running back with the football safely tucked under his arm. In response, Nelson quickly stepped off the bag and approached the edge of the infield grass when Larry's chest slid over the bag, and he caught a mouth full of dirt.

"Ha! Ha! Ha!" Pop laughed while slapping his knee. "The guy has good reflexes." In this fast moving game of baseball, Pop always wanted his team to be mentally alert. Even though Nelson's moves and the way he carried himself about on the field was different than the other guys, he did demonstrate his ability to play ball well.

"Hey Nelson! That's enough! C'mon over here!" Again Pop shouted before lowering his voice and focusing his attention on the guy standing next to him. "Mike! Tell Becky I wanna see her."

"Yes suh, Mr. Pop!" Mike's brown eyes were about to pop out of their sockets.

"Quick like a bunny!" Pop clapped his hands. He was anxious to talk to her. "I wanna see her now."

In a split second Becky broke through the line of all the other people standing around the table. After making an attempt to catch her breath, the short gal in blue jeans, red and white plaid blouse, and ponytail hustled to find the coach. "You wanted to see me, Pop."

"Yes, Becky. I want you to do me a favor."

"Sure. I'll try. That is if I can."

"Yes. I think you can. Come here. Get closer to me. This is what I want you to do." He motioned with his hand for her to bring her head down close to his so he could whisper something in her ear.

"Wow! That was fun. That guy running toward me sure got the surprise of his life when he met with mother earth." Nelson smiled with a twinkle in his eye.

"Ha! Ha! Ha!" Pop laughed. "I saw the whole thing. Thought it was funny."

"He sure had me fooled. I thought it was part of the test till I heard somebody say it was a practical joke some guy was playing on me."

"Anyway, Nelson. I want ya to meet Becky here." Pop turned around to look at her. "Becky! This is Nelson Swa ...whatever it is."

"Hi Nelson!" Becky extended her arm to shake his hand. "Pop would like me to show you around. Ya know. Kind a see what all the other guys are doing."

Leading Nelson on a mini cook's tour, Becky pointed out all the other players by name, along with a little background history. "Bill came from a well to do family." Pausing, she took a deep breath before continuing with her presentation. "It took a little work to bring him down to earth." Becky chuckled. "But we're glad he settled down and now has a more humble spirit."

Nelson smiled. "I bet."

"Don over there has been a good back up man. Or should I say utility player? An excellent ..."

"How can you remember all this stuff?" Nelson was amazed at Becky's knowledge about the team's history.

"Oh! It's not hard, once ya get to know them. Then there's Mike, our shortstop. He was born in the south. A minority with a chip on his shoulder. But let me tell ya, Pop is a patient, loving man. He doesn't give up once he sets his mind on doing something."

Nelson nodded. "I agree. But he sure ask a lot of questions."

"Yeah. Well don't let that bother you. He likes to get to know everybody. Please! Take no offense at that. He really doesn't mean any harm." Becky motioned with her hand.

They walked around the diamond and ended up in a van looking at all the baseball gear, before returning to the parking lot. Listening, with one ear open, Nelson learned a lot about the history of the team. Detail after detail, word for word, Becky didn't miss a thing. "Have to admit however, it got boring after awhile." Nelson felt nervous as each passing moment got to be more intense.

"And this is the rest room." Becky pointed to the building on the left. "It's a good thing they have showers in there. Following practice tryouts, everybody cleans up."

Nelson looked surprised.

"Go ahead. I'll get ya some towels." And when she returned, Nelson looked puzzled. "Something wrong?"

"Oh no! Not a thing!"

"Good! Come with me! We'll see if it's full." When Becky opened the door, she shouted if anyone was inside. A couple of fellows mumbled something incoherently. Satisfied, Becky encouraged Nelson to go on in, and that she'll meet him later in the parking lot.

"I really don't need a shower." Nelson pleaded with her almost to the point of getting on his knees.

"Pop insists. So go ahead. You'll feel a lot better after you've had a shower."

"I can't." Nelson turned his head back and forth looking serious. "I don't feel good."

"Great! After a nice cold shower, you'll feel even better. Go ahead." Without hesitating, refusing to listen to any more excuses, Becky started to push him inside.

Frustrated, Nelson took a deep breath in an attempt to regain his composure. "OK. You win. I can't go in there."

"Huh?"

"I'm not Nelson. My name is Nell. Nell Swanson."

"Huh?"

"Look! You wouldn't understand it if I told ya. I was raised with two older brothers. I'm a tomboy, and I like to play baseball."

Slowly the pieces of the puzzle started to fit together. Without the hat, an attractive gal appeared with a beautiful shade of long blond hair, blue eyes, hands well manicured, and no bulky jacket.

"But why?" After shrugging her shoulders Becky gave Nell a big hug.

"Baseball is for boys. Did ya ever see girls playing baseball in the major league?"

"Guest not!"

"Either have I. We're not strong enough. Or there's only one locker room. Or the guys just think that they're better than us gals. Besides, if Pop knew I was a girl, he wouldn't let me play." And as she continued to tell her story, a happy cheery gal mixed a smile with some tears rolling down her cheeks.

"Nell. You have a lot of courage. I'm proud of you for doing what ya did."

"Yeah! But my chances of playing baseball are over. I'm sure of that." She started chewing one of her fingernails in an attempt to calm her nerves.

"Now hold on. I'm not so sure about that." Becky encouraged her not to give up hope.

"But baseball is for boys. Pop has a boys baseball team." With more tears rolling down her cheeks, she started making up excuses. "Besides, I wasn't …"

Becky interrupted. "Listen Nell. I'm on your side. C'mon let's talk." And after giving Nell a big hug, they slowly walked away.

"Next! Whose next?" Pop asked, starting to feel the strain, as the day wore on with all the people trying out for the baseball team.

"Yes, Sir!"

"Name!"

"Ape, Sir!" He shouted, standing at attention.

"Pardon me, boy. But did you say Ape? Don't you mean Abe?"

"No, Sir!"

"Ape what, boy?" Pop grinned, thinking this got to be a good one.

"Ape, Sir! That's all! Just Ape. Folks call me Ape, nothin' else."

"OK, Ape it is." Pop wasn't convinced. "So ya wanna be a baseball player do ya?"

"Yes, Sir!" Ape answered promptly, taking a big swallow, while his Adam's apple went up and down on his long thin neck.

"How long have ya been playin' ball?"

"Nope! Never played before in my life. But I'm willin' to learn, Sir."

Pop looked surprised as he listened to his answers. "Oh! Can ya catch a ball?"

"Huh?" The boy grinned, showing his big white buckteeth from one ear to the other.

"Stand over here." Ape stepped back a few feet. "Fine! Right there. That'll be fine. Now here, catch the ball." Later struggling, Ape went through all the same exercises everybody else did.

A long day was finally winding down with lots of index cards stacked on the little table. "This should be the last of 'em." John added another handful to the pile.

"How ya gona score them, Pop?" Mark stared at all the cards scattered on the table.

"Probably has some secret formula." Darrell grinned at all the other guys.

"Maybe it's something scientific." Greg interjected.

"Yes suh! That's it!" Mike added his own opinion to everybody else's.

"It's very simple guys. As you can see, each play has a number assigned to it. The more numbers, the higher the score, the more likely that person has a chance to play on the team. Personality counts. How much does he love the game? Does he put forth his best effort to be a good baseball player? And how serious is he?" Then Pop's cheerful mood changed. "But the tragedy is I can't take 'em all. Some of 'em will have to look elsewhere." And then he reflected on his own love for the game, and the passion these boys and girls have for baseball that brought them out for the try-outs.

ELEVEN

The sound of a bullwhip echoed throughout the farm. Nothing else in the early morning hours beneath a dark sky could be heard. Only a light shining in the barn could be seen. Everybody else was sound asleep. And the sound of a whip cracking kept going like the cadence of a drum beating in a parade.

Suddenly, hearing an old familiar sound, Orville's mom tossed in bed trying to get a few more winks and ignored it. For a quick moment she stared at the clock ticking away on the bedside table. It read 4:30 a.m. so she rolled over and slowly closed her eyes. However, sleep left her. Soon, she was tossing again in an attempt to fight off the world of reality.

Once she was wide-awake, she sat on the edge of her bed and rubbed her eyes before stretching her arms toward the ceiling. While pondering the day's events, she heard the sound of a whip cracking again. Startled, she put on her bathrobe and rushed over to the window. When she saw the light shining in the barn, she immediately ran down the stairs, and rushed outside where the weak moans of a Boy crying blended in with the sound of a whip.

"Help! Help!" She screamed, running down the road as fast as her legs could carry her. "Please! Somebody help me!"

Inside the barn, with his hands tied spread eagle on a cross beam that supported the roof, Orville stood on an orange crate. No shirt. Just blue jeans and bare feet. His wrists were bruised and sore from the rope supporting a collapsing body. The marks on his back told the rest of the story.

"I told myself I wasn't going to let this bother me." The Boy courageously told himself to stand firm. Learn to ride above the circumstances. Just be a man is what his mother always told him. "It happened before and it'll probably happen again. Ouch! It just landed on my back again. Every time I feel the whip, my legs get weaker. I'm not sure how long I'll be able to stand up. A farm Boy should be tough. Every time my legs give way, I feel the pull on my wrist. They're sore now. I see some blood starting to ooze through the skin. But there's no way I can comfort my wounds, at least not now. Survival is the name of the game."

Orville loved his Uncle. He always looked up to him. He recalled how he was taught as a kid to honor and obey adults. "Ouch! There's that whip again. It almost left me hanging here, as my knees gave way. That's it. Love my Uncle. Who else would I have to turn to? But sometimes this is too much to bear.

"Unck prided himself in thinking he provided us with all the basics in life. Food. Clothes. A roof over our head. I hear him talkin' 'bout it all the time. Good health. Ouch!" Orville paused long enough to catch his breath every time the whip landed on his back. "There it is again.

"He taught me that work is good for the soul. Says it purifies the thoughts. Sometimes I don't think I have any thoughts left to purify. Ouch! Each time, the sting of that whip penetrates further throughout my body. Don't know how much more I can take. I can't wipe the tears rolling down my cheeks.

"Says he needs help. To keep the farm goin' he needs my help. It puts bread and butter on the table. I should be thankful for that. Ouch! There it is again." The impact of the whip almost knocked him off the orange crate. "Better that I work on the farm than go to school, he always says.

"But what about my life? Don't I have a life of my own? He says I do. And so I chuckle beneath these tears. Where is it? I don't see it. Ouch! Sorry! I have to take a deep breath before I try to regain my thoughts. That last one knocked the wind out of me. My thoughts are all his thoughts. It's like living in a straight jacket. I don't have a life of my own. After all! Isn't that why I'm perched on this crate? Arms spread out like the wings on an eagle, and tied with this rope like that used to tie a calf in a rodeo?

"I'm sorry. I have to go now. My body is getting weak. My thoughts are drifting. Little by little something inside me tells me to keep the faith."

As anger rose within him and gradually took control, Unck kept cracking the whip. This type of punishment must have been ingrained in him long ago when he was a kid. But where is love? Agape love? Is there a happy medium?

"I'll teach you to run away, Boy. When I was a boy my mother would do a lot worse. Could've locked ya up in a room all day. Or better yet a closet. Dark. No food. How'd ya like that?" Chuckling. "I didn't think so. In a few minutes this will all be over and gone. The rest of the day is yours. Of course, ya know there's work to be done around these parts. Don't be gone too long.

"My mom and dad would stand for none of this stuff you're doing. Either will I." And again he cracked the whip on Orville's back.

"Don't ya know what work is? Us farm folks always gotta work. No time for play. Baseball? And you wanna play baseball. You should learn somethin' from your cousins. Even cousin Louie doesn't do what you do." Again he slapped the whip on Orville's back.

"This'll teach you never to run out on me again, Boy. Feel like doin' this all day to teach ya a lesson. But now! I think I'll stop at fifteen. Fifteen times will be enough for now."

Mixed with sweat and tears rolling down his face and neck, Orville was gone. With legs like rubber, he hung from the beam. Though mumbling a few words incoherently, his thought process was blurred.

When Unck pulled his arm back getting ready to initiate the next blow, he felt a tuck of resistance. "That's enough John! Stop it!" Milton shouted, holding his arm.

Quickly, Unck yanked his arm away, thus freeing himself from the resistance, but not for very long. Milton grabbed him from behind, gave him a bear hug and threw him to the ground.

"Don't tell me what to do." John mumbled beneath his breath while struggling to get loose. "He deserves everything he gets."

"I think you're going too far with this thing John. Somebody's got to put a stop to it, and end it once and for all." Milton braced his legs to support his hold on keeping John pinned to the ground.

"Mind your own business brother Milton. This is my doin' and not yours."

Since Milton was the taller and stronger of the two, he quickly lifted John up by the seat of the bags, and while he was still kicking, tossed him out of the barn. Then, he locked the barn door behind him and tended to Orville's wounds.

Quickly, he searched for a knife. With so many rusty old tools laying around among lots of other things that had collected through the years, it was hard to find one. Finally, seeing one on the edge of the windowsill, he cut Orville down, allowing his own body to catch his so that it wouldn't crash to the ground. Then, he placed a blanket on a wheelbarrow, put Orville in it, and wheeled him outside.

Soon several other Uncles had gathered to watch Uncle John. While maintaining a firm grip on him, they looked in awe at the wounded Boy as Milton raced him toward the house.

Upstairs in bed, his mother treated his wounds. "Just an innocent Boy." Worried, with her hand on her cheek, she stared at his face. "A brave Boy. Lots of courage. Lots of love for his Uncle. Now he sleeps." Tears started to roll down her cheeks. She had mixed feelings. She loved her brother dearly, but also Orville, and was always caught in the middle between them.

"How ya doin' Ma?" Milton wrapped his long arms around her and gave her a big hug.

"Fine." She whispered, wiping away a tear from her eyes, forcing a smile. "Just fine."

"Should I call the doc?"

She whispered while nodding her head and looking at Orville. "Maybe you better."

In an attempt to spike the fever that burned within him, Ma placed a cold washcloth on his forehead. Several times, in the minutes that followed, she replaced it with a cold one. And while trying to control her feelings, she leaned over and whispered in his ear. "I love you Orville. Nobody else is like you. I love you."

Rocking in a swing outside on the front porch, John chattered excessively to himself. Out numbered by all the Uncles present, he wasn't going anywhere. Even though they all guarded him carefully, Orville remained uppermost on their mind.

Quickly the old Ford rolled up to the Hodge residence. Before Milt could turn of the engine, Doc Wagner was out of the car and up the stairs racing toward the bedroom with his little black bag.

Everybody stood quietly outside Orville's room. Soon all the Aunts joined the Uncles along with Lizzie. Silence. They were speechless. Their sad facial expressions were filled with thoughts about Orville.

Finally, Doc Wagner quietly and slowly opened the door. Removing his stethoscope from his ears, he moseyed on over to chat with Lizzie, his mother.

"How is he, Doc? Is he going to be OK? I can't tell whether he's just sleepin' or what. Please tell me what to do. I'll do anything I can to help him." She tried hard to maintain her composure with accompanying fears of breaking down.

Everybody huddled close around her and the doc. After all, they were a tight knit family. They've all faced many hardships together through the years, and like glue, stuck together through thick and thin. Now it was time to help the Hodge's. They wanted to know about Orville too.

"Mrs. Hodge." Doc Wagner continued to console her. "Come over here. Let's talk." The Aunts and Uncles stepped aside to allow her to pass. But they didn't go too far away. Instead, they stayed within ear shot of Lizzie and listened while Doc Wagner updated her.

Smiling, with a double chin, in a blue suit and vest, the chubby little man displayed a comforting tone in his voice. "He's a strong Boy, Ma'am. He doesn't go down easy."

"Yes I know. But what Milt told me. Hanging there! Sleeping!"

"I know, but he could've passed out from exhaustion. He put up a good fight. He tried to maintain a positive attitude."

Lizzie smiled. "Yes he did. That's my Orville." After sensing the comfort of a caring man, she changed the subject momentarily. "Do you have any kids, Doc?"

"Yes, as a matter of fact I do. A boy! Just like yours, only not as strong." Doc winked as he looked around at all the people in the room.

"Oh that's nice." She smiled and tapped his shoulder.

After a lot of small talk, the doctor pulled a watch out of his vest pocket and stood up. "Oh my goodness, how time fly's. Must be goin'. Continue to treat his wounds. Make sure he gets plenty of rest. And Mrs. Hodge."

"Yes Doc." She stood up, stared at him, and listened with great anticipation to what he was about to say.

"Give him some love. Lots of love. Sometimes it's the best medicine."

TWELVE

The pancake batter filled the bowl on the table in the corner of the kitchen. After Lizzie put a spoonful of lard into the hot skillet, she scooped up a ladle full of mix and made three liquid cakes that will eventually be added to the stack on a platter on the breakfast table. The thought of melted butter smothered in Maple syrup made everybody's mouth water.

A pot of coffee was perking on the stove. As the water climbed up the tube and dripped through the strainer quickly changing it to a black color, the aroma of the freshly brew filled the room. "Hmmm, good enough to start a man's day." Slowly, John inhaled the smell, grinning from one ear to the other.

In another skillet, Lizzie stayed busy turning the sausage links that were sizzling over a hot flame. Like a professional cook, she knew how to put on the finishing touches that made everything taste so good. When brown enough she put them on a paper towel that covered a platter, thus allowing the grease to drain off. Then, more links were added to the skillet. "Lot's of sausages. That's what the farmers want. They work so hard all day in the field."

A box of Corn Flakes stood in the center of the table next to a pitcher of cold milk along with some orange juice. The salt and pepper shakers were parked next to the sugar bowl. With plates and silverware all in place along with a napkin under each fork, breakfast was ready to be served.

"John, please say the blessing so we can eat." Lizzie folded her hands while her elbows rested on the table.

"Why sure! Dear God, thank you for this food. Amen."

Grinning. "That's what I like 'bout you John, short and to the point."

"I'm not much for pancakes today." Linda's eyes searched the selection spread out on the table. "Please pass the cereal."

"Why sure. Anything your sweet little heart desires, dear." Uncle John always treated her different than Orville. Boys were always expected to live up to certain expectations.

"Looks like another nice day today, John." Lizzie smiled while sipping her coffee. "Sure can get a lot done outside."

"Yep! Sure can." Silence filled the room for the moment. John looked around the room in search for something like a prospect looking for gold. "Hey! Where's Orville?"

"It's OK, John." Lizzie tapped his hand. "I let him sleep in this morning. Besides, he needs his rest."

"Needs his rest nothin'. He should be down here with us. There's work to be done around these parts."

"Please John. Just this one time. I beg to differ with ya."

"Nonsense! No Boy of mine is gona sit around this house and get lazy." Like all the other times, John got angry when he didn't get his own way.

"But John!"

"But John nothin'. Listen woman! As long as I wear the pants in this house, what I say goes. Now get that Boy down here now. Never mind, I'll get him myself."

"John, listen to me." Lizzie begged.

"Yes dad. Please listen to her." Linda pleaded with him while pouring some milk on her cereal.

"You stay outta this. Or you can go to your room."

"Listen John."

"No I will not listen." Soon a shouting match occurred.

"If you so much as speak to that Boy today, I'm going to hit you over the head with this here frying pan." Orville's mother was ready for war.

"Woman! I don't scare easy. Now where is he?"

"He's up in his room. I told him he could have breakfast later. And I mean what I say." Lizzie stood firm, holding the frying pan up high over her head.

"Nonsense. I'm gona get that Boy right now." John briskly pushed himself away from the table and stood up. Then, he walked toward the stairs where he proceeded to climb until Lizzie quickly stepped in front of him.

"Please dad! I beg you to leave Orville alone." Without hesitating, Linda rushed to give Aunt Elizabeth some help.

Pausing to reflect on his thoughts for the moment he replied in a soft tone. "Why Mama Hodge, I never heard ya speak to me like this before."

"It's OK Ma." Orville stood at the top of the stairs. I heard every bit of what ya said. You guys are always arguing."

Unck looked up the stairwell. "You get down here right away, Boy!" His voice started to escalate with a mean look on his face. "We've got work to do. Ya should've been up hours ago and had breakfast." Unck showed no compassion for the Boy's real needs.

Slowly Orville, in pain, walked down the steps holding his rib cage. When he reached the bottom of the stairwell, Unck grabbed him behind the neck with his hand shaped like a claw, and pushed him over to the table.

"John! You're hurting him! Stop it!" Lizzie shouted.

"Leave the Boy alone." Uncle Milton stood by the outside kitchen door. You've done enough damage already round here. We don't want anymore."

Surprised. "Milt! Ya can't just barge in here and run my family."

"Right now, all I'm interested in is the Boy."

Stubbornly, John ignored the warning. "Just sit down and eat, Boy. We've got work to do."

"You all right Boy?" Uncle Milton bravely took his place next to the Boy in front of John.

"Yeah! Sore, Uncle Milt. A little sore. But I'll be all right." Orville replied slowly in soft tones moving his eyes back and forth between Unck, Uncle Milt, and Lizzie.

Suddenly, there was a knock on the screen door in the kitchen. "Hey! Mornin' folks! Anybody in here?"

"Yes. Sure is, Uncle Dan! Come on in!" Lizzie yelled.

"Walkin' by I smelled sausage. Sure smelled mighty good." He looked around the room. "And now I see pancakes too." His eyes were ready to pop out of his head. "Makes a man's mouth water."

"Oh hush, you old man! Sit down and I'll get ya some."

Suddenly there was another knock on the screen door in the kitchen. "Hey! Anybody here? Can I come in?"

"Yes, Uncle John! Come on in!" Lizzie grinned, while shrugging her shoulders. There were several Johns in the family and often it got confusing telling them apart.

"Just happened to be walkin' by and smelled sausage cookin'." He wiped his lips with his tongue and looked around the room. "Sure would taste good. And I see ya have pancakes too."

"Sit down Uncle John, next to Dan over there, and I'll get ya some." Lizzie walked over to the stove and filled a platter full of hot pancakes.

Suddenly, someone else knocked at the screen door. "Hey! Folks! Anybody in there?"

Linda snickered.

"Yes, Uncle Mike! Come on in." Lizzie turned around to eye the intruder while continuing to make more pancakes, a favorite in the Hodge household.

"Heard a lot of talkin' goin' on in here, so I thought I'd stop by."

"Did ya happen to smell sausage cookin' too?" Linda chuckled, watching all the stuffed mouths moving with Aunt Lizzie's special recipe.

"Why, as a matter-of-fact I did." He paused for a moment. "And I see pancakes too." He smiled imagining the taste of Lizzie's pancakes with melted butter and hot Maple syrup in his mouth.

"Take a chair with the others, Uncle Mike. I'm makin' more sausage and cakes right now. Linda, could ya give me a hand?"

Before long several more Uncles joined the party around the

breakfast table at the Hodge house. Lots of small talk filled the room, as a bunch of hungry, hard working farmers satisfied their appetite.

"Now, where were we, John? What were ya sayin'?" Milton stared at Uncle John while chewing a mouth full of sausage.

"Nothin' much, Milt. Just a friendly chat." Uncle John realized when he was cornered. It was a no win situation for him so he spoke in a mellow tone. "Well I've eaten. And I've got lots to do. Please excuse me boys." And he walked away from the table.

Following breakfast Orville quietly moseyed on back up to his room. The pain in his back was an on again off again thing. His mother changed his dressings several times each day, carefully wrapping him with an Ace bandage that kept the gauze pads securely in place. "Sometimes I feel like one of those Egyptian mummies all wrapped up in a museum."

Back in his room, Orville got comfortable on his bed. Stretching, gesturing the discomfort on his face as he stretched the skin over his shoulder blade muscles, he reached for a magazine on the bedside table. A few more moves and he was ready to delve into some interesting sports articles. But it wasn't long before his thoughts drifted back to the day of try-outs with the Boys' baseball team.

Not too long ago he was with lots of other guys trying out for the Boys' baseball team. They called themselves The Boys on the Gold Coast because they originated from that neighborhood in Chicago, Illinois. Soon word got out that they were a great bunch of guys and fun to play baseball with. Orville agreed.

Like everybody else, Orville did his best to qualify. But like a lot of other test, nobody knew the final outcome till the test results were completed. The waiting game can be an agonizing experience. Soon Orville started second guessing himself. "Should I have hit better? Why did I miss so many pitches? The other guys were better fielders than I was." And so on. Negative thoughts started to out weigh all the positives. Sitting around in an empty room got boring, and he wondered if it was really worth it all.

Now came the long wait. Day after day went by with no news in sight. Though feeling sore, Orville made that painstaking trip down to the mailbox with great anticipation every day. And each day, maybe an electric bill, phone bill, or a couple of magazines, lots of junk mail, but nothing from the Boys on the Gold Coast. It was easy for him to get discouraged and feel sorry for himself.

Getting something in the mail was an exciting event. It didn't matter what it was, just as long as it was something. A letter with a person's name on it, or a little brown package with a key chain inside often felt good.

Orville can recall one day, as a kid, looking at the comics in the Sunday newspaper. Browsing down the page he came across an advertisement about a still picture viewer. In the picture it looked big and something every child would want to have. Along with it came three disks with five pictures on each disk, similar to looking at a beautiful scene in a View Master camera.

Continuing to move his eyes across the page, Orville finally saw in the lower right hand corner: print your name and address and mail it in to the following address with just twenty-five cents. "Wow! I sure would like to have one of those." And his eyes got bigger just thinking about what he could do with it.

Asking his Uncle for twenty-five cents was the last thing on earth he wanted to do. So, with an innocent look on his face he approached his mother. Even though times were tough, and money was hard to come by, she wanted the best for Orville, even though his Uncle wouldn't approve of it. With a little love and a mother's touch to an eight year old, they worked out an arrangement that if he kept his room clean for two weeks without being told, he could have the twenty-five cents. And it was a happy day when Mom and son sat down at the kitchen table to fill out the blank, tape the quarter to a piece of cardboard, place them in an envelope, seal it, address it, and put a postage stamp in the upper right hand corner.

And so the long wait began. Three weeks later a little brown box appeared in the Hodge mailbox. But when it did, Orville was racing down the road screaming, "Ma! Ma! It's here!" And quickly she rushed outside through the kitchen screen door with an apron over her dress, as if the house were on fire.

Shortly thereafter, Orville and his mother were sitting at the kitchen table opening the box that was about half the size of a matchbox. The little viewer that was nicely decorated and blown up to four times its original size in the comic strip, was no bigger than two thumb nails put together, and take away one thumb nail, and the Boy had the size of a disk that slides into a small compartment for viewing. However attractive it may have been in the advertisement, it was something to get in the mail that made Orville happy.

A few years later, Orville could recall shopping at the local grocery store and picking out some of his favorite cereals. High above, on a shelf, a colorful arrangement of boxes decorated the wall. He can still remember the storekeeper taking his claw on a long stick, and reaching up to pick out a box of Post Rice Krispies on the top shelf near the ceiling.

Cereal was a favorite breakfast treat for Orville, so he never had any problem opening the box and pouring the contents into a bowl before adding some cold milk. However, on one particular day, something else caught his attention. On the backside was an advertisement for some plastic baseball players.

Moving his eyes across every word on the back of the box, being careful not to miss anything, he learned about a chance to collect an entire baseball team for just three dollars and seventy-five cents plus three cereal box topes.

The assortment of players looked authentic and stood two and a half inches high. A detailed catcher held his attention for a long time. Then a right-handed pitcher with his leg kicked up high into the air ready to throw the ball. A lefty stood straight up with his hands together over the back of his head also ready to pitch the ball. A first baseman stretched his body with every aching muscle while extending his three-fingered mitt. A shortstop brought his hands together close to the ground ready to scoop up a grounder. The more he learned about this offer, the more excited he became. All the players were yellow plastic. For an additional three dollars and seventy-five cents, he could purchase an additional set made of blue plastic. Perfect. He would have two different teams, ready to play each other.

It wasn't long before he earned the money by making deliveries for a local cleaner. Working three days a week for a couple of hours each day and on Saturdays, he earned ten dollars a week. Once he had the money, he cut out the order blank on the back of the box, stuffed it into an envelope, made sure he put on the necessary postage stamp, and mailed it. Oh yes, and three cereal box topes were also included.

As a child, back in those days, three major sport events entertained audiences across the country. Baseball. Football. Basketball. Cable TV had not yet been born, and sports' viewing on the tube was limited. In the summer it was baseball, followed by football in the fall and early winter. Professional basketball wasn't very popular, as most sports-minded people focused their attention on the Big Ten Universities, not to mention other colleges. So Orville was in his second heaven when he thought about baseball.

Now that he had the players, what was he suppose to do with them? Well, it didn't take him long to organize a Cub baseball team. Listening to Cub's baseball on the radio all the time, he made a list of the players. Then he made scorecards. Yellow was one of his favorite colors, so they became the Cubs and played the blue team.

From a list in a local newspaper, he picked out the names of several players from an opposing team, and completed his scorecard. One day it might be the L.A. Dodger's, the next day the St. Louis Cardinals, and still another day, the Milwaukee Braves.

Looking at the pictures in his favorite baseball magazine, he liked the look's of the baseball diamond: the way the infield grass was squared off, the white foul lines, the curved edge that marked the beginning of the outfield grass, and the batter's box. The dugouts for the home team and visiting team also intrigued him. So, he got the wheels really spinning in his brain, and made a baseball field with dugouts for his newly developed baseball teams.

After school one day he moseyed on over to the local grocery store and brought home a couple of orange crates. Then, with a rusty old claw hammer, he removed all the nails and collected a dozen boards. With a handsaw, he made a square base measuring about thirty inches on all four sides. From the hardware store he purchased some penny-nails (as they were called) to secure the boards to the base. Some old molding wood, a half inch square that his Uncle kept in the barn, was used in places where the boards needed added support. A double wall was made on two sides to allow room for the dugouts. Cardboard from a box was cut out and used as a field. Finally, he painted the walls black, the only color he could find in the barn, and pasted navy blue construction paper over the support beams for the grass. The most fun was saved for designing the infield. With a compass he made the infield curve on a piece of gray construction paper, carefully joining a thin, one-eighth inch line from first to home plate, and third to home plate where another smaller circle was drawn. Bases and batter's box were painted on the paper. And, the Boy smiled from one ear to the other with his eyes ready to pop out of their socket, as he looked at the completed project.

The rules were the same as any other baseball game. Nine innings. Three outs and they changed sides to bat. A player must cross the plate in order to score.

To play the game, Orville took a spinner from another board game. All the necessary plays—single, double, triple, homerun, walk, and so forth were in place. It was fun to play.

From a book called the Rocking Horse Winner, there was a boy that loved to ride his horse. Every time he went up into the attic and got on his horse, he visualized himself riding on a racetrack. The more he rocked, the faster the horse would go, and he would win the race. The boy could do it for hours, and Orville felt the same way playing his baseball game.

When he wasn't busy working on the farm, or in school, Orville sequestered himself in his room playing baseball. It didn't take him long to get the field out from under his bed, get his players out of his shoebox, and make a scorecard on a piece of paper. Soon his thoughts were absorbed in the game and the minutes just flew by.

Orville loved to mimic the radio announcer, Jack Quinland, on WGN radio. "Hello baseball fans! And here we are again at beautiful Wrigley Field. The lead off man is on …he was hit by a pitch …the fans cheered …Back! Back! Back! It's outta here …the batter watched the ball." Carefully he placed his players on the field and spun the dial. It was fun to dream and he could do it all day.

Meanwhile, back in the real world, Orville started to feel the pain again nudging its way through his back. With a little help from his mom he felt fine again for the moment. However, the lingering thought about the Boys from the Gold Coast made reading a magazine impossible, so he put it away.

A week went by and still nothing. Everyday he anxiously walked down the road toward the mailbox. Sometimes, he stared out the window for hours, peaking through the trees, hoping to see the mailman coming. And when he came, he hustled his sore aching body out the door to greet him. And when the postman gave him nothing, he mumbled under his breath. "Darn! Another twenty-four hours to wait. It feels like eternity."

Following a long weekend he began to feel better and almost gave up on the idea of ever playing baseball again until one day he leisurely, just to keep pace with the routine, went to the mailbox one more time. Sticking his hand into the hot silver cylinder, heated by the sun, he pulled out a handful of envelopes along with a couple of magazines. Then, back home in the kitchen he carefully laid them out on the table. Most of them were the usual bills addressed to his Uncle; his mother hardly ever got anything. But he did notice one letter addressed to him. Moving his eyes to the upper left corner, he saw Pop's name. His heart started pounding, rapidly sending vibrations through his chest. Mixed emotions blurred his thoughts. Either way, it had to be good or bad news.

Nervously he opened the envelope. Inside he saw a one-page letter with three short paragraphs. Dear Orville, it read …Fear gripped his thoughts. Holding the paper close to his chest, while staring at the ceiling, he took a deep breath. Finally, he realized he should be a man. His mother said he should always be a man. So, he read on. Anxiously he skipped to the last paragraph that comprised two lines, and as his eyes carefully rolled across the page, tears started rolling down his cheeks. Congratulations! See you Monday at practice. Sincerely, Pop.

THIRTEEN

The black shinny Buick sparkled in the sunlight as it cruised down a country road. "Yes sir." Fred watched the speedometer with both hands planted firmly on the steering wheel. "They sure don't make 'em like this anymore. Fenders. Grill. Bumpers. Running boards. Pretty good for a car made in the 40's and still runnin'."

Forty-five miles per hour was top speed in those parts of Indiana. Slowing down, it took the curves like riding on air. The engine was so quiet the driver didn't know it was there.

He traveled a couple more miles among the open cornfields. Then, clusters of trees began to crowd the territory before he approached some scattered houses. Soon a gas station appeared, a few vacant strips of land, and finally a cluster of little shops. "Hmm. Must be Cedar Lane." He looked at his watch. "Didn't think it would come up so soon."

In town he made a right turn at the main intersection, and traveled another mile before coming to a small bridge of boards covering a creek on his right. The mailbox read Hodge, so he knew he was on target. After flipping on his turn signal, he slowly rolled over the boards and on up the hill toward the house on his left. Immediately, Ralph, the dog, who wouldn't stop barking, greeted him.

"Ralph! Ralph! Stop it!" Lizzie shouted as she rushed out the screen door on the side of the house. "You'll disturb the neighbors". She patted him on the butt.

"Nooo! Ma! She just wants to be petted." Uncle Fred stooped down to scratch him behind his ears. "That's a good boy. Yep! You can lick me all ya want."

"Well either way, come on in." Lizzie motioned with her hand. "Have some breakfast. Ya must be starved after the long drive."

He limped behind her into the house. "No. The trip didn't seem that long. I guess makin' the trip from over yonder so many times before; I just got use to it. Didn't seem long at all. But I sure could use another breakfast." He looked at his watch again. "Even if it is getting late."

"Don't worry 'bout the time. John is still getting ready upstairs. So you've got plenty of time."

After pulling up a chair and getting more comfortable, he rolled up his sleeves. "OK. What's for breakfast?"

"Waffles. You silly old man. Hot fresh baked waffles with bacon on the side." Sitting directly opposite him on the other side of the table, she reached over and placed a platter under his nose.

"Wow! With a little melted butter and some Maple syrup, my mouth can taste 'em already."

"So!" Lizzie broke off a piece of her waffle, stabbed it with a fork, and brought it up close to her mouth. "You're goin' to the apple orchard today."

"Yep! Thought it'd be a good idea for Uncle John to get away for the day."

"You can say that again. You know how hard it is to pull him away from the farm."

"Yep! Wasn't easy!"

"How'd ya do it?" Lizzie hoped to learn some big secret formula about how to influence her brother, and perhaps bring some real peace to her own mind.

Uncle Fred took a deep breath and stuffed his mouth full of waffles. "I'm glad ya asked. At first I wasn't sure if the trip would be a good idea or not. Then, I got a call from Uncle Milton."

"Oh?" Lizzie looked surprised.

"Yep! Said something 'bout this bein' an important day for Orville …"

"Shhh!" Lizzie interrupted, whispering, placing her finger over her mouth. "Don't wanna talk 'bout it here. Orville might hear what your saying."

"I gotcha. A secret."

She nodded her head. "Sorta."

"Anyway! So I thought it would be a good idea to visit Blake's Apple Orchard up in Michigan. I know it's early for apple pickin' time, but I thought it'd be nice just to visit with old man Blake and see how the trees are doin'."

Lizzie smiled while voicing her approval. "Well ya couldn't of picked a better time."

"Time for what? John asked, limping into the kitchen like the old man walking without a cane, quiet as a church mouse. "What ya all talkin' 'bout time?"

"Oh nothing, John. We were just sayin' it soon will be pickin' time again."

"Don't remind me, Lizzie. Times movin' fast enough as it is. Don't wanna think 'bout how soon we'll be pickin' again." While turning to get a good look at Uncle Fred, he sat down. "And mornin' to you. How've ya been lately?"

"Fine, John. Just skip all that formality stuff." Fred waved his hand.

"Just need another cup of java to get me goin' and we'll be on our way." Uncle John poured some coffee into a large mug.

After the usual small talk that lasted another fifteen minutes, the two Uncles were out the door. With a lunch pal in his hand, John got comfortable in the big car, while Fred moseyed around to the other side and got behind the big steering wheel. Soon the engine started to purr like a kitten as they backed out of the driveway. Lizzie waved good-bye from the kitchen screen door, and watched them slowly roll down the hill, over the creek, and on their way down the highway toward Michigan.

Meanwhile, after clearing the table back in the kitchen, Lizzie waited another five minutes before giving the all clear signal. "Orville! Ya can come down now! He's gone!"

Quickly, Orville came down the stairwell, skipping several steps at a time, and jumping with excitement. For once in his life he didn't have all the pressures of farm work with Unck on his back.

"What'd ya gonna do today, Orville?" Lizzie asked, pouring him a glass of orange juice.

"Don't know yet." It didn't take him long to get comfortable at the table. "Cousin Louie's comin' over. Says he wants to go bike ridin'. I said sure but where? Don't know he said, but we'll go somewhere."

"Here! Have some waffles. Ya didn't eat much this mornin'. Don't want ya to get hungry." Like a concerned mother she pushed a plate, stacked with waffles covered with melted butter and smothered in Maple syrup, in front of him.

Smiling. "Ya know I never go hungry, Ma. You're the best cook in the whole wide world. Sometimes I eat too much."

"Well never-the-less. Maybe ya'd like to go fishin'. Unck's pole is in the barn. He didn't take it with him."

"Nope. Good thought though. Besides, it's getting late. Fishin's better in the early mornin' or at night."

"It was just a suggestion." Ma got up from the table to pour herself another cup of coffee.

"Knock! Knock! Anybody home?" Cousin Louie tapped at the screen door.

"C'mon in Louie. You know you don't have to knock. Just walk in. You're always welcome here at our house."

"Yep! I know that." The medium height boy with the short brown hair plastered to his head, in blue jeans, was ready for a bike hike. "But my mom always told me to be polite."

"Well ya don't have to be polite here." Aunt Lizzie walked toward him with a cup of coffee in her hand. "Can I get ya something to eat?"

"No ma'am. I already ate. Thank ya anyway. We gotta get goin'. Time's a movin' along quickly." He looked at Orville. "How ya doin' buddy. Ready to go bikin'?"

"Yeah! Sure!"

"OKKK!" Louie padded Orville on the shoulder.

"Do ya know where we're goin' yet?"

Stuck for the right words at the moment, Louie stared at the ceiling and grinned. "Yeah! Sure! Got some ideas racing through my head, but we'll figure 'em out when we get goin'."

"Good! I'm glad somebody knows where we're goin' cause I sure don't." Orville wiped his mouth with a napkin, and walked over to give his mom a big hug and kiss on the cheek.

Outside, the Boys mounted their bike and soon were off. A flash of orange and a flash of chocolate color brown quickly disappeared down the hill. Suddenly, they braked before slowly rolling over the loose boards above the creek. Then they pedaled down the road to the next traffic light as if in a race before cheering fans. After making a left turn, and peddling a short distance, they were back on a familiar path in the woods.

Knowing the route from memory, they traveled faster and faster with Louie leading the way. Clearing some branches in their path, over a root peeking out of the ground, through a mud puddle, they went as if they were on automatic pilot. Coming to a Y in their path, Louie hung a right while Orville suddenly stopped.

"Hey Louie!"

Down a ways Louie quickly applied his brakes before putting one foot on the ground to support him and his bike. "Yeah? Whatta ya want?"

With both feet firmly planted on the ground and cupping his hands close to his mouth, Orville shouted. "Isn't this the way to Sherwood Forest?"

"Yep! But who said we're goin' to Sherwood Forest?"

Orville shrugged his shoulders while grinning. "I guess I …"

"Well don't just guess." Louie winked. "Follow me. Believe me. I know what I'm doing."

Over a knoll, up another slight embankment, and suddenly they dropped down a sharp hill. The Boys extended their legs straight out in front of them and prayed, hoping for a smooth landing at the bottom.

Through the woods on a winding path eventually the bushes got shorter till there were only a few scattered trees. Beyond them,

Orville recognized the backside of several stores all lined up in a row. Soon they were traveling down a side street lined with a brick wall on both sides beyond the sidewalk. At the first intersection Louie made a quick right hand turn and signaled for Orville, who was riding alongside him to stop. After dismounting their bike, they now stood in front of Ellen's Malt Shop.

"C'mon! Let's go inside." Louie motioned, waving his arm.

"Great! Cousin Louie! But I don't think so. I'm not hungry for a malt." With a streak of shyness, Orville didn't socialize well with other people. Consequently, he hardly ever went into town. Perhaps that's why working on the farm was a good excuse.

"Yeah! I hear ya buddy. Loud and clear." So Louie braced himself firmly behind Orville and pushed him into the shop.

High above the big picture window outside the sign read Ellen's Malt Shop. Nothing fancy. Inside, a long canary yellow wall was joined at the far side by a shorter one, and each decorated with a couple small landscape pictures. The ceiling, a plain arrangement of Celotex squares, supported two fans with three lights on each, shinning down on the customers below from its center. On the opposite side of the long wall was a long counter with stools secured to the floor. A dozen tables with Formica tops, supported by aluminum legs and complimented with four simple wooden chairs were scattered throughout the room. And at one corner a jukebox played favorite tunes all the time.

The ladies in pink dresses with white aprons stayed busy behind the counter making malts, preparing the burgers and French fries, along with other sandwiches and deserts. The sound of the motors mixing malts, a popular drink, in silver canisters was running constantly to accommodate customers.

Ellen's Malt Shop was a favorite hangout for many young people. Recently its reputation spread and drew large crowds from all over the county. Surely, the place was always packed with people having fun, listening to their favorite rock singer like Elvis Presley on the jukebox, and other songs.

After Don't Step On My Blue Suede Shoes and Love Me Tender, the mood shifted to Bye Bye Love sung by the Everly Brothers.

Meanwhile, on the floor teenagers jitterbugged to the fast paced music. Girls in ponytails tied with ribbons, wearing pleated skirts, white bobby socks, and black and white saddle shoes had fun. Guys in a sport shirt and slacks were more clumsy, but had just as much fun. The shop was small. People often bumped into each other, but laughed it off.

"Look at Patsy over there dancing up a storm." Kenny pointed to the gal in the center of the floor, drawing lots of attention. She was the envy of all the girls who wished they could dance like her.

"Oh! You mean the one with the pigtails?"

"You're darn right, George. Sure wish I could dance with her."

"I thought you liked Brenda."

"Yeah! Still do George. Back at school she and I always danced the Fox Trot together." Ignoring any response for the moment, Kenny was dreaming. "But right now I wish I was with Patsy."

After shaking his head with a grin, George excused himself. "Well I don't know 'bout you friend, but I'm gonna ask Sandra to dance with me." Boldly he walked over to the medium height gal with the long straight sandy color brown hair draped over her shoulders.

"Well excuse me." Kenny was offended.

"Hi Sandy! How are you?"

"Fine." She smiled while holding a glass of soda in her hand.

"Havin' fun?"

"Sure am." She blushed. "But it sure would be better if some-one asked me to dance with 'em." George was the best looking boy in the malt shop. The girls always went crazy around him. It was rare not to see him with a cluster of pretty girls gathering around him at school.

"Well say no more, Sandy." George started to sweet-talk her. "With those pretty brown eyes and cute smile, your troubles are over. Let's dance."

After taking her hand, he led her out to the center of the dance floor. He excused himself as they bumped into a few other people along the way. Music and the jukebox was a big thing at Ellen's Malt Shop, and there were lots of people dancing. Soon they were doing the jitterbug with everybody else.

George loved to dance. Anything he put his mind to he could

do. First, a right foot forward, then a twist of his ankle. Then the left and a twist. Wiggle his behind and start all over again. Holding hands, Sandy complimented all his moves. And they stayed with the beat of the music of Bye Bye Love sung by the Everly Brothers.

It wasn't hard to bump into other people on the dance floor, and George rubbed behinds with Barbara often while moving around the floor. When she felt his vibrations she merely giggled, shrugged her shoulders and moved on.

Barbara was another pro on the dance floor. When she didn't have a partner to dance with, she'd just get out there and dance by herself to her heart's content. In peddle-pushers knee high, red and white plaid top, and tennis shoes, she danced alone, bobbing to the beat of the music. The gal with short black hair and bangs was always in another world.

Following Bye Bye Love, came a moment of silence. It was unusual for the jukebox not to be playing somebody's favorite tune. However, tapping his spoon on a water glass, Steve sought everybody's attention.

"Folks! I have an announcement to make. We have a celebrity with us today. A special guess, and his name is Orville."

Everybody applauded with cheers.

"Yep! Orville just got chosen to play with the Boys from the Gold Coast."

"All right!" Louie shouted and clapped his hands, encouraging everybody in the room to join in with a big round of applause. Smiling faces gestured as if they already knew about the event.

"So! Let's celebrate!" Steve held up his glass of soda.

"Yeah!" The crowd cheered.

"Speech! Speech! Speech! We wanna hear a speech!" The folks chanted.

Blushing with a silly grinned, Orville wasn't accustomed to all this attention. Soon he was pulled out from under his chair by a couple of tough guys who assisted him up to the front of the room.

Thank ya all for likin' me and sayin' nice things 'bout me. I don't know what else to say." He grinned while staring at the floor to avoid direct eye contact with the crowd.

"Tell us how it feels to be a baseball player with all those other guys!" Stephanie shouted, from the center of the room.

"Don't know. Haven't played with 'em yet. All I know is practice starts next week."

Orville felt nervous standing in front of all these people. He wished it was over when Steve walked up to him. "This is for you, Orville. We're happy for you and want ya to have this." He reached over to hand him something wrapped in white paper.

Orville smiled, looking it over. "Thank ya Steve. And thank ya everybody." As he started to walk toward his chair Nancy shouted. "Aren't ya gona open it?"

To satisfy everybody's curiosity, even though they probably already knew what it was, he stood up in the center of them and nervously removed the wrapping. Everybody watched in awe wondering what it could be.

"A book!" He proudly held it up for everyone to see. In bold red letters against a blue background with the outline of a baseball diamond it read: Boys On The Gold Coast ... "Wow! I like this." Grinning. "And I'll be sure to read it. Thank you all."

As the folks started to scatter to their tables and stools near the counter while others to the dance floor, the sound of a spoon tapping on another glass echoed throughout the room. "Hey folks! Over here! Can I have your attention?" Ellen stood on a chair in a man's sport shirt draped over her blue jeans. Immediately, everybody stopped what he or she was doing to listen. "This is a great day. Let us celebrate. Soo! It's free malts for everyone. So enjoy!"

"All right!" One boy shouted to the background of laughs and lots of chatter. And soon the music was playing again while some folks danced.

"Congratulations Orville!" Carol stood on her toes, reaching to kiss his cheek.

"That a way to go buddy!" Steve was the first to shake his hand.

"Give it your best!" Richard, a good neighbor, padded him on the back. "I knew ya could do it."

"Good goin' buddy! Ya deserve it!" Louie felt relieved after keeping a secret bubbled up within him for many days.

"Hey cousin! Ya knew 'bout this all the time, didn't ya?" Orville blushed and grinned while staring at him straight in the eye.

"Let's just say I had an idea somethin' was cookin'. OK?"

"I knew ya was a good player all along." Barbara kissed him on the other cheek. He tried to back away, but couldn't as he was pinned in by people on all sides. "C'mon! Let's dance!" Before he could say no, she grabbed his hand and pulled him out on the dance floor.

The pace of the music slowed down to a two-step while the jukebox played Put Your Head On My Shoulder. It was something the shy little Orville might be able to handle even though he preferred not to dance at all.

"Take my hand Orville, like this." She took a hold of his hand. "Put your other hand on my waist." She paused. "Good, like that. Now watch me. One and two and one and two. Two steps forward and two steps back. Then, we do it again moving slightly each time in a circle."

The tall thin Orville moved clumsily at first taking big steps. Finally, after some more coaching along with some practice, his moves were in line as he started to sway his hips. Soon, his moves were smooth and easy and flowed with the music on the jukebox. "This is nice. Feels good to be dancin' with a girl." Surely, all the pleasant thoughts started to race through his mind.

"Very good Orville. I like dancin' with you." Barbara paused long enough to stand on her toes and give him another kiss.

Following the music, folks clapped their hands and cheered while some sat down and others continued to dance. In the midst of all the conversation with the music playing in the background, dancing was an on again off again thing all afternoon.

"C'mon Orville! Let's get a table." Barbara took his hand and led him to a table in a corner of the room.

"Gee whiz! School will be startin' soon, and I gotta get some new clothes."

"Ya look fine to me." Orville grinned, looking at her eyes.

"Oh silly. Don't ya know? A girl always likes to get new things."

"Whatta ya gona get?"

"Blouse tops. My mom says Nettie's Dress Shop always has a sale around school time. Maybe a new skirt. Some socks. And a few unmentionables that you don't need to know about." She blushed. "How 'bout you? Wouldn't you like to have some new school clothes?"

"Yeah! Sure!" Orville smiled. "But to be honest with ya, I never gave it much thought. Unck always said that what I had was good enough. Then he'd say, think of all the starvin' people in India."

"Oh Orville, I hear ya. But you're such a good guy. And hard working too." She looked at his freckled nose while holding both of his hands on the table. "Surely you deserve something." The soft sweet tones in her voice and the twinkle in her eye sent goose bumps running down Orville's spine.

"Excuse me folks!" Lillie interrupted, putting two huge chocolate malts on the table. "Enjoy! Ms Ella wants you all to have the very best." She stared at Orville with her eyes about ready to pop out of their socket. Then, before the heavy set lady in the black and white flowered dress walked away, she congratulated him one more time.

"Thank you Lillie!" Orville paused to think what he would say next.

"Now where were we? Oh yeah! Everybody deserves somethin' new for school in the fall. My mom says if we save our money, we can get somethin'. Might not be much, but it's something."

"Yep! Guess so, Barb. Hope ya don't mind me callin' ya Barb." He started to sip his malt.

"Oh no! I like that." She struggled, sipping some of her own malt. The thickness and different flavors are what makes Ellen's malts popular.

To accommodate him in getting the cold rich chocolate flavor down his throat, Orville started stirring it with his straw until he gave up and used his spoon. Finally, slowly, he was able to suck the delicious liquid out of his glass and into his straw.

"Hey! Did ya hear the one 'bout Johnny? Why'd he take his ruler to bed with him?"

"Don't know, Barb."

"To see how long he could sleep. Ha! Ha! Ha! Ha! Isn't that funny?'

"Yep! Sure is!" He accommodated her with a smile.

"Or how 'bout this one. Why do hens lay eggs? Surely, your

bein' from the farm. Ya oughta know this one."

"Yep! They lay eggs because they want to."

"Good! I like that! But no! It's because if they drop them, they'd break. Ha! Ha! Ha! Ha!"

"Yeah! That's it!" Finally, Barbara got a response out of Orville. Sometimes farm people were different. They acted like they were in another world.

The small talk continued. Barbara loved to chatter, especially about herself. However, she always had the courtesy to explore other people's feelings, stop, and listen to what they were saying.

Orville never was much of a talker. He just went about minding his own business. However, when in the presence of a pretty girl like Barbara, he did his best to be cordial, listen, and occasionally respond to the conversation. Then, all of a sudden in the midst of their conversation, his thoughts drifted off to a familiar tune on the jukebox.

It was the McGuire Sisters, who made their debut into the music world on the Arthur Godfrey talent show that was viewed by millions of people across America. Following his usual Lipton Tea commercial which always reminded people to take tea and see, he manipulated a needle on a monitor that responded to the applause from his audience. In those days most TV shows were broadcast live. Due to popular demand the McGuire Sisters took first place, continued to be loved by many people, and eventually spiraled their popularity to greater heights.

For the moment Orville was in a trance listening to the McGuire Sisters singing a song titled He. It talked about God and his control over the universe. Then it went on to mention that in spite of people's failure on this earth, He always had time to forgive them. As he continued to listen, the words started to resonate with Orville's own personal experiences in life. And he pondered the thought about forgiving those people who have wronged him.

Lost in her own stupor of conversation, Barbara continued to chatter. "Why did the chicken cross the road?"

But Orville didn't respond. Instead, he just stared at the wall.

She waited patiently until she couldn't take the silence any more. "Hey Orville! Did ya hear what I said?"

"Huh?"

Barbara shifted her body around to get more comfortable in her chair. "I didn't think so. Now pay attention. Why did the chickens cross the road?"

"Don't know, Barb. Maybe there were more chickens on the other side they wanted to be with. I don't know. Tell me."

"To get to the other side, stupid!" She joked about the riddle before changing the subject to something more serious. "Hey! Where were you? It looked like we lost you for a moment. Ya know what I mean? Like if you were on another planet." His facial expressions began to arouse her curiosity.

"Huh?"

"Where'd ya go? I thought I lost ya for a moment there."

"Oh! No where special."

Three hamburgers sizzling on a grill smothered in onions sent a delightful aroma throughout the restaurant. Diligently, Ellen turned them over with her spatula. A few more minutes and they were on a bun with some ketchup, mustard, and relish, along with some grilled onions. Add some fries to each plate, and they were on their way to some happy customers.

Ellen started this shop years ago with her husband Tom, when there was nothing else like it in town. In the middle of nowhere, other than a gas station down the road, and a general store in the next town, they thought it would be nice to have a little place where folks could rest their weary bones and chat a bit. Needless to say, the folks liked it, and has drawn large crowds ever since.

Even though money was scare, somehow the kids always found enough to drop into the jukebox. It became more popular than drinking Ellen's delicious malts, but not by much. Ten cents got a tune. Twenty cents got two tunes. For a quarter three of somebody's favorite hits. Surely it was a bargain. And it was always fun to sit around and talk. Often, on weekends, Ellen had to ask the folks to leave just so she could close the place down late in the evening.

And the party went on. People of all ages came and went at their pleasure. Most frustrating was finding a place to sit. Even though carry outs started to increase, no one wanted to leave. It was a good place to be with friends, talk about old times, and enjoy good food.

The dance floor stayed busy. Bumping shoulders and butts, while stepping to the music, really didn't matter. It was fun just to be around other people.

From a slow waltz or two-step to the beat of a jitterbug where the pace picked up, the folks danced the night away. The atmosphere was always upbeat. A happy feeling that made everybody feel good, and forget their troubles for the moment.

"How does Janet braid her hair?"

"Doesn't have pigtails like Patsy."

"Is Mike racin' again?'

"Did ya see the way she combed her hair?"

"I heard folks say Blanch got an inheritance from her uncle."

"Molly makes donuts all the time."

"Barney's been out fishin' again."

Small talk filled the room and folks felt good just talking about anything under the sun. But who said people had to get serious at Ellen's Malt Shop?

As Orville and Louie left Ellen's in the midst of lots of chatter and eating, the jukebox played another tune by The McGuire Sisters titled, Just For Old Times Sake. The faster moving beat raised everybody's spirit, while in one corner of the shop a girl argued with her mother because she didn't want to leave.

FOURTEEN

Back at River Front Stadium the noise started to escalate. Fifty thousand baseball fans blended their voices to support their star player. Cheers quickly dominated the boos.

The ball sailed toward the plate. Surely, a strike on a full count and another out. Curving slightly to the outside, Lee May hesitated, twitching his fingers while jerking his arm gesturing a swing. Finally, the ball echoed a loud thud sound when it landed in Randy's glove.

"Ball four! Take your base!" The ump pointed to first base, while Lee tossed his bat aside and trotted down the line.

Meanwhile, Randy Huntley, the Cub catcher, wasted no time dropping to his knees and throwing the ball to third. Immediately Santo stepped off the bag and stared at Pete Rose charging toward him.

Quickly, half way to third, Pete stopped dead in his tracks, wheeled around and raced back to second when he saw Santo coming toward him. Moans voiced the fans disapproval.

But Santo kept going, and so did Pete, like trying to pass somebody in a race. Then he threw the ball. It beat Pete to the bag. "He's out!" The TV broadcaster shouted to thousands of viewers.

Standing behind the bag, Beckert had the ball safely tucked into the web of his glove, long before Pete ever reached it. Then he dove, sliding on his chest several feet while Beckert brought his glove close to the ground for the tag. However, with his mitt firmly resting on the bag, again Pete dug his hand into the ground, just a fraction of an inch below the fielder's glove, thus wedging his hand between the base and the ground. "Safe!" The ump shouted, hutched over, spreading his hands to give the sign before a standing ovation from the crowd.

"Hey ump! Do ya need glasses? Look again! Think! I think he's out." Beckert politely challenged the umpire. "Do ya ever make a mistake?"

"Huh?" The ump braced his legs with arms folded.

"Never mind. I was only kidding." After tapping Pete's shoulder, Beckert threw the ball to first where Lee, who refused to budge, wouldn't take the bait and stray off the bag.

"Hello baseball fans! Jack Quinland here with Lou Boudreau over WGN-radio. Back here in Cincinnati you're listening to Cubs baseball. We're in the bottom of the ninth in a tie game 3-3, one out and runners on first and second."

Then River Front Stadium got quiet. For the moment baseball fans were speechless, watching Orville standing in the batter's circle.

"Don't know him, Barney. Who is he? Never saw him before in my life."

"I'm with ya, Harvey. Beats me if we're gona win this game with him."

"Marge! Where's he from?"

"Probably somethin' they dug up from the minors, Blanch."

Fans mumbled among themselves while many remained puzzled.

"What's Dave thinkin'?"

"You mean the manager?"

"Yep!"

"Probably doesn't know what to think. For sure he's second

guessing what's left on the bench."

"Don't see his name on my scorecard."

"Neither do I."

"Isn't there anybody else he could use? Maybe Pete Rose."

"Elmer! When did ya last have your eyes checked?"

"Hah?"

"Gee whiz! Ya can't hear either."

"Hah?"

"Never mind."

"Hah?"

"Look! Pete's already batted."

"Hah?"

"He's standing on second base."

"On first did ya say?"

"No. That's Lee May on first."

"Hah?"

"Never mind. Just watch the game."

Back on the field, Orville nervously swung a couple of bats over his shoulder while standing in the on deck circle. Then, after tossing one aside, he slowly walked toward home plate.

Silence resumed as fans stared at the Unknown Baseball Player. Even the commotion in the Cub dugout couldn't deviate their attention.

Then, like a shot from out of nowhere, Leo Durocher rushed out of the dugout shouting at the umpire. "Hey! Wait just a minute." He held up his scorecard, racing toward home plate.

Meanwhile, Orville just stood there with a bat resting on his shoulder when the umpire signaled with his hand, calling time. Uncertain about the reason, the Boy waited for further instructions.

"Ump! I don't see him listed on my roster."

After adjusting his trousers and tightening his belt, the man dressed in black struggled to get his own list out of his hip pocket. "I'll tell ya in a minute. Let me see what my card says."

Soon the other umpires joined the meeting at the plate.

Without hesitating, Dave Bristol trotted out of the Redleg dugout to join them. "What's up? Why the holdup?"

"Leo is questioning the Boys eligibility." Finally, the heavyset umpire scanned his list.

"Oh?" The Redleg manager looked surprised.

"He shouldn't be out here." Leo shook his head. "Ya just can't bring anybody out of your Club House to play ball."

Looking puzzled, Dave told Orville to return to the dugout. Confused and disappointed, the newcomer wheeled around and slowly walked back toward the bench. For the moment, his big hopes to play ball were dashed.

"My card says he joined the team last week." The umpire raised his chin, allowing his eyes to glance at the print from the bottom of his glasses.

"Oh! C'mon ump! Whatta ya talkin' 'bout? I don't see him on my list." Leo remained adamant.

The first base umpire concurred with the home plate umpire along with the other umpires. "Best that we remain quiet." No new thoughts from the three men in black were evident.

"Whose list?"

"My list, Dave. The one my secretary gave me."

"Maybe she didn't give ya all the scoop."

"Are you insinuating my gal makes mistakes?"

"Never mind Leo." The Redleg manager remained composed. "Whatta ya say ump?"

The umpire's eyes rolled across each line on his scorecard. Very methodically he studied each name. After flipping it over to look at the other side, he repeated the process. "I see his name right here …on the back side. Don't know why you don't have it on yours." He showed it to his fellow umpires before Leo looked at it.

"For all I know he shouldn't be here in the majors." Leo insisted on getting Orville removed from the game.

"Oh?" Dave was hoping the Cub skipper would hang himself with words.

"Yeah!"

The other umpires nodded their approval with the chief. "He's listed on my card."

Tucking his card back in his hip pocket, the third base umpire walked back to third on the foul line, as the other umps likewise returned to their original positions on the infield.

"You know darn well he belongs here, Leo." Dave argued,

ready to defend his star player.

"He's not on my list!"

"You're list is not up to date!"

"Yes it is!"

The anger escalated. Patience grew thin. Leo's jaws were rapidly chopping with his chest stuck out. Finally, the ump wedged his hands between them to separate them before boos and moans from the fans.

Following a few more harsh words from the man in black, reluctantly both skipper's returned to their dugouts. After pausing on the apron of the Cub dugout, Leo mumbled some obscenities. The umpire paid no attention.

With the silence gone, cheers echoed again throughout the ballpark when they all heard a familiar voice blare over the PA system. "Play ball!"

FIFTEEN

"Ball Four! Take your base!" The ump shouted before dusting off the plate.

A loud thud sound echoed off Randy's glove as the ball made contact with the leather. "Darn!" And while the team regrouped their thoughts, before facing another batter, the ace catcher of the Chicago Cubs threw the ball to Beckert, standing on the edge of the infield grass, just off the base line. Randy stood tall behind the plate. "I saw the ball at eye level sailing through the air uninterrupted."

Beckert raised his mitt to field the ball. The crackling sound made when the ball landed in his glove assured him that he caught it. While stepping to his left, he returned it to the plate. Randy dropped to his knees, held up his two-fingered pad, and trapped the ball in it with his bare hand. Then he side armed it to third.

To stay loosened up, the team often threw the ball around the horn between plays. And the outfielders did some quick knee bends or twisting exercises as well.

The ball sailed toward third. Nothing stood in its way until a big brown patch of leather appeared out of nowhere and interrupted its flight. Santo took two steps forward after judging his distance and fired the ball to first.

Ernie Banks stayed close to the bag. With one foot firmly in place, he stretched every muscle fiber in his body, reaching to scoop the ball up out of the ground.

"I feel the pulse of the game, just watching the ball, Harvey."

"I don't know how they do it. Moving that ball around, they make it look so easy."

"Some fancy ball handling, Fred."

"Just wish I could be out their with 'em."

"Keep dreamin', Harold."

"Too old for wishful thinkin', Barney."

Surely, the fans were entertained. With a hot dog in one hand, and a soda in the other, they were having the time of their life. Often their thoughts wandered off. Laughing. Talking. Having a good time. The score didn't matter. Just good old fashion fun and the hope that it would never end.

Back on his feet, Ernie side armed the ball to short. Nothing eventful, Don Kessinger didn't even have to move when the ball came sailing toward him. Extending his arm, the hot potato landed safely in the web of his glove. After picking it out with his bare hand, he tossed it back to Beckert, who stood only a few feet away near the second base bag.

Meanwhile, Billy Williams, the left fielder, did some fancy knee bends. With his hands firmly placed on his waist he stooped to the ground. Slow and methodical, like in spring training, he allowed every muscle to loosen up.

In center field, Don extended his arms straight out as far as they would go. In the shadows to one fan it looked like the formation of the letter T. Then, with his legs firmly braced he twisted the trunk of his body back and forth, first to his left, then right. He smiled with satisfaction as he massaged every muscle fiber.

Jim Hickman, the right fielder was anxious to play ball. Muscle exercises didn't interest him. After pounding his glove with his fist, he leaned forward, braced his legs, and got ready for the next ball to sail his way.

At second base Beckert quickly returned the ball to Randy behind the plate. As it sailed across the diamond, over the pitcher's mound, the ball passed Alex Johnson, the next batter, standing near the batter's box.

Kenny Holtzman circled the pitcher's mound, scanning his fielders, before stepping back on the rubber. Then, satisfied with a sign from his catcher, he went into an abbreviated wind-up and delivered the next pitch.

The ball sailed wide when Alex let it go by. Raising his arm to reach it, the Cub catcher barely had enough time before it tipped off the seam of his glove, and sailed to the screen behind him. "Ball one!" The ump shouted, placing his hands together behind his back, giving the sign.

Alex swung viciously on another fast ball. The loud thud sound as it landed in Randy's glove, left no doubt he missed the ball completely. And the fans voiced their disapproval.

"He should've hit it, Barney."

"Yep! The pitch dissected the plate."

"Blanch! Maybe the ladies could do better."

"I'm not so sure, Peggy. Those boys work hard. My husband says they practice, practice, practice, all the time."

"Ha! Ha! Ha!" Sarah laughed, over hearing the conversation. "With all that practice one would think he shouldn't of missed the ball at all."

"Don't be smart, Sarah."

"You mean cynical, don't ya?"

"Who cares? He missed the ball and that's all that matters."

"Whatta ya think, Larry? You're awfully quiet sittin' over there."

"Just thinkin'."

"Thinkin' 'bout what?" Harvey was always curious to know what the other guy was thinking.

"Don't ya know curiosity killed the cat?"

"Well I'm not a cat." He paused to regroup his thoughts. "And I'm not dead yet either. Now put that one in your pipe and smoke it."

"What was the first base coach sayin'?"

"Did ya see the way he leaned into the pitch?"

"I would've let it go by."

"If that catcher would just stop chattering, he might be able to hit the ball."

Small talk. Jabbering. The fans liked to hear themselves talk. And the more they saw, the more excited they got. Sitting on the edge of their seats, the plays were spellbound and filled with lots of action. They watched in awe, cheering their favorite team on.

"You'll never hit it, Alex. Forget it. Let it go by. Don't waste your time. The ball is outside. It's way off the plate. Believe me. So how's your mother doin'? Are the kids OK? Your ankle doesn't look good." The Cub catcher talked excessively. Rambling nonsense.

The next pitch left the mound spinning and traveling very fast. Half way to the plate it lost steam and started to slow down. However, Alex's mindset still focused on a fastball. His thought processes didn't change gear fast enough. Swing! "Strike!" The ump shouted, cocking his arm, giving the strike sign. The fans booed.

The Redleg batter couldn't believe it. "What'd I do?" He tried to rationalize an excuse. Without answers, he stepped out of the batter's box to regroup his thoughts.

The first base coach did what looked like a rain dance on an Indian reservation. Clapped his hands. Touched his cheek. Tapped the sun visor on his cap. Rubbed his left arm, then the other. Rapidly, he repeated the process several times. Over and over again he motioned. Surely, he was telling Alex something.

A curve ball sailed wide. The batter leaned into the pitch, attempting to compromise a bad decision. Practically standing on the plate, while Randy reached over for the catch, he swung, and some wood connected with the ball.

The ball shot up like a rocket, almost straight up into the sky. On the descend, the shortstop called everybody off as he raced in toward the pitcher's mound. Curving, curving, curving, the wind caught it. Don followed it. Bang! He crashed into Santo, who was also following the ball. The ball dropped between them. "Boo!" The fans couldn't contain themselves. Alex got new life. All runners quickly returned to their bases.

The Cub fans were outnumbered. Consequently the cheers

dominated the crowd. Mixed emotions reined. Surely, Alex was on his way to the showers until Mother Nature gave him another chance. Or was it poorly fielded?

"Ha! Ha! Ha! Ha1 Did ya see that, Barney? I'll be darn." Harvey slapped his knee.

"Talk 'bout luck." Arnie chuckled.

"Relax honey. It's only baseball. Whatta ya expect?" Feeling bored, Mary Anne looked at her watch. "Will this game ever end?"

"If this isn't luck, I don't know what is." Arnie wasn't listening to her. He begged her to come with him. To stop the pestering she finally gave in.

And the Redleg fans mumbled their approval in the midst of protest.

"Now that's good ball playin' if I do say so myself."

"He was lucky. There was nothin' Alex could do if Kessinger watched what he was doin'."

"Whatta 'bout Santo? He got in the way."

"I sure would like a date with Alex. Wish he'd date me …call me on the telephone." Sally's blue eyes twinkled on a smiling face.

"You're dreaming."

"No I'm not."

"What does a date have to do with baseball?"

"It's not like Kessinger to miss the ball."

"Santo should've called him off."

There are as many opinions about that play as Carter has liver pills. Thousands. The fans could argue all day and still not come up with any logical conclusion.

The next pitch sailed wide again, forcing Randy to step out of the box. Luckily the ball hit his chest protector and prevented the runners from advancing. "Ball one!"

Another ball grazed Alex's knuckles, as it hugged the inside corner and forced him to back away from the pitch. "Ball two!"

After pausing to catch his breath, Kenny delivered another pitch that sailed high over the plate. The replay on a TV monitor showed the ball at eye level with the batter. Randy extended his arm high enough to catch it, preventing it from sailing to the screen behind them. "Ball three! Full count!"

As the noise escalated in the ballpark, Alex stepped out of the batter's box, and took a couple of warm-up swings. After taking a deep breath to help relax his nerves and get a sign from the coach, he resumed a batter's stance back in the box.

On a full count, Alex was bound and determined to protect the plate. He put a stinging fastball in the seats over the visitors' dugout for some lucky fan. A slow ball rolled just inches off the foul line. Then a sharp hit liner toward the Redleg dugout.

"Duck!" Several players scrambled to get out of the way.

Without thinking, Orville put up his bare hand, as the ball took a funny hop, deflected off his hand and continued rolling back out on the field. "Ouch! Man! Did that hurt!"

"Hey, farm Boy! Ya all right?"

Several teammates clustered around Orville, as he shook his injured hand. "Where's the trainer? Get him over here!"

"It stings! Feels like strange vibrations running up my arm. Never felt like this before." Orville was in pain.

"Ya gotta lot to learn, Boy. Maybe ya never got hit by a base-ball before."

"Nope! I probably didn't."

"Hey! Move over. Let me see what's goin' on here." The Redleg manager pushed his way through the crowd. "Where's it hurt?"

Orville held up his hand.

"You from the farm, Boy?"

"Yep! Indiana, Sir!"

"Doesn't look broken to me."

"Nope! Don't think so either."

"I thought farm boys are tough."

"Don't rub it in Dave." Each teammate went down the line defending the new comer.

"You work on the farm?"

"All the time, Sir."

"Like what? Watchin' the big boys work?" Nobody appreci-ated his sarcastic tone.

"Milkin' cows! Pulling weeds! You name it and I've done it. Chickens and more ..."

"Leave 'em alone boss. He'll be all right."

Soon the trainer arrived and led him back into the locker room where he examined his hand. "Don't let that guy get on your nerves."

"Been through a lot Mr. Trainer."

"Just call me, Rob." The medical guy manipulated his fingers manually, looking for any possible breaks. "Hmm. No cuts. That's good."

"Yes Sir. Tough! That's what I am. Ready to play ball. You'll see. I'll show 'em." Grandiose thoughts raced through the Unknown Baseball Player's mind.

SIXTEEN

Life on the farm wasn't always pleasant for Orville. He wasn't allowed much of a childhood. He became an adult before his time. No time for fun. No time to play. Only work and school lay ahead. Uncle John called all the shots. When he spoke everybody listened. When he joked everybody laughed. He was a very controlling person. He lived in America with a European mindset.

One day while Orville was plucking corn off the tall stalks in the field, he overheard his Uncle calling all the men together. "Hey guys! How's it goin'?" All the Uncles groaned.

"Did ya ever here the story about Goldilocks And The Three Bears?"

"Not that one again." Uncle Dan complained.

"Oh no! I don't wanna hear it either." Uncle George moaned while shaking his head and staring at the ground.

"No wait! I didn't hear it."

"Ya did too, Uncle Fritz." Uncle Carl assured him. "Ya probably just don't remember. How could ya forget when that story was told over and over again? It was enough to make us all get sick."

More moans and groans. Feelings were mixed. It didn't really matter to Uncle John. He loved to hear himself talk.

"Well there were these three bears. One day, they all went out for a walk, while their porridge cooled. When they returned, they were mad."

"Gee! I wonder why!" Uncle Linz grinned. Once Uncle John made up his mind to tell a story it was settled. A no win situation. So, like many other times before, they decided to humor the man along.

"I'm glad you asked." He never realized that they were playing along with an old familiar story.

"Did they complain?" Uncle Joe asked. "What'd they do?"

"Papa bear groaned in a deep voice. Whose been eating my porridge?"

"Who ate it?" Curiosity aroused all the Uncles interest.

"I'm getting to that. Be patient. Then mama bear asked whose been eatin' her porridge."

"Who ate hers?"

"Shhh!" Uncle John motioned, placing his finger over his mouth. "I'm getting to that. Then baby bear asked whose been eatin' his porridge and ate it all up, and he began to cry."

"Poor baby bear." The Uncles felt sorry for him.

"Now wait just a minute guys." Uncle John motioned with his hands. "Mama bear then turned to him and said, shut up baby bear because I didn't make yours yet."

"Ha! Ha! Ha! Ha!" Uncle John laughed with a few of the Uncles, while the others gestured a silly grin.

"I think I heard this one before." Uncle Fritz looked puzzled, scratching his head.

"OK men! Time to get back to work." Uncle John gave the order, like an army sergeant clapping his hands. But they didn't care. Living under strict military rule in the Old Country was far worse than living in America.

It was early one morning. A rooster started to crow. The screeching sound echoed throughout the farm. The house remained silent when Orville reluctantly crawled out of bed.

Not long thereafter, in ankle-high unlaced boots, Orville tramped over to the barn. Rolling up his sleeves, he grabbed a stool and started milking the cows. Moving down the rows, one stall after another, each cow filled a bucket.

"Move that stool closer to the cow. Ya can't milk her bent over like that. You'll hurt your back." Unck followed him around everywhere. He was always right. Orville always wrong. If he tied his shoe looping the bow with his right hand instead of his left, he was wrong. Nag. Nag. Nag. There was no end to it.

"I'm sorry Unck. I thought I was close enough."

"Yeah!" The grumpy old man retorted, waving his arm. "Ya never do it right. Sometimes I think I'd be better off doing it myself. Will ya ever learn?"

After he finished milking the cows, Orville led them out to pasture. He struggled opening the big barn door. The weather beaten wood squeaked on its hinges protesting every move. After unhitching the ropes fastened to each cow's bridle, they instantaneously backed out of their stall. The cows knew where they were going. It was a routine habit.

"Nellie! Betsy! Mort! Ellie! Let's go!" Orville shouted, swishing each rump with his broom.

After leaving the contented cows in the pasture, he slowly walked over the hill back toward the barn. Now, his time was his own for the moment. The freedom to think was a blessing in disguise until his thoughts were interrupted. "Orville! What ya doin'? Where ya goin'?" The nagging sarcastic voice lingered deep within his soul, and never left him alone.

But he kept walking, hoping it wasn't what he thought it was. Later in his life he recalled Napoleon Hill, famous author of Think And Grow Rich, saying, the one thing man has no control over is another man's mind. How refreshing those thoughts were as he faced many difficult challenges in his life.

"Orville! Pay attention! Listen to me!"

Instead, Orville kept right on walking, hoping to avoid eye contact with the body behind the voice.

"Hey! Don't ya ever listen to me?" The voice kept getting closer until it was up against his ear. Suddenly, a hand grabbed his arm, forced him to stop walking, turn around and look at his opponent.

"Did ya get all the cows out?"

"Yep! Why don't ya go see for yourself?"

"Don't talk back to me, Boy. I'm your Uncle. I work hard to put food on the table for you, your mother and sister, Boy."

"Sorry Unck. I'm just tryin' to say that all the cows are out."

"I saw ya walkin' along doin' nothing, and was wonderin' what ya were up to." Uncle John was always quick to nose into other people's business, especially Orville's.

Uncle John was a hard working man and a good provider. But he was always telling Orville what to do. All work and no play was his motto. Whenever the Boy was reading a book or playing catch with a friend, feelings of guilt quickly swelled up within him. "Do something, Boy! Stop wasting your time!"

Back on the farm Orville heard the chickens chirping. The irritable sound got louder as he approached the pen. After closing the gate behind him, he entered the hen house.

Inside, the flock was ready to attack him. Not one chicken welcomed his arrival, as some of them clustered around him and started pecking at his hand with their sharp beak.

Elsewhere scattered throughout the hay, some of them laid content. White fluffy feathered birds with sharp crooked beaks. It would take an earthquake to move them off their nest.

In spite of the loud irritable sound attempting to scare Orville off, he searched for the feed pan. "Ah, there it is. Buried beneath some hay in one corner." Pouring some chicken feed from a big scoop into the pan, one bird continued to peck at his hand till it drew blood.

Before leaving, he pulled the long hose off a wheel outside the hen house, twisted the nozzle, and filled a water pan. It was important to keep the chickens eating and drinking all day, otherwise they wouldn't produce any eggs.

Finally, after taking a deep breath, the hard working farm Boy sensed that his work was done for the moment. However, without question a full schedule lay ahead.

At the breakfast table was a bowl of scrambled eggs, a stack of pancakes on a platter, and a pitcher of fresh orange juice along with some crispy bacon and smoked sausage, among other things.

The women always believed in a good hearty breakfast of nourishing food to start the day.

Children were to be seen and not heard. Silence was a golden rule in the house. So Orville, Sis, and Cousins just minded their own business, while the old folks moaned and groaned about the troubles of the world.

The big break from work was school. Rain or shine, the kids walked the mile down the hill and over the creek to the highway. Greeted by a big yellow school bus, they joined the other kids for the ride to the schoolhouse.

The children laughed and told jokes as they bounced along over the bumpy roads. Sometimes they were having so much fun that the bus driver had to settle them down before they got silly and hurt someone.

"Hey buddy! Don't be such a drab!" One kid said, encouraged by his friends.

"Yeah! Don't be such a bore. Get a life."

"Leave Orville alone." Cindy interrupted.

"Oh yeah?" Stan shouted, sticking out his chest.

"Leave her alone." Ben grabbed his arm. "She's a girl." Everybody got quiet when Ben spoke. He was the tough guy in the crowd, and strong with big muscles. He never shied away from putting people in their place. Most of the kids avoided him with fear and trembling.

Orville didn't mingle much with the other kids. His serious thoughts kept him focused more on work and studies. The fear of a shadow creeping over him kept him in line, minding his own business. Some of the kids thought he was anti-social. Later in his life, he regretted allowing these fears to control him.

But he did enjoy the bus ride. Looking out the window, he watched the other kids play. A girl jumped rope. To the tune of a song, her rhythm kept pace with each jump. Soon the other girls chimed in and sang with her.

Another girl bounced a rubber ball on the sidewalk. And when a friend came along, it turned into a game of catch.

Eyes rolled watching Billy do tricks with his yo-yo like around-the-world, walk-the-dog, and rock-the-cradle. Spellbound, they wished they could do them. He made it look so easy.

When little Johnny skinned his knee mom came to the rescue. A big hug, a kiss, and it was all over. Before long he was back out there peddling his bicycle again, and wearing a great big smile from one ear to the other.

Deep down inside Orville wanted to be out there with all the kids. He never felt like he was a part of the circle. As he stepped off the bus, he was quickly brought back into the real world. "Perhaps one day I will be like one of them. Hah! More wishful thinking."

After school it was back to milking cows. "Yep! It was back to the barn again. The same process started all over again. How boring." Reluctantly, the thoughts raced through his mind.

Following dinner he was back in the chicken house. Like a game of hide-go-seek, he felt around in the hay for some eggs. There were lots of them scattered everywhere. "We were lucky that there weren't any roosters. Just fresh eggs for hardworking people back at the house."

The chickens continued to peck away at his hand. Obviously, they didn't want anybody tampering with their pride and joy. While nursing his wounds he heard the screen door open behind him.

"Hey Boy! What's goin' on in here?"

"Not much, Unck. I'm just fixin' my hand."

"Let me have a look, Boy." Without hesitating, he grabbed his wrist and held it up to the light under his nose. "Hmm! Don't look like nothin' to me."

"But Unck!"

"Oh hush. Don't be such a sissy."

"I'm not." A weak voice displayed feelings of insecurity. "I wanted to stand up to him. My mama always told me to be a man, and stand up for what is right. Sometimes I think she was forced to be submissive to him because he provided a roof over our head. However, doubts and fears raced through my mind, reminding me that right now I wasn't doing a very good job at it."

"Whatta ya doin' in here?" Uncle John was always good at changing the subject.

"Gathering eggs, Unck. Just like I always do."

"Good. Thatta Boy. See that ya don't break any of 'em." After another personal dig he left the hen house, always making sure that he had the last word.

But Orville's work wasn't done yet. In back of the big house Uncle John and Aunt Martha had a big vegetable garden. They seldom ever went to the grocery store. Corn, potatoes, beans, and carrots grew in abundance. "We ate good on the farm, and it took lots of hard work to keep it that way." Orville remembered those days very well, toiling all day and all night.

Constantly Uncle John badgered Orville to weed the rows of vegetables. A hoe turned the dirt between the tall stalks of corn. On his knees he pulled the nasty weeds growing close to the beans. Carefully, he pulled the potato plants out of the ground for dinner.

"Hey Boy!" Uncle John called from his tractor.

Like a mosquito that would never go away, Orville hated the Boy stuff. "I heard it all day, all night, and even in my sleep."

"Clean up time. Let's go. Gotta clean up." The constant sarcastic reminders often made Orville feel like running away from home.

Back in the barn he grabbed a push broom and started cleaning out the stalls. Lots of cow manure. Enough manure to choke ten horses cousin Al often said, jokingly. Then, he filled the wagon that would eventually take it outside to be spread on the field. Lots of back breaking work.

While many of his friends had time to play, Orville kept right on working. Living on the farm under an iron hand, he very seldom ever saw his friends accept when he was in school.

Late in the evening, tired and discouraged, he moseyed on down a beaten path toward home, a welcome sight indeed. Inside mama sat comfortably in her easy chair reading a newspaper, while his sister painted her finger nails and listened to the radio.

The clock showed 9 p.m. when he started doing his homework. Usually, a couple of hours each night, he struggled to keep up with his studies. Looking at his report card, he was proud of a C+ average.

"The things ya wanna learn come from books." Uncle John often boasted, pointing to his head with a finger while twisting his hand. It's strange that he should say that, considering all the demands he placed on Orville.

The bedroom was his respite. Away from the hustle and bustle of the day, he could be himself. Again he remembered Napoleon Hill saying that old familiar phrase. "No body can control our minds."

Lying in bed, staring at the ceiling, there were no negatives to focus on. No criticism, even though he pictured constant nagging. "You don't do things right. It's better that I do them myself. What good are you?" It was hard to get it out of his head. Nosing around, he was always in the Boy's business. In the barn, on the field, or in his sleep, he was always there.

Helpless! That's the way Orville often felt. He had no life of his own. Raised on doubts and fears, it's a wonder that he ever turned out to be anything good at all.

SEVENTEEN

"**Y**a dress warm, Orville. Ya here? Don't want ya getting sick."

"Yes mama!" He shouted from his bedroom, as he got ready for a very exciting day.

"Did ya brush your teeth?" Lizzie will always be a concerned mother, even if she went overboard occasionally babying him too much. Shouting back, her voice echoed throughout the house. "The red toothbrush is yours. Don't forget to put the cap back on the toothpaste."

"Yes mama."

"What'd ya have for breakfast Orville?"

"The usual mama."

"Did ya drink all your milk?"

"Yes mama."

"Did ya have bacon and eggs? Your body needs good nourishing food. None of that junk stuff that makes you hungry the moment you leave the house, or in an hour."

"Some times mama."

"Some times what, Orville?" Often she'd talk so much that she'd forget what she said.

"How'd ya sleep last night?"

"With my eyes closed, mama."

She smiled.

Rules. Mama had lots of rules to follow. Do this and do that. Follow the rules and Orville was safe. Disobey and watch out.

Orville knew he was all right when he followed the rules. There was no safe place to be other than school. When the bell rang they all went to their classes. Listen. Be quiet. Follow instructions. The results were passing grades and a chance to move on up to more challenging opportunities.

Next to recess, Orville's favorite class was gym. Besides the routine stuff they did everyday like running around the gym on a green line, or tumbling on mats, he liked to play baseball.

Outside the school building, two of the biggest bullies in the class, Andy and Carl, always chose sides. With the handle facing up, George tossed the bat to Andy who caught it with one hand. Then, Carl placed his hand, about the size of a good fist, above his. Climbing the handle, each guy placed his hand above the other guy's until they reached the top.

"Great!" Andy shouted. "I'll take Art."

"Get over here Ken."

"Richard."

"Mike."

"John."

Orville wasn't the best player among all the guys. You can see that because he was always chosen last. He had to be picked. The gym class required it. His pals didn't have a choice. If they did, Orville would be watching from the sidelines.

After tossing a coin to decide who would bat first, the boys scattered out in the field. Orville always played in short right field. Very few guys ever hit into right field, and besides, who ever heard of a shortstop between first and second base? "I think they put me there just to humor me along, and keep me out of their way. They thought I'd be happy there."

When it was time for Orville's team to bat, he always batted last. It was no surprise. But he felt good holding a bat and taking a couple of warm up swings.

"Wait a minute!" Paul shouted, standing near the fence. Immediately, he and some of his buddies scattered away from the fence off the left side of home plate.

"He throws his bat." Mike looked at Ben sarcastically with a goofy look on his face.

In spite of unpleasant circumstances, Orville's heart was in the game. Through the years he developed a real liking for baseball even though he got no respect from his pals. "My heart was burning with a passion to play baseball. I longed to be a regular player on the team. I wanted to be in the field catching fly balls, and a star player hitting home runs and bringing the guys home with the winning run. I relished the cheers from the fans. I was deeply hurt always being misrepresented by my pals."

"Relax!" Paul shouted to all the guys along the fence that quickly scattered. "No body's gona get hurt."

"Ho! Ho! Ho!" John joked. "Look whose talkin'." The guys laughed with fear and trembling. They remembered too well, the many times before when he threw his bat against the fence after hitting the ball.

"C'mon!" Jack complained. "Let 'em hit one. Let's get this game going."

"That's right Jack." Tony padded him on the back. "You always come to his rescue."

"I just wanna play ball. Coach Wicker will be over here soon, and gym time will be over."

Orville stood firmly in the batter's box and took a couple of warm up swings. He could never figure out what he was doing wrong. He held the bat right, choked up on it, and watched the ball sailing toward him from the pitcher's mound. Perhaps he needed stronger arms like all the other guys had.

The twelve-inch soft ball arched its way toward him. Then, he swung viciously. Quickly it sailed toward second base. Easy. A fellow classmate caught it on the fly. Another out. He did this all the time. A grounder to the shortstop or popup was the same. What's the difference? An out is an out.

At recess his time was his own. Fifteen minutes to walk

around the school grounds and watch the other kids. His social skills weren't the greatest either, but he sure wished he were part of them, someone on the inner circle having fun.

Occasionally some of the kids would gather to play ball. In overalls with a tattered ball and splintered bat, they'd choose sides. Naturally, Orville wanted to play too, so he'd mosey on over to join them. "Hey guys! What ya doin'? Can I play?"

"Ha-ah-ah-ah! Yeah!" Chuck laughed, looking puzzled. Orville noticed he was stuck for just the right words at the moment. It wasn't often that he'd catch one of his pals off guard.

"Yeah! You can play Orville. We're just about ready to choose sides."

The sides were picked, but he wasn't one of the lucky ones. "Hey Chuck! No body picked me."

"Ahhh! Ahhh!"

"He meant you can bat after Fred." Kenny interrupted.

"Yeah! After Freddie you can bat." Chuck smiled.

It was three up and three down. The innings passed quickly, and he never saw a bat or threw a ball.

He didn't play the outfield either. As the boys took their different positions, often Orville just stood behind second base in short center field. And the ball never sailed toward him. "Sometimes I feel like the guys planned it that way on purpose just to keep me out of their way. Now I'm starting to get paranoid."

There wasn't any organized youth baseball in those days. Baseball games were played on corner lots in overalls with tattered baseballs and splintered bats. An old piece of cardboard served as bases. They just had to watch out for rusty old nails chasing a ball toward the fence. It sounds like something taken from the pages of The Little Rascals.

Summertime was busy on the farm. If Uncle John had his way Orville would be working all the time. Lucky for him, mama always stepped in and saw to it that he would get some time to be with his friends. It wasn't much time, but some time used sparingly to play with his neighbors.

Down a beaten path, Rich and Orville found an empty lot that they frequented many times. It started with a simple game of catch. Soon it caught on and other guys in the neighborhood joined them.

It wasn't long before they were playing baseball. A softball quickly traveled around the infield. From third to first, to second, to home, to short, and back to the pitcher.

Two-man-in was their favorite game. One guy came up to bat while another waited his turn. For sure the guy on base had to make it home after the next guy hit the ball otherwise he was automatically out. They didn't have a catcher. Rotation started with the pitcher, and worked its way around from right field to left field. Then around the infield from third base to first. It was fun to play ball. No body was discriminated against.

Occasionally they split up into teams and played a few innings. Orville's neighbors eventually became his closest friends. They didn't have to impress anybody. It was just time for some good old fashion fun.

Orville liked to take long walks when time permitted him to do so. Through the woods, down a beaten path, away from all the hustle and bustle of life, his thoughts wandered into a different world.

One day, while weaving his way through the trees, he stumbled upon the backside of an abandoned gas station. It looked like the perfect place to get away. But abandon buildings always looked suspicious to him. "Why was no one there? How long has it been vacant?"

To satisfy his curiosity he slowly and quietly crept around the building to get a better look. Like a church mouse, he didn't want to be discovered. It felt like he was carrying something valuable, as if he just discovered gold in California and didn't want to get caught.

There was nothing unusual about this structure. It had big white dirty concrete blocks on all sides. A big picture window next to the front door. Pressing his nose against the glass, his eyes started to search the inside. In the dark he saw an old wooden desk like Miss Pryor, his first grade teacher had, collecting dusk. A few papers were scattered on the floor next to a chair lying on its back.

In front of the station was a concrete base about five feet long, six inches off the ground with a couple of steel pegs peeking through. He assumed this is where the gas pumps once stood.

Most intriguing to him was the backside of the station. A small window, boarded up, ten feet off the ground at one corner was the only opening to the inside. The remainder of the backside was a concrete wall about fifty feet long. Only rusty old nails along with a few hooks that supported some ladders at one time were scattered on the wall.

Once Orville's curiosity was satisfied, he raced home to get his tennis ball, and an old baseball glove his mom got him for his birthday a year ago. Then, it was back to the wall.

As his interest in baseball started to develop, he threw his ball against the wall. Quickly, it returned to his mitt. He threw it again and again and again, and each time it quickly returned to his mitt. Occasionally, it bounced off a nail and sailed high into the air. Soon his mind began to wander into another world, and it was fun to dream.

Using his imagination he pictured the crowd cheering as he walked out to the mound. He loved hearing the announcer say, "Number sixteen now pitching!" More cheers from the fans.

The TV announcer said, "Hello fans! Welcome to Cub's baseball over WGN brought to you by Coca-Cola. Today's starting pitcher for the Chicago Cubs is Orville Hodge." And in the background were cheers coming from all the fans.

Meanwhile, Orville continued to throw his ball against the wall, and every time it rebounded back to his mitt he got excited.

"Number sixteen fans is getting them out every time. Your watching live action right here before thirty-five thousand fans over WGN-TV." More cheers followed after every play on the field.

As Orville continued to dream, he pictured the fans reading the scoreboard. Orville Hodge it read. Ten wins. Three defeats. Strike out king. Pitched the home run ball once. No walks. Welcome lefty.

With no limit to the thoughts racing through his mind, his imagination ran wild. "I continued to throw my ball against the wall. The more I threw it, the more I didn't want to go home. I threw the ball to my heart's content. I could do it all day." Surely, Orville was in his second heaven.

Like any pitcher, he leaned forward and stared at the wall.

Placing his hands behind his back, he nodded his head hoping to confuse the batter. Then, bringing his hands together at his chest, he kicked his right leg up high into the air, and threw the ball. After the ball returned to his glove he shouted, "Strike!" And again he pictured all the fans cheering him on.

A couple more pitches and it was all over. He circled the mound, listening to the cheers when the batter returned to the dugout after taking a third called strike.

He continued to pitch to three more batters. Stooping to field a ground ball, one got by him for a single. The fans booed. One player hit a ball back to the mound that nearly knocked him off his feet. He threw him out at first. The next guy swung viciously at three pitches and missed. Goose bumps ran down Orville's spine watching them strike out.

Another time he was the team catcher. After signaling where he wanted all the fielders to stand, he squatted and threw several balls to the wall. Again his imagination ran wild. He pictured himself wearing all the necessary catcher's gear, which included shin guards, breastplate, and facemask. One time he caught a ball by his knee, stood up, and threw to second base. When he heard the fans cheer, he knew the runner was out. The ump gave the out sign confirming it.

When the team's fastball pitching ace walked out to the mound, Orville braced himself for some hard throws. With one knee firmly resting on the ground, he held up his baseball glove, and caught every pitch that quickly sailed over the plate. Traveling very fast, the next batter never saw the ball coming. Soon it was three outs and time for another inning.

Being a catcher intrigued him. Squatting. Holding up his glove as a target for the pitcher. Letting the ball bounce off his chest protector. Dropping to his knees to catch a ball and hold the runners on base. Wow! Fun! But who ever heard of a southpaw behind the plate?

Orville threw his ball. It hit the wall and quickly returned to his mitt. Every time it hit the wall it returned to his mitt.

As the star pitcher, he stared at the wall, and leaned forward with the ball in his hand behind his back. Then, bringing his hands together at his chest, he kicked his right leg up high into the air before throwing the ball. On the return, he pictured a fastball landing in the catcher's glove, which is really his own glove. And there were more cheers coming from all the fans.

Other times he was fielding a grounder. At third he hustled to scoop up a bunt and throw out a runner racing toward first base. He caught a sharp hit liner to the infield or a towering fly ball to center field. It was fun to dream.

Then, Orville played first base. A ball rebounding off the wall quickly rolled toward him on the ground. Well positioned on the edge of the outfield grass, he quickly brought his glove down close to the ground, scooped it up, waved off the pitcher, and raced toward the bag. The ump gave the out sign. Fans cheered. It felt good.

Another ball quickly sailed toward him. The southpaw batter hoped to line the ball over his head and bring the guy home from third. Leaping in a split second, the ball landed safely in the web of his glove. Without hesitating, he threw the ball to third. Meanwhile, the runner quickly wheeled around and dove for the bag. Lucky for him he was safe. The fans booed.

Lots of baseballs were hit to the infield. Orville loved to place his foot firmly on the first base bag, take a big stretch, and catch the ball, and beat the runners only by inches.

To his surprise many balls took a funny bounce off a rusty nail on the wall, and sending it high into the air. "Great! What a good opportunity to catch fly balls."

Then it was time to play center field. After pounding his glove several times, he raced in to catch a fly ball in short center field. Other times he was pinned against the wall leaping for a catch. Occasionally he missed a few. But it didn't take him long to get back on his feet for some spectacular plays.

In right field the batters tried to test his patience. Often the ball rebounded off the wall sending it away from his usual position. Thus, racing into the right field corner, he caught a ball on the run, and sent an angry batter back to the bench.

Most of the fly balls sailed into left field. Again, after pounding his glove several more times with his fist, he repositioned himself by stepping to his right, forward a couple of feet, or to his left, and caught the ball every time. And cheers from all the fans spurned him on for more spectacular plays.

In time he created his own team. Jerry played first, Larry second, Billy in centerfield, and so on. They always played the Chicago Cubs, Orville's favorite team. His imagination continued to run wild and it was fun to dream.

Before each game, during batting practice, the team loosened up. Like a game of hot potato, he quickly threw the ball to the wall. With some fancy footwork, without hesitating, he caught the ball and threw it back to the wall. The ball made its way around the infield. From third, to first, to short, to second, to the catcher and back to third again, where it started all over again.

Following the ball around the infield got him excited. The batter hit a ball that traveled quickly on the infield grass. Quickly, the shortstop scooped it up, tossed it to second, where the fielder wheeled around and threw to first. Yes! And there Orville was every time, throwing a tennis ball against the wall. On the rebound he was the shortstop, second baseman, and the guy stretching his long leg off the bag at first to catch the ball.

Another ball rolled down the third base line into the fielder's glove. Standing up to regroup his thoughts, he took a couple of steps forward and fired the ball across the diamond to first. Orville was everywhere and couldn't do anything wrong. It was fun to dream.

But all good things must come to an end. Feeling tired and hungry as the day was rapidly coming to a close, reluctantly, he picked up his tennis ball, grabbed his baseball glove, and went home.

Down a path and through the woods, his thoughts remained in another world. Baseball was his key to another life. A life he often wanted to belong to in the future. He wanted to be somewhere else. Perhaps playing baseball to his heart's content. Lost in his thoughts he almost tripped over a branch not watching where he was going. Then, suddenly his thoughts were interrupted by a familiar sound. "Hey Boy! Where ya goin'? What ya doin'?"

EIGHTEEN

"We traveled to Chicago, Uncle Milt and I. It was my first trip to the big City since I left there as a kid a few years back."

The big wheels on the ten-wheeler spun faster and faster. It was a smooth ride and felt like riding on air. Looking out his window, Orville saw the rows of beans quickly go by.

From inside the bus the driver had the best view. Sometimes Orville wished he were the driver. Through the big windshield he saw the broken yellow center lines on the highway quickly pass by. The Boy was intrigued, looking at how the man handled the big steering wheel when they went around corners.

"I'm not use to riding in luxury. Air conditioning made us forget about how hot it was outside. Tinted glass. Soft cushy seats that could easily put me to sleep." With bulging eyes looking around at everything and grinnin', from one ear to the other, Orville was in his second heaven.

As the bus approached the City they passed Soldiers Field, The

Natural History Museum, The Aquarium, and beautiful Buckingham Fountain, before entering the downtown area.

Cruising down Michigan Avenue, they turned left just before the bridge, and went through some convoluted underground passageway before entering the bus depot. Slowing down almost to a halt, Orville saw the big sign read: GREYHOUND BUS TERMINAL.

The depot was busy inside. People hustled about making last minute arrangements, getting tickets or saying goodbye to loved ones and friends. The shops were crowded with curious seekers looking for things to purchase and take back home. Suitcases stood everywhere. Even getting passed the benches where people waited their turn to board the bus was difficult. Lots of chatter echoed throughout the bus station.

"Attention please! Ladies and Gentlemen! Now arriving at gate six is number thirty-seven from Cedar Lane, Indiana." The loud voice over the PA system startled everybody.

Just outside the terminal the bus waited. Then, once the traffic light turned green, their driver turned the big steering wheel as they slowly started to roll. After passing several other parked buses, number thirty-seven veered to the right into another diagonal stall.

A greeting party of family and friends anxiously waited their arrival. When the big bus door finally opened, people eagerly got off with open arms. For some folks it was a long ride from New York City through Pennsylvania, and eventually here to Chicago.

Again the driver intrigued Orville. For the moment he paused and kept his eyes clued on him. Methodically he opened three or four doors on the side of the bus. Then, he took out lots of trunks and suitcases, and placed them on an oversize cart. And, as Orville's eyes continued to roll, looking at all the other buses coming into the parking area, suddenly he felt Uncle Milt pulling him into the station.

Uncle Milt was like a good friend to Orville. "I should be so lucky. When the workload back on the farm got rough, Uncle Milton always came to my rescue if I was treated unfairly. I don't know why, but he was always there."

To Orville's surprise one day at breakfast, following his morning chores, Uncle Milt barged into the kitchen. "Mornin' Liz, John, Martha, folks." As friendly and sociable as he always was, he couldn't remember names.

"Mornin' Milt." Not looking at him, Liz scrambled some eggs in the big frying pan over the stove. "Pull up a chair and sit down. Your eggs are ready and will get cold if ya don't eat 'em."

"What's so good 'bout it?" John's grumpy look always gave people a negative feeling at the breakfast table.

"Every morning's good John, if ya look at the good side of things."

"My-my. You're always so positive, Milt." Martha interrupted, smiling.

"I suppose that's where the good part of my day comes from." Another sarcastic response came from the head of the family.

"Hah?" Milton asked, looking puzzled.

"Oh C'mon, Milt. You know what I mean. With all the work we have to do around here, just thinkin' 'bout you is positive enough for me."

"Ha! Ha! Ha!" Uncle Allen laughed.

"Ya men better eat up before all this good food gets cold." Lizzie walked back to the stove to get more eggs.

"Yes, I agree." Martha left the table to help Lizzie with breakfast. The ladies of the house always stuck together and prepared some nice meals for the hard working men.

"Ha! Ha! Ha!" Milt laughed. "You're always lookin' after us old men, ladies. That's what I like about you. Feed us and then send us out to work our head's off." Shifting his voice to mimic a deep base tone. "Yah! Yah! Yah! It was real hard work. Ha! Ha! Ha!"

"Stop laughing Milt and sit down and eat your eggs." Aunt Martha looked at him square in the eye, while pouring his coffee and waving a spatula in his face.

"Yeah, I know. Or it will get cold."

"You bet." Uncle John mumbled, stuffing his mouth full of French toast.

Soon Uncle Milt got comfortable at the breakfast table with the usual chitchat. "How ya all doin'? Linda? Al? Orville?" Ann stayed out of the conversation while sitting at the other end of the table, looking at a magazine.

"Hi Uncle Milt. Got any new jokes to tell us?" The twinkle in her blue eyes always caught his attention.

Smiling. "Yes Linda. As a matter of fact I do."

"Go ahead Unck. We're all ears." Cousin Al chuckled.

"OK! One day there were these two ants. Another ant came along and now there were three ants. Then one ant said to …"

"Not that one again. If I heard it once, I heard it a thousand times."

"Oh you're just an old grump, John. Loosen up and maybe you'll get a life." Grinning. "And who knows, ya might like it."

"Don't tell me about life, Milt." John got defensive.

"OK! That's enough." Liz interrupted. "Eat up! There's lots of work to get done." Lizzie was always right.

Looking at Orville. "Hey Boy! How ya doin'?"

"Fine, Uncle Milt."

"Thatta Boy. That's what I like to hear."

"Yes sir."

"Say! Whatta ya doin' today?" Silence. "Not much." Holding up his hands. "How 'bout you and I go to a baseball game?"

"Baseball game?" Surprised. Orville's eyes nearly popped out of his head.

"Yes! A baseball game. The Cubs are playin' the Milwaukee Braves today at Wrigley Field in Chicago."

"Baseball! No sir! We've got work to do. We're farmers. He stays right here." Pounding his fist on the table, Uncle John voiced his anger. "Orville stays right here. He's goin' nowhere today. Do you understand?"

"Oh hush John. Leave the Boy alone." Lizzie felt strong standing next to Milt.

And so that's how Orville got to the Greyhound Bus Terminal in Chicago. Uncle Milt and the Boy were going to a ball game.

Outside, the traffic was bumper to bumper. Taxicabs, city buses, trucks, and cars cluttered the street. Occasionally a horn expressed the feelings of an impatient driver.

Weaving through the crowd, Uncle Milt and Orville hurried along walking toward State Street beneath the glittering lights of the Oriental Theatre. After stopping long enough to stare into the big picture window at Vaughn's to look at a display of castles and miniature knights in shining armor, Orville felt a tuck on his arm urging him to keep pace with his Uncle.

At another corner they stopped so Uncle Milt could regroup his thoughts. Meanwhile, with a hand shielding his eyes from a bright sun, Orville saw all the big signs down the street. Marshall Fields, Goldblatts, Mandel Brothers, Sears, and Carson's department stores all decorated the downtown area where shoppers browsed to their heart's content. Looking the other way, like book ends all lit up, was the State Lake Theatre and Chicago Theatre, which were popular movie houses.

In the center of the intersection a police officer in a navy blue suit directed traffic. The silver badge on his hat glistened in the sun. Waving his white-gloved hands signaled for vehicles to stop, turn or keep moving straight ahead. Occasionally he blew his whistle to get a driver's attention.

A horn blew and brakes squeaked when the old farmer in jeans with a bib, straw hat, and muddy boots limped toward the officer. "Pardon me sir. Could ya tell me where Wrigley Field's at?"

Puzzled, the man in the blue uniform brought all the traffic to an immediate halt. It was lucky no one got hurt. Removing his hat, he scratched his head. "Listen, old timer. Ya don't belong out here in the middle of all this traffic. This ain't the farm."

"Just wanna know where the Cubs are playin', officer." Even though he looked stupid, Uncle Milt could be just as stubborn as the next guy.

Then, they moseyed on down Randolph Street with the crowd. In business suits and fancy dresses, they hurried along only to pause long enough to stare at the two strange creatures from another time in history.

"Who they lookin' at, Unck?"

"Don't know, Orville."

With brief cases, a purse hanging over a shoulder, and swinging arms, the people continued to hurry along. Strollers hugged the buildings to avoid being trampled. Still, people could not help but to stare, giving them the strangest look.

"Hey buddy!" A pedestrian shouted, while quickly weaving around them. "Get a horse!"

"Who brought them out of the wood work?" One lady paused long enough to ask a friend.

"Move over old timer." A man in a business suit said, quickly pushing his way through between Uncle Milt and the Boy.

"Don't pay any attention to them folks, Orville. Just keep walkin'. Remember, it's always best to mind your own business."

Orville remained curious. There was so much to see. He never saw so many people before in all his life back home on the farm. He never saw so many stores and cars, or the lady rushing to catch a yellow cab. Even a stray dog raced across the street. He's lucky he didn't get killed.

At a bus stop they climbed the steps into the big green monster. After dropping some coins into a coin box, they took their seat half way down the isle. Naturally, Orville wanted to sit by the window.

The window's edge met his chin, so he had to sit tall in his seat if he wanted to look out and see anything. With so much going on in the big City, he didn't want to miss a thing.

For a twelve year old, again the bus driver intrigued him. He liked the way he steered the bus, turning the big wheel, moving away from curbs into the flow of traffic. It was fun to watch him push the little handles down on his change purse on his belt producing dimes, nickels, and pennies, so he could give change to the passengers. He even felt the motor vibrating in the floor as the bus struggled to carry a heavy load of people.

Leaving the loop, a name for downtown Chicago, the bus rolled across the bridge over the Chicago River. The big bridge bounced as they reached the center, sending chills down everybody's spine. Below a tour boat cruised along allowing the gawking viewers to see all the sights. Further down, a train on a double-decker bridge, kept pace with them crossing the River.

As the bus continued to move along, a variety of shops came into view. Away from the hustle and bustle of the downtown department stores, everything from A to Z could be purchased at one of these shops.

In the big picture window of Adolph's Meat market, a butcher was placing choice cuts of meat in white trays. Ribs, Chicken, Roast Beef, among other things was enough to make any mouth water just looking at it.

Inside Klein's Drug Store noisy teenagers read comic books, while angry customers approached the cash register. As Carl filled a prescription in the back room, things often got out of control in front of the store.

Tall steeples of various churches peeked through the concrete jungle, reaching out toward the sky. Holy Name Cathedral stood tall at Chicago Avenue. Crossing North Avenue, Orville saw Moody Memorial Church. Uncle Milt told him that his mama met his daddy there. "Wow! My old neighborhood must've not been too far away."

Soon they passed the Historical Society, a museum full of Chicago history along with our sixteenth president, Abraham Lincoln. A mile down Clark Street was another museum filled with butterfly collections and a variety of insects.

Stretching his neck, Orville felt like a giraffe whose head was far away from its body. There was so much to see in the City.

Below his window just outside the bus, cars and trucks passed them by. Occasionally an angry driver sounded his horn when the bus butted back into the regular flow of traffic. Turning the big steering wheel, their driver did lots of moving in and out of traffic.

Meanwhile, people continued to board the bus at every street corner. Soon, it was standing room only and lots of chatter to go along with it.

"Ernie oughta hit a home run today." A fat man manipulated an unlit cigar in his mouth. Rules of safety prohibited any rider from smoking inside the bus.

"Yes sir." A middle age lady with a weak voice replied, staring up at a man's face.

"He better, otherwise he strikes out most of the time. I just wish he'd hit a single once in awhile." The passenger's face turned red as he got more into the conversation about baseball.

"Yep! You said it best. I don't think I could say it any other way."

"Who they playin'? The Braves?"

"Who?" Another man questioned, with his ear up close to another lady's face.

"Lou Burdette pitchin'?"

"I thought it was Spann."

"Ya got good seats?"

"The best in the house."

"The ball almost hit the wall. He should've caught it. Instead he crashed into the wall, and missed the ball completely. We should've won the game." The gentleman shouted, waved his arm and almost tipped the picnic basket in another lady's lap.

"Nooo!" The passenger standing next to him listened in awe.

"Hey folks!" Suddenly, a bus full of passengers got as quiet as a church mouse. Startled, people froze, staring at the driver. "Next stop, Addison! Wrigley Field! Everybody out!"

After getting off the bus, Uncle Milton and Orville weaved through the crowd toward the entrance of the ball park. Baseball fans scattered in all directions while the people at the concession stands begged for their attention.

"Extra! Extra! Read all about it!" A boy shouted, wearing a blue apron, holding up a Herald American newspaper, bumping into the crowd.

The headlines read: CUBS PLAY BRAVES. And accompanying the boy who so rudely held a paper up in front of Uncle Milton's face, were the other guys also peddling off theirs on other fans as well. All the major newspapers were there; Sun-Times, Tribune, and Daily News. Take your pick. Don't go to the newspaper stands, and they'll come to you.

Near a fire hydrant a small band played in mellow tones, Chicago My Kind Of Town, and Take Me Out To The Ball Game. A trombone, French horn, and tuba, blended in nicely with a high pitch trumpet. Orville paused long enough to stare at the trombone player. "Where did all that brass go when he drew his hand up close to his mouth?" Puzzled. Orville stood catatonic for the longest time trying to figure it out.

"C'mon, Orville. No time to waste. We gotta get to our seats." Uncle Milton jerked him along, nudging his shoulder.

"Programs! Scorecards! Pencils! Get your scorecard here." The man standing on a stool almost lost his balance holding up a dozen scorecards.

"Unck! Can we get one?"

He wasn't listening so Orville took his hand and pulled him toward the concession stand. "I like the pictures on the cover."

"Not now. We'll get one latter, inside."

Inside the ballpark Orville couldn't believe his eyes. Lots of people were scrambling to get to their seats. Young and old alike, men and women, stepping on each other's toes while walking through the rows of seats. Some men carried a big silver box strapped over their shoulder, shouting as they walked along, selling hot dogs. Likewise, other people were selling ice-cold soda pop and popcorn. One gentlemen poked a lady's chin with the big box strapped over his shoulder.

High above centerfield there was a big scoreboard with flags on poles waving in a breeze. Uncle Milton said that all the baseball teams were listed up there. Orville saw big numbers after each name.

"What's that big screen for, Uncle Milt?"

"It's to protect the folks sitting behind home plate, Orville. Lots of baseballs rebound off a bat and fly back there." The Boy's eyes followed that screen all the way up to the roof hanging over the upper deck.

And the baseball field. "Wow!" Orville thought. "I never saw anything like it before." It was smooth as silk with rich green grass. Brown dirt on the infield without lumps that looked like it was just shifted through a screen.

"What are the big white lines for, Unck?"

"Those are boundary lines, Orville."

Puzzled. "What are boundary lines, Uncle Milt?" The twelve year old was inquisitive and full of questions. Seeking answers, he could tell that Uncle Milton was getting upset. Sometimes, he preferred to be left alone in his own adult little world.

"Any ball that lands outside those lines, Boy, is not in play."

"Then what happens, Unck?"

"It's a foul ball and they do it all over again."

"From the beginning? Start the game all over again?"

"No silly! Never mind. They just start where they left off."

"What's in those big white boxes around that base with the point on it for?"

"It's the batter's box, Orville. Man you're just full of questions, aren't ya Boy?" Uncle Milton smiled, shaking his head with all five of his fingers spread out on top of the Boy's head.

"Nope! Just wanted to know what all that stuff is for."

"Well ya just keep askin' all those questions, Boy, and I'll do my best to give ya the answers."

Orville liked the uniforms. Pin strips against a white background. Knee high socks. Big numbers on each player's back. "Wow! I wish I had a baseball uniform like that."

As his eyes continued to roll around looking at everything, his thoughts were suddenly interrupted by a loud voice over the PA system. "Good afternoon, ladies and gentlemen! Here is today's line-up for the Milwaukee Braves!" Boos immediately echoed throughout the park.

"What ya doin', Unck?" Orville stared at the scorecard opened on his lap.

"Writing down the name of each player as the announcer reads them off."

"Oh!"

Following the line-up, everybody stood up and faced the American flag whipping in a breeze high above the scoreboard. Then, a band played The Star Spangled Banner, the national anthem. Short as he was, Orville stared at the people's faces and saw long, serious expressions waiting for the music to end. On the last note, a military band marched off the field. And while the fans sat down, an old familiar sound echoed throughout the park. "PLAY BALL!" Then, the crowd cheered with anticipation for an exciting game to begin.

Halfway through the game Uncle Milton bought a couple of hot dogs smothered with ketchup, mustard, relish, and onions. The Boy from Indiana eagerly stuffed his mouth full before gulping down some ice-cold soda.

And it was fun to watch 'em play ball. Folks often said this was a young man's game. The ball traveled very fast. Only with a sharp mind, quick eyes, and a good pair of hands, could a player keep up with the pace.

The ball left the pitcher's mound traveling very fast. Connecting with some wood near home plate, it quickly rolled on the ground toward the shortstop, who scooped it up, and threw across the diamond to first.

Another ball sailed into the right field corner.

"Foul!" The ump shouted.

From third, to first, to short, to home, to the pitcher, and back to the guy standing on the first base foul line. Smiling, with bulging eyes, Orville followed the ball. Watching one player side arm the ball to a teammate, listening to the crackling sound of the ball as it landed inside a glove, he pictured himself being one of those players someday. A lot of wishful thinking for a twelve-year-old Boy who loved to dream.

A fly ball to left field. A throw to second, to first for a double play. A slow roller toward third. The players made it look so easy. And it kept Orville along with all the other baseball fans, sitting on the edge of their seat throughout the game.

The numbers on the scoreboard kept changing. There were big zeros through the first three innings. Occasionally a number one appeared. Maybe a number two if they were lucky. Men with strong arms put the big white numbers up against a black background, like placing screens in a window frame.

Throughout the game Orville watched with great intensity. There was so much to see. Lots of thoughts raced through his mind.

Later, as the big wheels spun faster and faster on the Greyhound Bus traveling across the highway toward Indiana, he couldn't keep his eyes open any longer. Snoring, with his head tucked in one corner of the seat against the window, he was off in another world. Baseball filled his thoughts, and it was fun to dream.

NINETEEN

At 6 a.m. Wally walked into the post office and greeted his fellow carriers, who were already busy sorting stacks of mail for their route. "Mornin' Bud, Cathy, Diane, Neil, and Kelly."

"Ya always say somethin' to those guys, Wally. What's the matter with us? Don't we count?" Jenny asked sarcastically, while placing some mail in bends for the different routes.

"Oh Jenny! Ya know I get around to talkin' to all you folks. It's just my way of doin' things."

"Yeah. Well get out of my way with your way stuff, so I can get these distributed." Debbie carried a tray of mail over to route one. The short little blond with blue eyes was a strong-willed assistant clerk in the small post office. Stubborn. She always got her way.

"If ya weren't a Kennedy, I'd have a few words with ya." Wally smiled. The name Kennedy always carried a lot of clout.

While continuing to sort the mail, Laurie, another clerk, took bundles of newspapers around to all six stations. Before putting letter size envelopes into the different slots, it was best to put in the newspapers and magazines first. That way they can be wrapped around the envelopes which makes for easier handling on the route.

"What's this?" Wally asked, looking at a bundle lying on the floor by his feet, before staring at Laurie.

"What does it look like? Telephone books?"

"Don't be funny, Laurie. I know what it is. I was just wonderin' why today. We normally don't have Gazettes on Tuesdays."

"Yeah! You're right. But this is a special edition."

"What's so special 'bout it?" Cathy interrupted.

"Haven't ya read the headlines? Gee whiz! The whole town's talkin' 'bout it." Bud held up the front page.

"Let me see that." Neil grabbed it out of his hand. As his eyes rolled across the page it read: Cedar Lane High School Team beats Boys from the Gold Coast. Then in smaller print the article described the events at Sherwood Forest State Park. Finally, after pausing for a few minutes from sorting his mail, he mumbled. "Hmm! Must be some big thing. So much so that it ended up with a three page article."

News around Cedar Lane wasn't unusual. And like a close knit family, everybody in the community wanted to get in on the act. It's just that an extra edition of the Gazette made for some extra work at the post office. The post office was always moaning and groaning about work. But then, why work at the post office? Good question.

Across the room on some four-wheel carts, Lloyd, the postmaster, leaned over and reached for some more trays of mail. Then, he turned around and placed them on a table for the girls to take around to the different stations, in addition to bundles of magazines that came out of another cart. There were five carts in all filled with a variety of magazines, letters, and periodicals. "Mule work. That's what I call it. Lots of mule work." And he always kept busy taking them off the truck on the dock in back of the post office, and later returning them empty to that same truck.

Back at route number three, Wally reluctantly bent over and cut the twine off each bundle. Then, with a small stack resting on his arm, he cupped each one individually as he placed it into the different slots. "These folks will be happy today." Usually by the time each carrier was loaded up and on the road in their postal jeep, a peace and contentment took over that made the job well worth it. Newspapers, then magazines, then letters, and the job were complete. Colored plastic markers in various slots reminded him of a parcel going to a specific address. Once he was loaded up, Wally walked around to the right side of his postal jeep, got inside, and started up the old engine. This vehicle, like many others of its kind, was better then ten years old, and took some coaxing before the engine would start. Finally, purring like a kitten with a few coughs and sputters now and then, he rolled out of the back lot.

Cruising down the various streets was a postal carrier's dream. Away from the constant chatter at the post office along with arguing, petty gossip, complaints of all kinds, and a boss looking over their shoulder, were things a letter carrier eagerly left behind. Now, he was on his own, working at his own pace and loving every minute of it.

Wally's route took him to a popular residential section behind the stores on Main Street. Delivering mail for over twenty years, he had all the streets memorized. With his eyes closed he could see them: Maple, Mulberry, Elm, Ester, Sedgwick, and more.

In the small rural town the houses were all scattered on acre lots. None of that stuff found in the big cities with wall-to-wall houses stacked up next to each other like on a checker board. Some folks call it a concrete jungle. Here, the homes were set back on huge lawns. Framed two story homes with a front porch or other accessory. Lots of trees like Oak, Maple, and Weeping Willows surrounded the landscape. There were resemblances of a Paul Revere lamppost before a walkway. Yes, the neighborhood had personality.

Chugging along, Wally rolled over to a mailbox, usually a hot silver cylinder baked in a hot sun, flipped open the door, placed mail inside, closed the door, and moved on. Red flag up, reminded him of letters to take back to the post office.

In twenty years, Wally knew all the residence and boxes without having to look twice. And he knew the names as well since most of the people have lived in Cedar Lane for many years. It was a stable community, safe, and healthy. Just passing the familiar landscapes the names raced through his mind. "Parker, Hansen, Nark …yep, they're all here." Folks often thought Wally was a pillar in the town and hoped he never retired. It was like having an old friend as a neighbor.

Looking at the different homes along his route brought back many stories to Wally's mind. A wedding. New baby. Business venture. New car. There were always lots of things to talk about.

Up on a hill at the end of Mulberry Street lived the Olson's. Frank was a retired engineer. He worked many years with Abbott Lab. Helen still works for the same company in their Human Resources department. Frank keeps busy raising Angus Steers. With three grown kids out of five still living at home, there's always lots of activity around the house.

As the postal jeep rolled away from their mailbox, Molly Olson backed out of their garage in her green Chevy. The folks were always surprised to see them living like average people. They still drove a five-year-old car. Wore clothes from a church bazaar or a garage sale. Dined out with the other farmers. There was nothing out of the ordinary. And today, she was on her way to Lee Anne's, Set It Right Salon.

Slowly her Chevy made a right turn at Main Street before pulling over to an empty parking meter. After getting out of her car, she placed a couple of nickels into the meter, thus assuring herself that she will be inside at least two hours. Looking up at the big picture window, she saw the sign read: Set It Right Salon surrounded by a fancy drape, so she went inside.

"Good mornin', Molly!" Olivia greeted her with a smile. "My don't we look nice today. Certainly not the usual clothes you wear to the office each day."

"Oh nonsense, girl. Don't be silly. Whenever I'm home I always wear these black snug fitting bottoms, knee high, and this blouse with red polka dots on a white background with a low V-neck collar. Silly girl, I wear it all the time."

"Either way, ya look very nice."

"Thank you dear." Molly blushed with a smile.

"I notice your hair's in a ponytail today. Unusual for you, isn't it?" Olivia grinned while turning her head to look out of the corner of her eye.

Smiling. "Oh yes!" She motioned with her hand. "I like it. Don't you? Though I don't often wear it this way, it is comfortable for the summer."

"Oh?"

"Yes. But that's why I'm here, Olivia." She closed her eyes for the moment while she kept talking. "It's getting long. I need to get it cut. It's driving me crazy."

"Well come on over. Let's set you down in this chair." Olivia walked down the aisle between chairs on both sides of the store, motioning with her hand. "Peppermint will take care of you today."

In the back of the shop, beyond the chairs, a couple of ladies, with their heads buried in big silver canisters, that reminded people of the Cone Heads on Saturday Night Live, a popular TV program, ignored their surroundings for the moment while glancing at some magazines. The loud noise of the hair dryers made it impossible to hear anyway, even though a third lady sitting across from them was fast asleep, with her chin resting on her chest. Occasionally, Cinnamon, another hairdresser, came by to remind her that her head was coming out of the dryer.

As Molly Olson got comfortable in a chair, Peppermint placed a folded piece of white tissue paper around her neck, before draping her entire upper body, below the neck with a white-flowered sheet.

"Short ta-day?" Peppermint asked, in a southern accent while chopping viciously on some gum.

"Yes. Ya know what I want." She paused long enough to give Peppermint time to think about it. "And wash it and set it, please!"

"Oh my goodness. Do I see a few gray strands in front of your ears creeping in?" Peppermint's tangy voice often irritated the other patrons.

"Shhh!" Molly whispered, taking her hand out from under the sheet and placing her finger over her mouth. "I wish you didn't notice either."

"Well, I'll be! What did ya expect honey? I'm the hair stylist. I'm lookin' right at your head. I mean hair. I gotta notice everything." Peppermint continued to attack her gum vigorously like on a tough piece of steak at a restaurant.

"Oh never mind. Just get on with it." Molly repeated, waving her hand.

"Of course!"

"Did ya see all those people at Sherwood Forest State Park the other day?"

"No, Molly. Were ya there?"

"Nope! But all the folks are sure talkin' 'bout it. Everywhere I go that's all I hear."

"Sure must be somethin' important if everyone's talkin' 'bout it." Peppermint continued to work up a soapy lather on Molly's head.

"Be careful with that stuff, Peppermint. I don't wanna get any of it in my eyes." She paused for a moment. "And everybody was eatin': Hot dogs. Soda. Ice cream. Even Mama Rice's fried chicken got lots of takers."

"Put a towel over your eyes. I'm washin' your hair. There's some soap that's bound to get in your eyes." There was a brief pause in the conversation. "Fried chicken! Mama Rice! Sure wish I could have some."

"The boys were havin' fun. All of 'em playin' baseball. Don't know what the boys liked about old man Pop. That's what they called him. Pop. But it keeps 'em out of trouble playin' ball."

"Oh?" Peppermint poured a pitcher of warm water on a head perched over a washbowl.

"It's hard talkin' to ya while staring up at the ceiling. Anyway! WKUC took movies. Folks say later we can watch it on TV."

Following the rinse, Peppermint trimmed the edges of her hair. Then, with bobby pins and clips, she made the curls. After dabbing her hair with a special permanent formula, Molly moseyed on over to join the other ladies under the silver canisters. Now, she was a Cone Head with the rest of them.

Turning on to Elm Street, Wally saw a little brown two-story frame house on the corner at Wallace Street. Once the mayor's house of long ago, Lester and his wife Gertrude now raised two kids there. As a retired health nut, Lester always enjoyed the two-mile walk into town. Today, he was going to have his ears lowered.

"Hope they put ya to sleep, Lester." Mel joked, smiling when he walked by.

"Always Mel." Lester winked. "Always thinkin' of my comfort, Mel. Never hurts a bit."

Down a couple of doors, Lester moseyed on in to Sam's Barber Shop. "Mornin' Sam!" After the greeting, he took a chair near a shelf full of shampoos and tonics ready to grease up a guy's hair and scalp with.

"Be right with ya, Lester. Just finishin' up with the old timer here." Carefully with a pair of scissors in one hand and a comb in the other, Sam put the finishing touches on Alfred.

Lester took a deep breath. "Take your time. I'm in no hurry, Sam. Got all day."

Following his haircut, Alfred stretched his legs a couple of times while standing near the cash register at the counter. "Feels like I've been sittin' too long." Then he reached into his overall pocket for some dollar bills.

"That'll be two bucks, Al." Sam pushed the buttons on his cash register.

"Two bucks!" Al shouted. "Outrageous! Why, I remember the day I got a hair cut for a dollar. My Pa always said he got one for a quarter. That is after Ma got tired of cuttin' his hair."

Sam remained calm, cool, and collective. He heard the story many times before. "Yeah. I know Al. But times have changed. Things are different now."

After placing the newspaper down, Lester got up, wobbled over to the barber chair, and got comfortable.

Sam clipped the black and white pin stripped drape around his neck. "What will it be today, Lester?"

"The usual. Ya know. Neck clean and sideburns left on. I don't want long sideburns. But I don't want 'em straight across from where the ear joins my head either. Give me just a little dip." He pointed to his ear. "And cut some off the top as well. I like it short."

In his hip length smock, Sam pumped up the chair raising Lester's head to his own eye level, before combing his hair. Then, after placing his comb on the counter in front of the big mirror, he turned on his electric razor, and over the buzzing sound started to chat. "So what's new?"

"Not much Sam. Other than the baseball game over at Sherwood Forest the other day."

"Yeah. Heard some of the other guys talkin' 'bout it. Folks say they drew a large crowd."

"They sure did." Lester grinned.

"Were ya there, Lester?"

"Saw every bit of it. Me and my son."

"Didn't Gerdy go?"

"You know Gerdy doesn't like baseball. Besides, at her age she has very little patience with kids."

"Sorry I asked, Lester." Sam shrugged his shoulders and took a deep breath during a pause. "So! How was it?"

"Great! Those boys played a good ball game. Wouldn't mind if they come back and do it again."

"Who won?"

"We did, of course. That's what the talk is all about. Didn't start out that way though. Yes sir, Bob! Within three innings it was three zip."

"Cedar Lane High?"

"Nope! That's the bad part. The Gold Coast Boys got an early lead. Unfortunately, later on, that lead was five zip."

"So what's so exciting 'bout that?"

Laughing. "But it didn't last, Sam. Our boys came from behind and beat 'em anyway. Yes sir, Bob! Good clean fun!"

"Well that's good to hear." With lots of folks in his chair everyday, Sam listens to lots of small talk. Town gossip. Sort of puts a deaf ear to it. Becomes oblivious to his surroundings.

"Video camera. They were neat. WKUC videotaped the whole thing. So you'll be able to watch it on TV, Sam. Won't that be great?" After catching his breath, he paused long enough to allow for a moment of silence. "You should've seen it. They had this guy out in centerfield sitting in a little Johnny house with a camera. Had a huge lens on it. And he got some good shots."

"How's the hair look on the sides? Should I take any more off before I do the top?"

"Looks fine, Sam." Lester moved his head around to get a good view at different angles in the big mirror in front of him.

Sam, then gently positioned his head by holding his jaw before lowering the chair slightly. "Good."

"And the cars. There were lots of cars there. The parking lot was full. The overflow parked on the grass. And the police had their hands full."

Following Lester's haircut, Sam put a little axle grease in his hand, rubbed them together, and applied it to Lester's hair. Trying to keep his bobbing head still while massaging it into his scalp was tough. Finally, with his long black comb, he parted it on the side, and laid it out nicely on his head. "There ya are Lester. Good as new." And he removed the drape while lowering the chair.

After a couple of knee bends, he stretched his arms briefly before getting out his wallet. "And what are the damages today, Sam?"

"Like the other guy Lester, two bucks."

Sam's was a popular hangout for many of the old timers. Whenever they wanted to catch up on the latest gossip, they'd visit Sam's. And when Lester left, the shop already had three other gentlemen waiting to get their ears lowered.

Over on Dickens Street, Aunt Sofie was locking the front door on her little blue house when Wally drove up. "Mornin' Wally!"

"Mornin' Aunt Sofie! Out for your mornin' walk are ya?"

"Nice day for walkin', Wally." She shielded her eyes while staring at the sky. "But I'm off to the bank. Ya know. Gotta take care of that stuff. Every week."

"Yep! Know what ya mean." Wally chuckled. "Sometimes I let mine get behind."

"Guest that's part of getting old, Wally."

Folks would never know it's a bank in Cedar Lane. Tall, two story building with Greek gothic pillars parting the big picture windows on four sides. It's not that. Or plush carpet with polished wood desk and ladies dressed in their Saks Fifth Avenue best. It's not that either.

Instead, a plain wood door next to a small window with vertical bars and a sign that reads Cedar Lane Bank, decorated the front of a small building. Blink too many times when passing, and the folks might not see it.

Inside, Aunt Sofie walked across the title floor of the small foyer underneath a ceiling light with three bulbs concealed under a glass shade. To her right was a small table where patrons filled out the necessary forms. Not too far ahead of her was a wall that separated the bank office from where the patrons did their business up front. A small window, also barred, with a counter, allowed Aunt Sofie to stand and chat with Audrey, the bank teller.

"Good mornin', Aunt Sofie. Nice day today, isn't it?" Audrey greeted, with a flat affect in her voice. Bankers always looked serious. More like death warmed over, as if their best friend just died. Nothing ever excited them. They had a white complexion, thinking that a good sun tan were the curse of death. And always wore a black dress with a white laced collar along with black two inch laced shoes.

"Yes it is. I hope the sun stays with us all day." Sofie returned a cordial reply. Banking was always serious business.

"What can we do for you today, Aunt Sofie?"

She placed her big purse on the counter and opened it. "I gotta get some American Express Travelers Checks. I'm going to visit my daughter in Texas."

"Oh? How much?" Audrey rounded her lips while dropping her jaw. Not too many people living in Cedar Lane took long trips. And when they did, usually the whole town knew about it.

"Probably need two hundred dollars. Do ya think that will be enough for my trip?"

"Depends. How long ya gona be gone? Does this include your ticket?"

"Heavens no, Audrey." Aunt Sofie puckered her lips. "My daughter is paying my way. All of it. All I want is some spending money."

Audrey nodded her head. "Then I would say two hundred dollars is enough."

"OK! I want two hundred dollars in travelers checks, please."

"Good, Aunt Sofie! In what denominations?"

"I never thought of that, Audrey. What do you suggest?" She stared at the teller looking puzzled.

"If it's just spending money, I'd suggest the smaller the better. Certainly no larger than a ten."

The bank patron didn't hesitate. "Good! I'll take it. Two hundred dollars in tens."

After Aunt Sofie completed the necessary form and handed it through the window, she took ten brand new twenty-dollar bills out of her purse and shoved them through the window. Audrey carefully counted each one of them.

"Thank you, Aunt Sofie. I'll be right back." Then she took the money, along with the form to the back corner of the room. Meanwhile, listening, Aunt Sofie heard some noise on a machine, but couldn't recognize it. On returning, she handed Aunt Sofie a small plastic billfold with some traveler's checks inside.

"And I thank you very much, Audrey."

"You're quite welcome. Oh, by the way. Did ya here 'bout the boys playin' baseball over at Sherwood Forest the other day? Folks comin' in here are talkin' 'bout it all the time."

Surprised. "You know Audrey, I did here 'bout it. I wasn't there. But at my age, I have more important things to think about."

"I know. I was just wonderin' what you thought 'bout it."

"Didn't think anything 'bout it. Oh, I'm sure it was good for the boys. They need somethin' to do. If my husband Otto were still alive, he surely would've gone to the game. He loved baseball—the boys. I probably would've gone with him. Good day." And she hurried out the door.

It didn't take Wally long to know when he passed the Powell residence. With three kids there was always lots of chatter. Toys thrown out the window. Arguments that echoed throughout the neighborhood. Lights left on at all hours of the night. Yes. Everybody knew where the Powell's lived.

"Where ya goin', mom?" Five-year-old Elaine asked, in her shorts.

"Honey! Mommy has to go to the grocery store." After tapping her cheek she turned her around. "Now you go back to your room and get a shirt on. You can't walk around this house lookin' like that."

"Would you buy me some cereal, mom?" Elaine stuck out her bottom lip.

Mother smiled. "Why sure, honey. What would you like?"

"Some Corn Flakes." The sweet little girl with a cute smile was irresistible.

"Yes, sweetie. I'll buy you some Corn Flakes." Her mother chuckled while tapping her on the bottom. "Now get up to your room and get a shirt on."

"Mom. I want some soda." Billy interrupted.

"Me too." Jane echoed.

"I want a toy, too." Elaine held up a spinner-top in her hand.

"Can I go with you?" Jane asked.

"Me too." Elaine interrupted. "I wanna go with."

"You never buy me any candy. I want a candy bar."

"Can I get some peanuts?"

"Why do I have to wear these pants? She never has to wear them."

"Because she's not a boy." Mother rushed toward the door shouting. "Tony! Help! Get down here! These kids are driving me crazy."

Soon Pam had her lists and was out the door. "Thank heavens." She muttered after taking a deep breath, feeling relieved.

At the grocery store, Papa Munchie in a long white apron with a bib dragging on the floor, just finished ringing up Mrs. Stones order when Pam entered. "Ah! Hi! Mrs. Powell. Be right with ya."

"Oh, take your time Papa. I've got the time."

Walking down the narrow isle to the back of the store, she picked out a dozen sausage links, a pound and a half of ground beef, and several slices of ham for some sandwiches. Not able to resist the aroma of fresh produce, she filled her shopping cart with some carrots, radishes, green beans, and lettuce. Back up front, she asked papa to use his claw on a long stick and pick out a box of Corn Flakes from all the other cereals displayed in different colored boxes. A loaf of bread, gallon of milk, a dozen candy bars, and her shopping was complete.

"Yes Mrs. Powell." Papa Munchie muttered. "Let me see what we have here." And moving his large hands that showed many years of hard work, he placed the food at the other end of the counter as he rang each item up on the cash register. "That will be $6.54 please."

"Be patient with me." Slowly, she bent her knee to support her purse on her thigh, while struggling to get out her money.

"That's OK Pam. Why don't you put your purse on the counter? That way it might be easier for you."

"Thank you."

"Did ya hear 'bout the game at Sherwood Forest the other day, Mrs. Powell?"

"Hasn't everybody?"

"I suppose so. Everybody comin' in my store talks about it. There ain't nothin' else they wanna talk 'bout."

"I was there, Papa Munchie. The whole family and me were there. It was hard keepin' the kids sittin' still. But otherwise, it was nice to see all the boys havin' some fun."

"Yes, I agree. Wish I could've been there. But ya know, somebody has to run the store."

"Yes. Took Tony back to the days when he was a boy. Playin' baseball on corner lots. He hopes the money goes to a good cause around these parts."

"I think it is, Mrs. Powell."

"Oh?" She looked surprised.

"Folks say, it's gona start up a youth baseball team. Right here in Cedar Lane."

People often gathered in Papa Munchie's store just for the conversation. Pleasant atmosphere. Friendly people. Forget their troubles. Free coffee and sweet rolls. Simple. Nothing fancy. Just a nice place to be.

As the day went on and Wally got near the end of his route, it was time to gas up, before returning to the post office. So, up ahead, he slowly rolled into Ma and Pa's Gas, the place where everybody went to fill up.

Limping out to the pump, Pa greeted him. "The usual Wally?"

"Yep! The usual!" Wally replied in slow laborious tones, after a hard day's work. He was tired.

"The usual it is." So Pa pulled the nozzle off the hook, spun the handle on the side a few times, and placed it into the spout on the jeep. "Want your windows cleaned today, Wally?"

"Nope! Don't need it. Thanks anyway." While listening to the bell ringing as his gas tank filled up, he placed a rubber band around some envelopes. "Say! Have ya heard 'bout the baseball game at Sherwood Forest the other day?"

"I don't wanna hear it, Wally." Pa shouted, with a mean look, staring at the jeep. "Everybody comin' through here today, yesterday, and forever, is talkin' 'bout it. Grant you, they're a good bunch of guys, but I'm tired of hearin' 'bout it. Ma and I support the boys in every way we can. But when ya got lots of cars comin' through here all the time, it gets a bit tirin'. Ya know what I mean?"

Soon Wally was driving an empty jeep back to the post office. Another day's work was done. However, on the way back he couldn't help but thinking to himself. "Must've be mighty important to have everybody in town talkin' 'bout it. Must've been a big day."

TWENTY

The sound of church bells echoed throughout the neighborhood. Even on the farm, that melodious sound penetrated into the hearts and minds of all the folks sitting down at the breakfast table.

It was Sunday morning and all was quiet around town. The shops were closed. Occasionally a car might be seen traveling down Main Street, but that was rare. No cluster of cars feeding parking meters. No shoppers stopping to chat on the sidewalk in the middle of the day. No smiling faces. It looked like a ghost town in an old John Wayne western.

Even life on the farm was still. No loud tractors tilling the soil or spraying crops as it slowly rolled across the field. Tending to the animals was an unavoidable necessity, however, putting all things aside, it left for a quiet, peaceful day.

For one day, the little white church with the steeple in town became the center of attention. Loud and clear, Horace pulled the long rope that rang the bell, calling the folks to gather for worship. And gradually they responded, as the cars filled the small lot across the street.

The ladies loved to show off their new hat. Usually made of straw with a wide rim and colorful arrangement of flowers, caught everybody's attention. A flowered dress, three inches below the knee, beige nylons with a straight seam, and white heels, completed their wardrobe.

On the other hand the gentlemen didn't care much for all that fancy stuff. Having one suit hanging in the closet back home was enough, not to mention that it usually was black or dark brown. White shirts all looked the same regardless of who was wearing them, and the same necktie went to church every Sunday. Yep! The men were all a good look-a-like. But no one cared. Just having something to wear was good enough.

The kids were another story. Boys wore slacks and a sport shirt. Girls a nice flower decorated dress just like mom wore. Getting them to wear a hat took some coaxing. The real task was keeping them proper looking because the young folks always found church boring and often got into trouble running around.

In pairs, the senior members entered the church with the misses grabbing an arm. Slowly, walking up the steps, they were greeted by the clergy. "Good mornin', Chuck! And how's Mrs. Brown today?" The Reverend shook his hand. And one by one they entered the church. The Riley's, Hamilton's, Wilson's, Hodge's, Parker's, and the list goes on. The whole town was there.

Like any other small town church the inside was plainly decorated. Pews were a dozen benches. The Uncles made a pulpit and placed it on a dais with two chairs and a flag at each corner. It was nice for the folks in another church down yonder to donate an old piano, now sitting in the corner where Mrs. Hunter played to her heart's content. A small table, with a beautiful arrangement of flowers brought in every week, in front of the pulpit always caught the people's attention. They couldn't wait till the service was over, so they could smell them.

Looking at all the faces in the pews told of many years of hard work. Wrinkled with age. Responding to the different temperatures under a hot sun to severe cold. Bruised marks on their hands. Coming from different backgrounds. Surely, everybody had a story to tell.

As people reverently walked in, Mrs. Hunter played Bless Be The Tide That Binds. Softly the mellow sound got people to thinking while they meditated over the words. She played it through several times till everybody found their seat. Exact time in starting wasn't as important as all the folks being there.

"We're a hard workin' people." One farmer remembered. "Dad always said to be honest. Yep! We eat and we sleep, and most of all we live by the Good Book."

When Mrs. Hunter finished playing, everybody sat quietly. Silence felt its presence throughout the room. No chewing gum or talking was allowed, less a person get their hands slapped.

Freedom of religion is what these folks wanted. Many of their ancestors came from oppressed countries where liberty was denied, including the right to worship God. Even though everybody didn't attend church, for those who did, felt an obligation to set aside work on Sundays and just be there.

Randy, the pastor's son and recent college graduate, left his chair in the front row to lead the congregation in a hymn from behind the pulpit. "Let us all stand folks." He motioned by raising his hands. "And sing Holy! Holy! Holy! Lord God Almighty. The words are on a sheet of paper Mabel gave you all at the door." Following the hymn everybody eagerly sat down.

"Thank you, Randy." Pastor Meyer spoke in a deep bass voice, slow and methodical, typical of any pastor. "Elsie will now come up here, and let us know what will be happenin' here at Harvest this coming week."

In a pink dress, out of character with all the flowered patterns on the other ladies, and a plain white straw hat with a blue ribbon hugging the rim, she walked up to the pulpit. Standing on her tiptoes, she struggled to stand straight up so that all the folks could see a smiling face on a short body.

"Thank you, Pastor. It's nice to see you all out here this morning on this bright sunny day. This Thursday, at the Davis house …" And she continued in her high-pitched southern accent to give a run down of events from a small Bible study group at the Davis house to Wednesday night service along with other important events taking place later in the week.

Old man Blake needed no introduction. He merely stood up from wherever he was sitting. "We'll now take the offering." Then he sat down. That's it. Plain and simple. Straight to the point. No ushers. Randy started to pass a plate at one corner of the room up front, and it continued to zigzag through each row.

When all was quiet once again, Pastor Meyer approached the pulpit. "Let's pray. Dear God, we thank you for this time together …speak to us now, as we listen …Amen." And everybody whose eyes were closed with bowed heads suddenly came alive.

"These are hard times. I don't think anybody can deny that. The harder we work, the harder it always appears to get. There doesn't seem to be any end in sight. No light at the end of the tunnel, if ya think 'bout it."

"Yes sir. Amen to that." A gentlemen moaned in the third row.

"Yes brother." The Pastor concurred. "Workin' hard on the farm. And I don't mean to exclude you hard workin' folks in town. It takes a lot to keep your shops goin' too. But out there on the farm, the work never ends. Sometimes we feel like we're in despair. Sometimes we feel like given up. But brothers and sisters, I say to you. Please! Don't give up!"

"Yes sir! Amen!" Again the sound echoed from the man in the third row.

Soon the same thoughts started racing through other peoples mind's as they listened. It brought back many sad memories: Seeking a place to live. War. Struggling to make ends meet. Never ending toil and hardship.

Old man Wilson, the senior resident, who could hardly stay awake listening at the age of eighty-two, saw lots of changes taking place through the years in Cedar Lane. "I remember when there was hope in these parts." He forced a great big smile. "Yes. Those were the good old days. But now …" And a smiling face turned to look at him. "I don't know what's comin' next."

Fudge's dad recalled how he saw his pa, Fudge's grandfather go bankrupt. He had to sell lots of his machinery. Eventually he had to give up the land that went along with the farm. It was a sad day in Cedar Lane.

A couple of folks thought about old Tom. He's gone now. Past away a few years back. But they all recalled how he struggled. Inherited the farm from his dad, who got it from his dad. Grandfather after grandfather after grandfather, folks thought about how the Vetter's got the farm years ago. Maybe before the Civil War. Yeah. Chasing Indians off the property. Clearing the woods. And just to think of poor old Tom. How he struggled. Never had enough cash to make the necessary repairs. Eventually, everybody knew what happened to good old Tom.

"But I say folks, don't give up. There is hope. The good Lord put us all here for a reason. So whatever you do, don't give up.

"Now, let us turn our attention briefly to some successful people. What immediately comes to your mind when you think about successful people? Business. The home. Perhaps a neighbor. I sense those wheels are again turnin' in your brain. I bet a lot of ideas are beginning to surface right now.

"Let me be more specific. Who do you think about when you think about successful people? Marilyn Monroe. John Wayne. John F. Kennedy. I'm sure the list goes on. But when you think about these people, did you know that they had bad days too? Highs and lows just like you and me. You see folks, we only see them at their best. We never see them at those discouraging moments in their life when they were ready to throw in the towel. Yes. Go ahead and say it. Ready to give up."

Listening to the preacher talk, Sylvia was bubbling over with questions. The pretty twelve year old with the pink bow in her brown hair, absorbed it all like a sponge drawing water out of a pale. "Mom!" She whispered, leaning close to her ear. "I had no idea those people were like that. Does that mean even though we live in hard times, we can be as successful as they are?"

"Yes!" Sylvia's mother whispered in her ear while placing her finger over her mouth. "We'll talk about it later."

Then the little girl's face lit up with a smile. Even the look in Sylvia's eyes shown satisfaction for the moment. So she re-directed her attention back to the Reverend standing behind the pulpit.

All eyes were focused on the Preacher. With a listening ear they paid strict attention. Very carefully they did their best not to miss a single word. Some folks even took notes.

"A-A-A?" The old timer yelled, cupping his hand close to his ear. "What's that you're sayin' 'bout success? Nobody's successful you say." Polly, his granddaughter, felt embarrassed sitting next to him.

Losing their thought of concentration for the moment, the folks turned around to get a better look. "Whose that?" Mildred whispered, putting her hand close to her mouth.

"I don't know." Martha replied with a whisper, searching around the room with her eyes.

"Homer did it again." Dan tried to keep his voice down so no body would notice he was mumbling. "Bet the guy didn't hear a word the Preacher was sayin'."

"Nope." Chuck was always agreeable. It didn't matter who was doing the talking.

"Nobody thinks I'm successful, but I am. Even if I'm as poor as a church mouse." Homer stood up on his wobbly knees.

"Oh dear! What'll I do?" Polly thought, biting her nails.

"Sit down! The gentlemen in the back row shouted. "I can't see a thing."

"Yeah! Me neither." His friend echoed.

"Ya need a hearing aid Homer. Where is it? Sittin' on the shelf back home." Elmer tried to be polite.

"I think success is what ya want it to be. You can be feelin' high with success. Or you can be feelin' low with success. Either way ya look at it, it's up to you." By now Homer wasn't making any sense at all. Always hearing the wrong thing, he got misdirected. It's no fun getting old.

The gentlemen sitting behind Homer politely leaned over, took hold with both hands on his pants, and pulled him down. Then he whispered in his ear a few words that apparently he was able to hear up close. Immediately he got comfortable while Polly turned around to thank him.

"Let's take a look at Joseph, the one with the coat of many colors in the Old Testament." The Reverend tried to get his message back on track.

"You may recall Joseph had some jealous brothers. His father Jacob gave him a coat of many colors because he was born to him in his old age. His brothers didn't like that. In fact, they thought he stole all the attention away from them.

"Eventually, Joseph was sold into Egypt. To satisfy his brothers, they took his coat of many colors, dipped it in a goat's blood, and told their father Jacob, that some ferocious animal has devoured him. And so Joseph was left for dead.

"Here is somebody folks, that was his father's favorite. Surely, somebody that was destined for success. But now it doesn't look that way. Instead, he meets with resistance from some jealous brothers. It looks like it's all over for Joseph. But let's move on.

"Now left in a strange land, through interpreting dreams correctly for Pharaoh, Joseph became governor of Egypt and in charge of distributing food throughout the land during a seven year famine. People came from all over to get food, for you see folks, other countries didn't store up a supply like Egypt did during the prosperous years. Smart I would say. Wouldn't you?" Amen's echoed throughout the room. "And guess what? That's right! His brothers now came to Egypt seeking food for themselves and their father Jacob, who was back home.

"Folks! You can read the rest of the story for yourself in Genesis. But the point I wanna make here is that he didn't hold a grudge against them. He didn't seek revenge. He didn't say, Ho! Ho! Now it's my turn. Now it's my turn to get even. No! He did none of that. Instead, he forgave them. He forgave them because he loved them. Now a man in his position. Successful. Well liked by the Pharaoh. Could've given them a hard time. But no! Instead he forgave them."

Everybody sat quietly listening to the preacher. Not a sound was stirring throughout the entire room. All eyes were glued on the man behind the pulpit. The O'Leary's. Leasmon's, Westberg's, and more all sat with their hands folded in their laps. In the next row, the Hodge's, including all the Uncles, likewise sat quietly. He had everybody's attention. Even Orville sat puzzled, with a disturbing look on his face.

Lots of things raced through Orville's mind. "Yeah it's easy for you to say that Preacher. Can I forgive my Uncle? Do you know what I've been through?" A tear started to trickle down his cheeks when his eyes welled up. "I almost died on that beam, feeling the sting of that whip. Were you ever on the receiving end of a bull whip?" Smiling, he tried to hide the tears." Uncle Milton! I like him. He rescued me.

"I'm supposed to love my mother, Uncle, and all the rest. But how can I? How can people expect me to love my Uncle after all that?" Mixed emotions raced through Orville's mind.

Meanwhile, back in the church, the Preacher continued with his message. "I know what you all are thinkin', folks. Forgiveness is the last thing on earth you wanna do. I wanna do. But when we look at the big picture, it might not be so bad. Think about it for a moment.

"I know you all have been through a lot. Keepin' your shops goin'. Maintaining the farm. Tryin' to make ends meet. Yeah. We've talked about it before and it's on our minds again.

"But think again. Didn't Jesus forgive? Isn't that the reason He came to earth in the first place? If He forgives us, how much more can we forgive each other?

"We must go about our business with a cheerful heart. In spite of our circumstances, we must persevere. We must stick together and make it work. I personally know each one of you. I'm a farm boy just like most of you. I know you folks have done it before, and can do it again. So let's make a difference. Amen!"

The message brought smiling faces with peace and contentment among the crowd. There was always something the Reverend said that made them feel good about themselves. Life hadn't changed that much in the hour they were in church. But inside each person there was something to feel good about. It was like a shot in the arm that reenergized them. Got them all ready to carry on. Maybe that's why they went to church.

Outside the church building the folks gathered in the parking lot for a brief time to chat. Many people worked long hours during the week, and saw each other only on Sundays. A job might keep some people away consistently or an illness in the family. Either way, all were welcome when they could attend. Nothing special about the conversation. Lots of small talk. "How's your Aunt Jane, Dolly?"

"Caught any fish, lately?"

"She was so young to have that kind of an operation. Was it really necessary? Did she see more than one doctor?"

"I didn't know he had a heart attack!"

"Yes! Mike repaired the church roof last year."

"Maggie makes the best apple pie I've ever eaten. Makes my mouth water just thinkin' 'bout it."

"Oh? I didn't know he's goin' to college in the fall."

"Is Blanch OK? She looks so thin."

"That's a nice dress you're wearin', Polly. Is it new?"

"She's so cute in curls. Look at her blond hair and blue eyes. She looks just like her mother.

"I didn't know he was killed. When did that happen?"

"Did ya here she almost won a thousand dollars? Wish I was that smart."

It felt so good just to share with other people. That traditional get-to-gether in the church parking lot, following the morning service every Sunday was like the frosting on a cake. It was that something extra that made life special.

TWENTY-ONE

The building was an oversize barn that stood in the middle of a bare lot. It didn't look like a barn on a farm, with the usual A-frame roof creased in thirds, and a tall silo parked along side it. Rather, the straight walls angled slightly outward from the ground and reaching toward the sky, joined an overlapping A-frame roof at the top of the wall.

For many years the gray structure saw lots of activity. A pulley, perched on a rope, squeaked while another rope hosted hay up to the attic. Cows munched on some oats. A boxed in horse stall overflowed with corn. Swinging on a chain, a lantern shed some light over a blacksmith putting a horseshoe on Blackie, a favorite horse. Outside, it overlooked many miles of corn and bean fields joining the sky in the distance.

Now, the farm looked tired, like a marathon runner struggling to win a race, or an elderly person with a wrinkled face unable to walk across a room without assistance. A loose board, caught in the wind, swung on a rusty old nail. A plastic sheet replaced a broken window. Cobwebs laid undisturbed in corners and crevices along the big wooden beams supporting the ceiling. The walls, stripped of paint by the weather, exposed the naked wood.

Down the road, a mile or two yonder, Mr. Baxter got ready for a trip to the old gray barn. Humped over the emerald green fender, he checked for loose wires under the hood of his truck. "Try it again Elmer! Let her rip!"

Without hesitating, a muddy boot pushed down on the gas pedal while turning the ignition key on the dashboard. The engine grumbled and after a couple of rotations died. Again more gas and she sputtered and died. More gas. Finally, after a cough and a sputter she started purring like a kitten.

"Thought she'd never start Elmer." Old man Baxter slide into the driver's seat. "We gotta get movin'."

"What's your hurry Pa?"

"Gotta get these cows to market Elmer. No time for wastin'."

Slowly, the truck rolled off the dirt road and joined the busy highway. Traveling at thirty miles per hour they took in a breath of fresh air, while scanning the fields that once produced a money crop that allowed for a good living. Now, they laid bare, like a wasteland, forsaken, and brought back lots of memories. Thinking about it, a tear trickled down old man Baxter's cheek.

Around a curve on the highway they cut through a forest. Tall trees blending into the landscape provided a path for walking and thinking. It was a nice respite from the troubles of the world and a haven for the birds. "One day a deer bolted deeper into the forest when I and a friend approached him." Elmer loved to just sit back and daydream.

Back out in the open fields, they saw more wasteland that was once rich farmland producing lots of corn. "Yes siree Bob. Things aren't the same around these parts anymore. Ya might say times are a changin'." Old man Baxter felt secure living in the past.

"Oh?"

"Yep! You're too young to remember, Elmer."

"Yah?" The tall teenager in overalls and straw hat with the tattered edge looked puzzled.

"Boy! Today we go to the auction to sell off the last of our herd, probably to some big corporation. Use to be we went to market to get money for more farmin' needs and eventually some more calf's or another herd." The tired farmer wiped the sweat off his face with a red and white polka dot handkerchief. "Yes sir! But not anymore! Now the farms are closin'. Selling out!"

Trucks from all over the county rolled into the lot. Mostly pickup trucks with boarded up sides to create a pen for livestock. Murphy's Trucking loaned its GMC, a bigger version of a pickup truck, to help with the hauling. The large semi's waited on the other side of the barn to haul the corporations prized possessions off to the stockyards in Chicago.

"Hey Burt! Move it over to the right!" Clyde shouted, standing next to a line of trucks, motioning for him to get in line.

"Which way, Clyde?" Art rolled down his window and drove up beside him.

"Park it! Over there! Behind those five trucks already in line. It'll be a while before they get to ya. Go get a cup of coffee. Maggie is servin' coffee in the back of the barn. Got some delicious sweet rolls and donuts to go along with it.

"Mornin', Clyde!"

"Not you too, Baxter!"

"Yep! Just like the rest of 'em! Gotta sell!"

"Sorry to hear that, Baxter." Clyde stared at the ground looking sad and deep in thought.

"The more I think 'bout it, the angrier I get. Use to walk the floor at night. Couldn't sleep! At least I didn't take it out on ma wife like Carter did. Bad temper that man has."

"Park it, Baxter! Get some coffee with the others! Over there!" Clyde pointed to the corner of the lot. Suddenly, a loud horn blew. A driver got impatient waiting behind a stalled truck in the line. "Never mind! Quickly! Pull it in here!" Clyde struggled, motioning with his arm while directing the traffic. All morning they came, his buddies, like one big happy family. He loaned his barn out for the momentous occasion, and gave of his own time to help them.

"But Clyde!"

"But nothin'! Just do as I say!" He continued to shout over the loud noise of truck engines and the smell of gasoline fumes.

At the front of the line, Oscar put his truck in gear and slowly backed it up to a path boarded up on both sides that led into the barn. Then, Rafeal, nicknamed 'The Cowboy', reached over and lifted the gate on the back of Oscar's truck. A whistle, along with a slap on the behind from an old board, started the herd moving into the barn.

Inside the barn four rows of benches in a half circle faced a pen where the herd entered and excited, following the bidding. Once a lively place, the farmers gathered to sell their livestock and catch up on the latest gossip. Now, the locals were selling off their herds for survival. The times were changing. Farming wasn't any fun anymore. "We started payin' to go to work, and that just ain't right." One farmer moaned.

One by one the cows were led into the circle from the pen. Each had a numbered tag on his ear. A strong cowboy in a plaid shirt, blue jeans, boots, and hat, turned them around allowing the buyers to view them from all angles.

The bidding began with the auctioneer quickly babbling off numbers from the tip of his tongue. "Forty, forty, forty, forty! Do I hear forty? Forty, forty, forty, forty!"

A man in the front row raised his finger from a hand dangling between his legs.

"Yes I do. Do I hear fifty, fifty, fifty, fifty? Going! Going! Going! Do I hear fifty, fifty, fifty, fifty?"

Another man raised his eyebrows.

"Yes I do. Sixty, sixty, sixty, sixty. I hear sixty, sixty, sixty, sixty. Gentlemen! Sixty, sixty!"

The man in the back row jerked his head.

"Very good. Sixty-five, sixty-five, sixty-five! One more time. Sixty-five, sixty-five, sixty-five."

Auctioning off the herds took all morning. Briefly, stopping to sip some coffee or soda and catch his breath, the auctioneer then continued to babble off some more numbers. Sitting still like statutes in a park, the spectators hardly knew who was responding to the calls. The farmers had a style of doing business all their own.

On the third row up toward the center, a group of Cedar Lane farmers sat together for the last time. Staring down at the herd, farmer Jones was oblivious to his surroundings. With his arms folded he mumbled to himself. "Times certainly are a changin'. My pa would never think this day were a comin'. The farm goes back many generations to my great-great grandfather. Now it goes to the big guys. The corporations." Tears rolled down his cheeks watching one cow after the other led out of the pen into the big truck in the back. The large calloused hands that saw many years of hard work, gripped his elbows. Chewing the corner of his lip, he moaned. "Sometimes I wonder if it was worth it all." Doubts and regrets flowed through his mind for the moment.

Moving down the row, old man Homer almost fell off the bench snoozing. Hunched over with his chin resting comfortably on his chest, he rolled forward. "Hey! Homer! Wake up!" Ollie said, grabbing his shoulders to block the fall. "Wake up old timer. You're missing out on all the action down in the pen."

Earlier, Homer sat wide-awake with all the other farmers when the auction began. However, as the big hand on the clock moved around passing all the numbers, his mind wandered off into a different world. Homer gave up farming a couple of years back due to poor health. Since than, Missy, his life long partner operated a chicken ranch. Everyday, she toiled among four thousand hens, gathering eggs and preparing them for the market. Forced to succumb to rising prices in the futures market, Missy, like her neighbors was soon paying to work. "The chickens had to go!" Homer moaned.

Over the hill beyond a cluster of trees, off a muddy road, Clarence backed his truck up close to the chicken house. He applied the brakes and gave her more gas until Lester signaled for him to stop. Finally, a rusty old door rolled up on a track and four men came out to get some cages. Then, going inside, the hired hands grabbed some chickens by the feet and placed them inside cages before carrying them back out to the truck. Following a short break to chat with the other farmers, and sip some ice-cold soda, they were off with a loaded van to a soup factory in another town.

Harrison, Frank, Stewart, Johnson, Tucker. Tired with age they all sat motionless. They were the pillars of Cedar Lane and well known. Every Tuesday they warmed the bench at the auction. Lintz, Archer, Hodge, Nolan were all there except old man Parker. His place on the bench remained vacant. It was a memorial to a hard working farmer who passed away last year.

Meanwhile, back in town, Lucy, slowly walked down the steps

of her bungalow supporting her plump body with a cane. With not a care in the whole wide world, it might take her all day to reach the car, moseying down the sidewalk in her black two-inch laced shoes.

"C'mon honey. We don't have all day." Mabel encouraged her, leaning against the car fender with her arms folded.

"Oh hush, Mabel. Waitta you reach my age. I'm doin' the best I can. You should be so lucky, you youngster."

Mabel rolled her eyes. "Huh! I'm only three years younger than you are."

"At sixty two, this plump body is full of arthritis, Mabel. The way you move around, you're still a young chicken."

"I have my own problems too, Miss."

"Call me Lucy, please!"

"Lucy!" Mabel sighed. "Sometimes ya talk to me as if I were one of your pupils."

"Oh hush, Mabel. Get over here and help me get into this car." Lucy braced herself on the car frame while stepping on the running board of the old Buick. Finally, a push and a shove and she was in the back seat.

Cruising through the neighborhood at 10 m.p.h., Mabel ignored the cars behind her tailgating and sounding their horn, while engrossed in some conversation. Thirty miles per hour was the posted speed limit in town.

"When ya gona get rid of this car for a four door, Mabel?"

"Stop grumbling, Lucy. As long as she's runnin' and getting us around town, I'm not buying another car."

"I'm getting older, Mabel, and this body's havin' a hard time getting into this car."

"If ya had your own car maybe this wouldn't be happenin'."

"Now you know very well, Mabel, if I could I'd have my own car. Had to get rid of it. These fat legs and swollen ankles aren't what they use to be." After shedding a tear. "Sometimes it's hard havin' to depend on other people to get around. Use to be more independent."

"I'm sorry, Lucy. I know it's hard on ya." The best of friend's for many years, they often badgered each other for nothing better to do, then made up.

"Oh think nothing of it, Mabel. You're probably right. I should just stay at home." She wiped a tear off her cheek with her handkerchief. "C'mon. Let's get goin'. We've got lots to do today."

It was a peaceful ride through town. The children were in school while the older folks busied themselves with work and household chores. Mabel loved to drive and be in control behind the steering wheel of her car. Slowly, at 25 m.p.h. in a 30 m.p.h. zone, they stopped at every corner. Finally, thanks to an impatient driver behind them, they crossed the intersection. They gawked at the houses set back on lawns, camouflaged among the trees. After a couple left turns and a right, they approached a dirty old gray structure weather beaten with many years.

"Give her the horn, Mabel."

"No I won't." Mabel protested, while gripping the top of the steering wheel with both hands. "I'm as anxious as you are, Lucy, to get goin'. But ya know how the sound of a horn makes Blanch angry."

"But she don't know we're here. It'll take her forever to realize that we're here." Lucy rolled her eyes with frustration. "OK! Get ready for the long wait, just like all the other times when we pick her up."

"Oh nonsense, Lucy. Stop talkin' like that." Mabel sighed. "Look! There she comes now!"

The screen door slammed shut behind her as she slowly walked down the steps toward the car. Hutched over, like the Hutch back of Notre Dame, her bowed legs struggled to carry her torso with the help of a cane. Losing her balance momentarily while stepping off the curb, she grabbed the car door. Finally, after allowing her butt to do the walking, she maneuvered her feet into the car and soon they were on their way.

"Hello, Mabel. Hi Lucy. Mornin' to ya both."

"Mornin' Blanch!" A half smile concealed Lucy's true feelings.

"I know you're angry with me Lucy. Ya always are. These legs don't carry this old body the way they use to."

"I'm sorry Blanch. It just reminds me of all the times I use to wait on a bunch of fidgety third graders."

"You should forget 'bout all that Lucy. How long has it been since you retired teachin' school?"

"Many years. And don't remind me."

"Your hair looks lovely. When did you get it cut, Blanch?" Mabel hated arguments. The positive force in the group, she never shied away from an opportunity to change the subject.

"Thank you. Had it done last week."

"Who did it?" Lucy cordially shifted her mood during the conversation.

"Birdie did it over at Curls Shop. I always go to Curls. That is when I can get a ride."

"They always do a nice job on hair. Been goin' there for years myself. Wanted Birdie to do it, but every time I go, she's off. Instead I get Connie. But she does a good job too."

"Lucy, you oughta try Curls." Blanch suggested, struggling to twist her body around to get a better look at Lucy in the back seat.

"And your dress. I never saw you in that one before. I like navy. Don't see too many like it anymore with the big black buttons down the front. Did you add the black belt with the big buckle or is it part of the dress?"

"Skip with the compliments, Mabel. Let's get goin'. By the way, where's Angie?"

After a few more turns on the open road, and a mile outside of town, they pulled into Angie's driveway. Like a spring chicken, the seventy year old hopped into the back seat on the driver's side. The health nut that walked two miles every day come rain or shine, hot or cold, with the thin body, never looked better. "Eat right, exercise daily, and get a good night's sleep are rules to live by, my mama always said." Constantly, she offended her friends reminding them of this rule.

The carload of retired schoolteachers chattered all the way to the farm. Mostly small talk, they loved to reminisce about the good old days in the classroom. There were lots of stories to tell. The little boy who wet his pants was heard over and over and over again. Everybody wanted to see the girl's appendix scare that changed colors when it rained. Or the junior high class that loved to sing four-part music. Sopranos, altos, tenors, and bass' blended nicely at the concert given twice a year in the big assembly hall. Everybody in the community loved to attend the concerts whether they had kids of their own or not. And, the ladies always enjoyed laughing when they heard a good joke.

Down Walnut Road, up and down the hills, the ladies saw the mailbox ahead decorated with the blue and white balloons flopping in a gentle breeze. Cars parked everywhere as the folks sought out bargains on the Parker farm. Today, in another auction everything had to go.

The front lawn was dotted with makeshift plywood tables supported by sawhorses. People walked up and down the isles taking notes of everything up for bids. Numbered tags identified each item. Shortly thereafter, an auctioneer moseyed on over and began the bidding.

"Oh my goodness." Mabel mumbled, dropping her jaw while placing a hand on her chin. "She's selling her sewing machine."

"Goodness gracious, land sakes alive!" Angie agreed with her. "I can still remember her sitting up nights mending patches on Mr. Parker's trousers, or hemming a skirt."

"Listen child." Lucy interrupted. "She should've gotten rid of that old machine long time ago."

"Oh?"

"Yes! Electricity has come of age. All those nights just sittin' there peddling that pedal just to make that thing go."

Across the isle on another table was an assortment of threads on different spools. Every color imaginable was at the spectator's fingertips. And yard goods. Scrapes of material to make a dress, top, or anything else a lady's heart would desire, along with lots of buttons. It was a paradise for any seamstress.

The pots and pans spread out on another table brought back lots of memories as well. "Mama Parker made the best cinnamon rolls. Makes ma mouth water just thinkin' 'bout the aroma filling the room as they baked in the oven." Mabel licked her lips.

"I beg your pardon to differ, Mabel." Angie retorted. "I recall mama Hodge, down the road or two, makin' delicious cinnamon rolls. The folks say the locals always ended up at her door step for somethin' to eat."

"We don't wanna argue with ya, Angie." Lucy chimed in, hoping to avert a fight. "Good foods all over the place. It's just that Mama Parker's are one of the best."

"I like her Beef Stew." Blanch remembered. "She always used fresh vegetables. I can still recall her standing over a hot stove dumping beef chucks into the boiling gravy, along with some carrots, potatoes, and peas from her garden. Hmm! I can still taste it."

"Her spaghetti was another favorite of mine." Mabel continued the scenario. "It wasn't just a bowl of pasta under a hot sauce. Instead she mixed the sauce, her secret recipe, into the pasta, added some mushrooms along with some onions, and baked it. And, with some hard rolls, I could eat it all day."

"Her red meatballs along with some rye bread satisfied many appetites on a cold day. I envied all the folks who sat at her table. Sometimes I wish it were me."

"Oh Angie! Ya make it sound as if no body else knew how to cook." Mabel started to think that things were getting out of hand and wanted to change the subject.

"See that large pot over there?" Lucy pointed to a 12-ounce pot at the end of the table that drew a large audience. "Havin' coffee with her many times, I saw the donuts floating in a hot grease in that pot. Simple, brown on the outside, chewy dough on the inside with a little powder sprinkled on top. I'll miss 'em. Makes me hungry for them right now."

"Yes!" Angie sighed a deep breath while scanning the table. "Soon they'll all be gone. Poor Mama Parker. What will she do next?"

"I don't know, but where's my pocket book?" Blanch uttered. "I want those cooking pans over there. Maybe she left a secret recipe in one of 'em."

"Oh nonsense, Blanch. You should be so lucky." Mabel tried to be practical. "Mama Parker never wrote anything down. You should know that. All her favorite recipes came right out of her head steeped in tradition."

Across the lawn some of the gents grinned with pride, as the auction just ended on some old power tools. The tag on a bench saw read sold in big capital letters. Ben had a couple youngsters load a jigsaw into the back of his pickup truck. Ralph struggled carrying a chest full of hand tools. "These old bones ain't what they use to be." He muttered. Everybody took home an assortment of nails in little brown bags. "Nails, as useful as hearing a rooster crow."

Hank muttered. "Can always use 'em. Somethin' on the property is always falling apart. A nail here and a nail there. Ain't nothin' a nail can't do when it comes time to fixin' something."

Meanwhile, back in the Parker barn, the folks gathered to auction off an old John Deere tractor. Tears started to roll down their cheeks just thinking about all the times they saw it in the field. Next an ice cream machine, and finally a lawnmower.

"Most of the stuff went dirt cheap." Uncle Burt remembered. "Wonder how much money Mrs. Parker will get for all this stuff."

"Yep!" Andrew muttered, agreeing with everybody. "And soon the Parker farm will be history just like the rest of us."

Again, back at the big house that resembled a barn the auction continued. One by one. 'The Cowboy' led in a cow or a hog. Soon it would be horses and cattle. Nothing was forgotten about. Everything had to go. Next to an empty space on the bench, old man Hodge sat in a daze with his arms folded. Meditating, he thought about his own once prosperous one hundred acres of farmland.

"Gotta get to work, Lizzie." The fast eater always had work on his mind. "And tell that Boy to get out here. No time to waste."

"You mean Orville, John?"

"Whoever! These young folks don't know what work really is. Huh! They should be so lucky." Limping through the door, he soon was in the barn starting up his tractor.

But now the one hundred acres was gone. Sold off to many hungry land developers, it was filled with new homes on individual lots. Suddenly the Hodge residence was engulfed with lots of neighbors.

"Hey! Hodge! What ya thinkin'?" Old man Blake jerked his arm.

"Nothing much." Old man Hodge remained stoic, staring out into space.

"Ya look like your deep in thought, as if ya just left the planet earth."

"Maybe I did." The worried face mumbled.

"Don't wanna here it. Got enough troubles of ma own."

"Like what?" Farmer Jones, like most of the other farmers sitting on the bench, tried to remain calm. They already knew what was taking place. Now, in reality, they couldn't care less about their fellow workers.

"Labor! All my help is gone." Blake muttered, in a soft monotone voice to anyone listening. "All the young folks are leavin' the farm. Lookin' for greener pastures, I suppose. Hard for me to get good help to work on the farm these days."

When the auction ended they all gathered down at Bubbles, a favorite water hole in town to share their feelings. "Yes siree Bob. This use to be a place buzzing with activity."

"Don't be so glum, Paul." Larry moaned, while sipping his beer. "Things could be a lot worse."

"Nothin' can get worse than this." Tony shared his own sad depressed feelings.

"You said it. A man use to make a good livin' in these parts, but not any more. No sir. Corn. Beans. Hogs. You name it. Gone. We had so much to take to the market."

"Gentlemen!" A voice echoed among the solemn moods throughout the room from a stranger standing near the door.

Suddenly, the room got quiet. All beer mugs stood idle on the table. Jaws dropped on worried faces as they all turned around to look at the stranger.

"Change men! It's all about change! We must learn to adapt and change with the times. Think about it. Everything must work for the good."

TWENTY-TWO

L ike a thief in the night, change gradually crept over the town of Cedar Lane and left its mark.

The people didn't like change. By not thinking about it they thought it would merely go away on its own. But it didn't. So they put up a wall of resistance.

"Oh! It's never gona happen to me." The young man starting out in life was so confident.

"I'm so busy sometimes I don't know which way is up and which way is down." The busy housewife never had enough hours in her day. She never gave retirement, death, or whatever a second thought.

But time will tell and it did as people were forced to realize that things would not always be the same. And so just as Cedar Lane changed through the years, so did the rest of the world.

Things weren't any different for Linda Hodge either. The home-grown girl from Cedar Lane experienced the same heart rendering changes that every body else did. Once a busy farm girl, now an adult, it was time for her to move on and have a life of her own.

Linda never left Cedar Lane. Old time friends were lasting relationships. Besides, city life never did appeal to her. So, she married a childhood sweetheart, Frankie Cox, from a farm down the road, settled in a small farmhouse in town, and raised two children.

Even though larger department stores started to spring up along some shopping malls, Linda's homespun philosophy never waned. "Save your money for a rainy day. Besides things were getting way too expensive." So, from morning till night, she spent endless hours in the kitchen preparing meals from scratch, or busied herself at a sewing machine. It wasn't the electric kind where folks merely pushed a button. No! Just a peddle on the floor where she had to constantly remind herself to keep her foot goin' up and down. Needless to say, sometimes it felt very good for her to put her head on a pillow at night along with those aching wrist, ankle muscles, and aching back.

The furniture in Linda's house was never new. They always had the usual hand-me-downs from the old folks accept for a new mattress once in awhile, cause the hole in the center of the old one was so big that often a person found themselves sleeping on the floor.

Their car saw many years of hard work as well with lots of miles accumulated through the years. "I got sick and tired of always hearin' my dad, or Uncle John to some folks, say over and over again the times he fixed it. Or the constant reminder that it was his father's car, and his father's before him, and so on."

Frankie, her husband, didn't have the proper schooling. Instead, he spent most of his time on the farm. Whenever there was work to be done, no matter what time of day it was, he'd stay home from school and work on the farm. Luckily for him he had a good mechanical aptitude. Quickly, he got use to fixing things. Some years later, now married to Linda, he developed a small business and went around to the different farms fixing things. "Brought in enough to put bread and butter on the table." He never shied away from boasting about his own pride and joy.

And so the Cox family was like a Rockwell painting. Hard work. Good health. Honesty. Go to church on Sundays. Live in a home in the country and enjoy the American way of life.

To compliment their family income and stay in touch with

the community, Linda opened up a small flower shop in town. Mama Rice put her baking aside many times to help out in the shop. Other ladies also volunteered of their time to help Linda. The town gossip filled the store with lots of chatter daily.

"Mornin' Ms Hanley." Mama Rice greeted, pulling out a large sheet of green paper off the big roll to wrap a pot of flowers.

"Hi Ma." The customer struggled limping down the two steps supported by her walking cane while sniffing the air. "I always like the smell of fresh flowers in your shop."

"Why thank you. Linda always likes to hear that. What ya lookin' for today?" She looked around at the assortment of all the different colors in nicely decorated pots. "Nothing special. Maybe some Lilly's. Maybe some African Violets. Maybe some cut flowers. Perhaps some Roses or Carnations. The fragrances in here are breath-taking."

"Well good. Look around. Let me know if ya need any help. I'll be over there putting some corsages together."

"Yesum! Will do." As she continued to browse around the shop the little bell above the door jingled, signaling that another customer just entered the shop.

"Mornin' Beulah."

"Mornin' to you too, Mama Rice. I didn't know you stopped baking. Always did like your fried chicken."

"Yeah! That's what they all say." After pausing for just a second. "Anyway. What ya lookin' for?"

"Glad you asked, Ma. I want some Carnations. A dozen or so will do just fine. Some white some red. Let's see what ya got."

"Over there." She pointed toward the cooler. "Look around. Help yourself. When ya got your mind made up, let me know."

Approaching the table, Betsy was bubbling over with talk. More interested in small talk than flowers. "Ma. Did ya hear 'bout Janet's knee? Heard she had surgery last week. Marians kennel business is doin' OK. I went to the Rodeo last weekend."

Like one big happy family in a small town, the flower shop did well. Nothing ever went out of the shop that Linda wouldn't want herself. If it did, they should bring it back. Linda always prided herself to make good on every sale.

However, looking around the town, times have changed. Some

of the old favorite stores were gone. A few changed hands, but just like Linda's flower shop, new shops soon opened.

"Like the stores, people changed too." Many thoughts raced through Mama Hodge's mind as she rode through town one day, looking at all the shops. "Not many old timers left anymore, Rodney."

"Yes Ma'am. I hear ya." The driver mumbled, as the big black Buick cruised down the street at 25 m.p.h.

"This is crazy, Rodney. I can't afford you. I can't afford this car. I'm not use to all this luxury. Did you know that?"

"Nonsense, Ma. I hope you don't mind me callin' ya Ma. When I talk to ya, I feel like you're just like my own mom. Ya make me feel so good just bein' around ya."

"Thank you, Rodney. Your so sweet." Ma chuckled.

"Uncle Herbert said ya deserve the best. That's why I'm here, Ma."

"Yeah. Sure. Just cause old Herb did so well workin' for the Railroad, and now lives in Chicago, doesn't mean he should throw all his money away on me."

"Nice day today, isn't it?" Rodney tried to focus the attention on a more positive subject.

"Yes, Rodney. Will the sun be up all day? What's the forecast?"

"Sunny today and hot."

"Take me to the Park, please." Ma interrupted, with a tear rolling down her cheek.

"Ya really wanna go, Ms Hodge?"

"Yes. I'm sure. Just take me to the Park, please." As she spoke her eyes welled up with more tears.

Slowly the car rolled around Mulberry Drive. Up ahead, beyond the field dotted with trees, laid the history of Cedar Lane.

"Pull over, Rodney. Near the gate will be just fine."

"Yes Ma'am."

Close to the wrought iron gate, Ma patiently waited for Rodney to walk around the car and open her door. Then after grabbing his arm, she slowly stepped out of the car. Old age has changed her ability to move about freely. But her mind remained as sharp as a tact. With a slight tremor in her hands, she proceeded to lift the latch and open the gate.

"Let me help ya, Ma." Rodney held her hand.

"That's all right. I can do it myself." The lady still had a stubborn streak in her. The folks say that came from working on the farm with a lot of tough Uncles.

The wrought iron fence that surrounded the Park stood the test of time. Weather beaten, if it could talk, it probably would fill a history book about Cedar Lane. The gate squeaked softly when she opened it and stepped inside. Slowly, walking down the winding cobblestone path, she looked at the many markers, dotted with clusters of trees and flowers, as she held Rodney's arm that helped support her weak body. Just thinking about it, her mind began to wander into a different world. Moving around a big Oak tree, she paused to observe the simple stone.

"Would ya like to sit down, Ma?"

"No Rodney. Just let me be for a moment, please." Again, she tried to hold back the tears, but it was no use.

Glancing at the stone it read: Frederick Hodge, born 19—. Quickly, she looked at the trees, refusing to finish reading as the memories flowed through her mind. "Apple farmer. Loved his orchards. Talked to his trees everyday. Thought with the right pep talk they'd grow more. Always encouraged John and me to visit the farm."

"Would ya like a handkerchief?"

"No, Rodney. I'll be all right."

Slowly, they continued to walk down the cobblestone path meditating. As the path curved ahead, they paused on a small bridge overlooking a pond long enough to stare at the goldfish below, swimming around searching for food. So peaceful and quiet, they wished they could stop the clock and stay there all day.

Near a small flower bed Ma saw the next stone that read: Dan Hodge, born 19—. Again she looked away. Pleasant memories quickly swept through her mind.

Uncle Dan loved to be around other people. That was unusual because most farmers loved to get lost among the cows or in a cornfield. He often thought more about other people than himself, and did his best to help them in his own little way.

"Most important to Dan was his providing transportation to loved ones who lived in the big city." Ma remembered. The Hodges had widows with small children who lived in Chicago, and had no way to get around without the help of public transportation. Frequently, Uncle Dan brought them out to Cedar Lane in his old Plymouth on holidays, for a time of fun and fellowship with friends and family. "May his soul rest in peace."

Next to a small fountain that the town graciously provided to the Park, laid a plague engraved with the name of Walter Hodge, a great Uncle to ten kids. People often stopped long enough to admire the mermaid holding a fish spraying water out of its mouth. Looking at the surrounding grass, if too tall, folks might miss the plague completely.

Uncle Walter was the oldest of all the Uncles, a forerunner to the others coming over from the Old Country, and eventually settling down in Cedar Lane, Indiana. Not too far down the road from Ma, Uncle John, and Aunt Hodge, he farmed a small stretch of land himself. Later, parceling out his land, he helped build Ma and John Hodge's house with all the other Uncles, and it was a momentous occasion.

"Let's go, Rodney. I'm spendin' far too much time here. Must move along." Ma nudged him with her free hand while leaning on his arm.

Even though people shouldn't live in the past, it sometimes does them good to pause for a moment and reflect. Fond memories often bring folks closer together in a world of reality far more than they could ever imagine.

"Uncle Mike is gone too. Where is he, Rodney?"

Through a cluster of bushes deep in another corner of the Park laid a stone labeled, Uncle Mike, born 19—. A cluster of tall bushes enclosed a marked grave where people could go and reflect on a great man. He always liked privacy and felt other people would like it as well.

Like most farmers, Mike was a hard worker. Even though he never received many accolades throughout his life either, he loved to work and deeply felt it was the obligation of every man to put in a good day's work. "The mark of a good man is his willingness to work." The folks can still picture him saying those exact words today. He was the jack-of-all-trades. There wasn't anything he couldn't do on the farm. His only draw back was being too quiet.

More work and less talk was his motto throughout his life.

"We've see 'em all, Rodney. All I wanna see for one day. Let's go. I—"

"But Ma."

"Don't interrupt, Rodney. Get me outta here. Isn't that the gate over there?' She pointed to an exit sign on a maintenance shed. Now, weak and feeble, often her memory slipped.

"But Ma." Rodney insisted. "Don't ya wanna see your favorite?"

"Oh yes. I almost forgot. Please take me to him."

A newly marked grave, only a couple of weeks old, laid on the edge of an open field. Like those already there, this vast countryside will mark the history of many more in the future.

"I can't take it any more, Rodney." The tears that filled her eyes clouded a blurred vision. "I'm tired now. I must sit down. My wobbly knees will carry me no further."

"Yes, Ma." He assisted her over to a bench near the marker.

On a simple stone, all it said was Milton. Nothing else. He wanted his legacy to be that which he left in the hearts of those he came in contact with. The way he lived was the way he wanted to be remembered. Even though Ma loved all the Uncles, she missed him the most.

Ma often visited Milton's grave the least because it was hardest for her to adjust to his passing away. Milton took Orville to his first major league baseball game. Saved the Boy from a terrible beating. Protected him as much as possible and encouraged his future.

There were other Hodges in the Park. Even though Ma often placed flowers on their graves, and liked to spend more time there, the grieving process became overwhelming. So she slowly walked with Rodney's assistance back to the car.

Traveling over the wobbling boards that covered the creek on up the hill, there was no more Hodge farm. Gone were the days when all the Uncles gathered. The aroma of hot coffee perking over a hot stove. The small talk that got them caught up in the latest gossip.

Down a deserted path the barn stood empty. Cobwebs formed in the corners. The tools on a bench stood dormant ready to collect dust and rust with age. And, there were no more stalls to clean.

There were no more cows grazing in the field. They didn't have to concern themselves with lush green fields of grass, and rotate the location of the herd to keep them eating. No milking in the early morning hours and evening any more. No constant checks by the Board of Health to maintain a top notch dairy farm.

Ma missed the fresh eggs. Taking care of chickens could be a nuisance. Keeping them eating was an awesome task. Candling and washing eggs kept everybody busy. Now, the empty hen house offered only memories from the past.

It was fun to watch the corn grow. From breaking up the soil to planting seeds, to watching them pop up out of the ground, and grow taller than eye level, even the kids had fun playing hide-go-seek in the corn field. Watching the farmers harvest the crop and fill the silos. The folks loved to listen to an old tractor chugging along in the field. Or watching a pheasant fly out of a row of corn after being stalked by a dog. No more. There will be no more toiling by the farmers in the field. Only a for sale sign was left, perched on a splintered post in a bare field.

The roof leaked. A pipe burst. Thousands of pigeons nested in the attic of a silo. A tattered wire draped on a pole to the barn offered no electricity. But it didn't matter. No signs of life lived there anymore.

For Ma, Uncle John, and Orville's Aunt, life was different now. Uncle John could move around even less than Orville's mother. Confined to a chair, all he did most days was just sit around and moan. For a man who was always busy most of his life, reading the newspaper was boring. And his appetite wasn't any better. Not eating much, he lost a lot of weight over recent years. Luckily, Connie, a grand daughter who lived in town, came out frequently to assist getting him dressed, in and out of bed, along with helping both of them meet other basic needs.

Orville's Uncle tired easily from listening to the radio. As far as he was concerned, television never existed, even though the family gave him one a year ago. At eighty-eight years of age, though his mind wavered, he still always found time to do a lot of complaining.

Next to the farmhouse, which stood empty now for years, the Hodges lived in a small trailer. A small bedroom, bath, and kitchen were all the couple had. Linda insisted that they move into a trailer park, where they could meet friends and be around other people. But John would have none of that.

Unck was the last of all the Uncles. For as hard nosed as he was, it was surprising that he outlived them all. There must be something to that old saying, work hard, eat good, and sleep good, for farmers adhered to that kind of a life style all the time, and Orville's Uncle was no exception.

Besides his health, Unck encountered other problems. Money. He never could afford any insurance, nor did he want it. "Their all money hungry. Why do they always complain about money, yet they maintain some of the fanciest offices around? Just drive through any big city. You'll see." So the Hodges struggled to live on a social security income.

But their money woes didn't end there. The bank still had an interest in their farm. Without a cash flow there was no way they could maintain the payments. Naturally, that bothered the bank. They weren't interested in a farm that no body else wanted. All they wanted was cash, and often made things miserable for Orville's mother, Aunt, and Uncle.

"John, I wish you'd eat more. You hardly touched your breakfast." Lizzie glanced at a newspaper while sitting in the small living room.

"Don't need to eat when I'm not hungry, Ma."

"Yes, I know. But ya know what the doctor always says—."

"Oh fiddle faddle on the doctor. What does he know? He's not me. He should mind his own business." Uncle John raised his finger, getting ready to give another long speech.

"Nonsense, John. You know your health is important."

"What ya eaten, Ma?"

"A sandwich. It's lunchtime. Since ya didn't eat much breakfast, I thought ya wouldn't be hungry for lunch."

Suddenly, the doorbell rang and interrupted their conversation. Slowly, Ma walked toward the door.

"Ms Hodge?"

"Yes, I'm she."

"May I come in? I'm Carol. Carol Ross. I'm from The Farmers Trust and Savings Bank here in town."

"Yes. Sure. Why not?" Anticipating the nature of the visit,

Lizzie felt nervous and angry. "I get so many nasty phone calls and letters from you people. This is probably the next thing. I haven't spoken to a real live person in my house yet."

"I'm sorry. I'll only be a few minutes. I promise. I just want to share a few things with you and your husband." The middle-aged lady with short brown hair was well dressed for church in a blue dress.

"He's not my husband. He's my brother. And if ya wanna talk to him and Martha, they're in the living room over there." Ma pointed with a shaky finger. "That's what they all say, only a few minutes." Ma mumbled underneath her breath. After pausing to regain her thoughts, she led Carol into the living room. "This is the lady from the bank, John. She wants to talk to us."

"A-A-A?"

"Don't worry, Ms Ross. He probably can't hear a word you say anyway."

"That's OK. I'll be brief."

Ma nodded, looking worried.

"Ms Hodge. We need one hundred thousand dollars in order for you to keep the farm."

"What else is new?" Through the years Orville's mother developed a cynical attitude toward the business community.

"I know that's a lot of money, and you don't have the money right now."

"Oh?"

"We at the bank have been tryin' to come up with a way to help you make your payments."

"Oh?"

"Yes. We thought 'bout selling the farm, but nobody wants it."

"Yes. Go on. What else is new?"

"We thought 'bout leasing it, but that wouldn't work either."

"Yeah!"

"So the best we could come up with is if you just give it to us. It's sort a like a gift and it will free you up from any further debt on this property. We'd sell it to a land developer and give you something for it. Might not be anywhere near what it's actually worth, but it would set you, the misses, and your sister here all up nicely in a home."

"Nursing home?"

"Something like that, Ms Hodge. I'm sure you'll all be comfortable for the rest of your life." Ms Ross tried to be helpful with their situation.

"No way! I heard that! That is the last thing on earth I would ever want to do. Do ya here me? You! Ms, Ms, Ms, whoever you are." John shouted while struggling to stand up.

"I'm sorry Ms Hodge. I didn't want to get your husband, brother I mean, upset. All I'm tryin' to do is help. But we're running out of options and time."

Lizzie took a deep breath. "Yes I know, Ms Ross. Could you give me a little time to think 'bout it?"

"Yes. Of course. Take all the time you need. Here's my card. Give me a call in a couple of days." Then, Ms Ross stood up and bid them all farewell as she walked toward the door accompanied by Mama Hodge.

"She's got a lot of nerve." John complained. "Who does she think she is barging in here and demanding that we give up our farm?"

"Shhh, John!" Orville's mother whispered while placing her finger over her lips. "She didn't come barging in here. She knocked."

"I don't care." John's angry feelings started to escalate. "She has no business tellin' me what to do."

"But John. She's from the bank. The bank can do anything they want. They could kick us off this land without even talkin' to us."

"Well that's a fine how-do-you-do. Work hard all my life. Now I'm an old man. Can't do much anymore. Hard to stay on my feet. And she's tellin' me to pay up or get off my land. So whatta we suppose to do now?"

Lizzie took a deep breath and gave it some thought. "I don't know, John. Something will work out. I'm sure." With Uncle John now up in years and not well physically, often she did all she could do to maintain her composure.

"I don't know what this world is comin' to." John moaned, and held on to the furniture as he slowly walked into the other room.

Again the doorbell rang. This time John grabbed the door handle to support his feeble body before answering it. "Yeah! Who is it? If you're sellin' somethin', we don't want it." He shouted, not even knowing whom it was on the other side of the door.

Again the doorbell rang.

"John! Don't ya think ya better answer it?"

"Yeah! I suppose." Reluctantly he approached the door. "Better see what they want, and get rid of 'em."

When the door opened, Uncle John stood stung for the moment. Orville, the Boy he hadn't seen for a long time, was now coming home. Even though his sight was failing him, somehow, he always knew when it was his nephew.

"Unck! Can I come in?"

"Sure! Make yourself at home." Unck slowly turned around and walked back to his chair in the living room.

"Who is it, John?" Ma asked, and when she saw him, she rushed up to him and gave him a big hug as the tears started to roll down her cheeks. "Orville! It's so nice to see you. How've ya been? What brings you back here?"

"Sit down, Boy. Don't just stand there."

"Thanks, Unck."

"Can I get ya somethin' to eat? Oh never mind. How 'bout a sandwich? Got some ham in the kitchen. Maybe some ham on rye bread with some mustard, maybe? And how 'bout a soda? I bet you'd like some potato chips to go along with it."

After the usual chitchat to get caught up on the latest gossip, they all settled back for some serious conversation. Word got around that Ma, Aunt Martha, and Unck were in some real serious financial trouble. Orville has done quite well playing baseball, and with a love so strong for each of them, he handed Unck an envelope. "And so Unck, I'll talk to Linda. She'll help you set this up and we'll stay in touch." After a big hug for the man who set up so many road blocks in his way, like a minefield ready to explode in the army, Orville was gone.

"What ya thinkin', John? Sittin' there in your easy chair, starin' out the window. Ya look like ya just saw a ghost."

"Yep! I did. Don't understand it. Don't understand a lot 'bout life. Why me? Why does he wanna help me? Surely, I can't be deservin' of it. Like an unexpected blessing to a sinkin' ship. Makes me think 'bout a song Orville once told me 'bout called He ...forgives ..."

TWENTY-THREE

Back at River Front Stadium it was the Cincinnati Redlegs playing the Chicago Cubs. The bottom of the ninth and a tie game: 3—3. Two men on the bases and one out. Home team fans were sitting on the edge of their seats. Visitors hoped for extra innings and new life.

Alex choked up on his bat while staring at the pitcher. Squinting, he struggled to locate the ball in the southpaw's hand. Finally, from out of nowhere he saw a ball sailing toward him.

"The pressure is on. I have a full count on me, two guys standing out there on the bases, and the whole team in the dugout depending on me."

As the ball crossed the plate, Alex swung viciously while the fans dropped their jaw watching in awe. It connected with his bat. Randy dove for it. But the ball rolled out of his glove and hit home plate before bouncing back up into his glove again. "Out!" The ump shouted. "Safe! Foul ball!" Quickly the man in black changed his mind.

Without hesitating, Leo raced out of the dugout. "Are ya sure ump? Looked to me from where I was sittin' my man caught it." The Cub manager stuck out his chest with a flapping jaw, while rapidly spitting out words. After the third base coach pushed him away from the ump, his temper cooled and he reluctantly returned to join the rest of his team on the bench.

The next ball sailed deep into the left field corner. Williams never took his eye off the moving object. After realizing it had a commanding lead, Billy dove for it while extending his arm. Sliding several feet, the ball barely touched the tip of his glove, before bouncing on the ground. Then, rebounding, it landed back in his glove. The fans went wild when he quickly stood up and held the ball up high in his mitt. But it didn't matter. The ump already gave the sign.

Jim Hickman moved slightly to his left to catch the next fly ball in short right field. Two out. The runners remained on their bases while the fans moaned.

As the next batter slowly stepped out of the dugout and walked toward the plate, fans took advantage of a pit stop. "What goes in must come out." Baseball fans were convinced, and hot bodies took in a lot of liquid that day.

Other fans lined up at the concession stand for more food. Hot dogs smothered in ketchup, mustard, and onions, couldn't satisfied everybody's appetite. Some folks went back to their seats with an arm full of peanuts, popcorn, crackerjack, and ice-cold soda.

Meanwhile, back in the Redleg dugout the boys moved around. Everybody stood up. Some paced back and forth while a couple guys lined up by the drinking fountain. Puzzled, Orville remained seated on the bench. "Time to move, Boy." A teammate encouraged him to join the flow of traffic.

"But where do I go? What should I do?"

"Don't ya know, Boy?"

"No! I don't know."

"Follow me."

As they strolled toward the other end of the dugout, a Robert Mitchum like voice suddenly interrupted their trend of thought. "Hey Boy! C'mere!"

Orville looked around. He heard a voice, but couldn't trace where it was coming from.

"Over here, Boy!"

The fellow behind him pointed to the coach, standing with one foot perched on the bench, halfway down the beaten path. Then Orville stepped out of the line and joined him. "Ya wanted to see me, coach?"

"Yeah! Sit down! Let's chat!"

"OK!"

"Where ya from, Boy? Can't say I know ya. Ya remind me of a kid from outta nowhere." The coach scratched his chin with a puzzled look on his face.

Joined the team last week. Don't ya remember? I saw you there." The Boy tensed up.

"I can't remember everybody I see."

"Oh?"

"Never mind!" The coach always got angry when some wise guy tried to challenge him. "Now you're a professional league ball player. Ha! Ha! Ha!" A cynical laugh didn't help the situation. Instead, it was more like adding coals to an already burning fire.

"Yes sir."

But how'd ya get here? Can't say that I know ya. Must've been born with a silver spoon in your mouth. Kinda like who ya know, and not what ya do.

"No Sir! You'll be surprised. Life is full of surprises, Sir."

TWENTY-FOUR

As Orville's thoughts remained deeply engrossed in the game, suddenly he felt a slap on his shoulder. "Hey Boy!" The Robert Mitchum voice greeted. "Don't say that I know ya. Never saw ya before in my life. Who are ya?"

Slowly Orville turned around to stare at a silly grin. He felt insulted, scared, and reluctant to speak. "Or—Or—Orville, Sir!" Mama always taught him to be polite.

Glancing at his scorecard, the coach rolled his eyes down the page mumbling. "Orville. Orville. Orville. Oh yeah! Here ya are. Hmmm! Toward the bottom." After scratching his chin. "Don't know ya."

"I joined the team last week, Sir. Don't ya remember? I was the guy that…"

"Had lots of things goin' through ma mind. Can't remember everybody I talk to." The rude interruption startled Orville.

"Orville Hodge, Sir! Orville Hodge!" The nervous Boy repeated himself, avoiding direct eye contact with the monster figure, while his thoughts remained in the game.

"Ya look thin Boy. Turn one way and I might not see ya. Doubt if ya can hit Boy."

"Six foot Sir." After a moment of silence. "And strong. And don't call me Boy coach. I can hit …ya wanna see?" Orville was getting ready to fight.

"OK! Ya can hit! But ya look weak. Doesn't look like ya can hit the south side of a barn."

More insults. Doubts raced through his mind. Orville didn't sound very convincing and rolled his eyes in disbelief.

"Where ya from? How'd ya get here? Can't say that I know ya." Gradually the man with tough skin, potbelly, and whiskers started to mellow.

"From the farm, Sir! Indiana, my mama says …"

"Yeah! I know all that." The sarcasm in the coach's tone was unsettling. "But who are ya? Really!"

"I—I—I'm …"

"No! After shaking his head and waving his arm. "Are ya somebody's pet?"

"No Sir."

"Is Babe Ruth your dad?" The other guys chuckled, while listening to the coach ask all the questions.

"Huh! I should be so lucky." Orville thought. "No!" The newcomer shouted in the coach's ear.

"Mickey Mantle's dad?"

"No way!"

"Yeah!" The coach grinned.

"Keep talking. It's getting good." Grandiose thoughts started to race through Orville's mind.

"Belong to some big business guy?" More questions. The inquisitive coach never ran out of questions. No such thing of curiosity killing the cat here.

"I—I—I …"

"Like Gene Audrey or Ted Turner? Ya know what I mean?"

"I'm tryin' to tell ya coach." Even though butterflies started to churn in his stomach, Orville tried hard to remain calm.

"So you're from Indiana?"

"Yep!"

222

"Ha! Ha! Ha!" The coach laughed. "Ya look like something that just came out of the woods. Tall. Thin. White complexion. Like a skeleton."

"I never did tan well. Born in Chi-ca-go, Sir! But didn't stay very long. Grew up on a farm in Indiana."

"Doesn't everybody come from the farm?" He pointed his finger at all the other players sitting on the bench. "Just about everybody here originated on the farm."

"Due to circumstances my mama always said." After taking a deep breath. "She sure worked hard."

"Who?"

"My mama!" Orville shouted. "My mama, Sir!" The Boy was getting ready to defend her from all the insults.

"OK, Orville. I'm sorry." The coach gestured with his arm, sensing the mood.

"So what else do ya wanna know?" Though cautious, gradually the Boy felt more comfortable.

"Ya some rich kid? Ya know, like a wolf in sheep's clothing. I know a guy who walked around through office buildings in overalls shining shoes. Then, at the end of the day he changed into a suit and tie. Drove away in a Cadillac. Wow! Sure fooled me!"

"No Sir! Not me, Sir! Wish I was …"

"Oh?" The coach probed one foot up on the bench. "Tell me more Boy!"

"No silver spoon in my mouth."

"Oh yeah! I bet." The coach still had doubts about Orville's whereabouts.

"No foolin' Sir. Never went to Harvard. No famous dad who could shoot me to the top. And money? No way! Never saw much of the stuff."

"So where ya from Boy?"

"My mama was born in 1910 and raised in Charos, a small Rumanian town near the Russian border. She use to tell me about the Russian soldiers terrorizing the town at night riding through to water their horses."

"Oh?"

"Yep! Most of the folks were hard workin' farmers. Never got enough food and very little meat. Besides government provisions, folks were forced to steal off the vegetable wagons in the field."

"So you from Russia Boy?"

"Nope!" The coach wasn't listening. "Skip the Boy stuff. I already told ya I didn't like it."

"So where ya from Boy?"

"I'm getting to that …"

Although Orville tried to oblige him, the coach made him mad, especially when he just wanted to focus on the game. But talking about all the stories Mom told him, made him nostalgic.

Throughout the village, thick black smoke spite out of chimney tops from houses clustered together. No electricity. The fireplace was the only source for heat and cooking. "And let me tell ya, the winters were mighty cold. I can still picture everything mama told me." Goose bumps ran down Orville's back just thinking about it.

"Jean! Get the pot. Go outside and fetch some water out of the well. You'll be lucky if you get to go to school, even two years Jean. We need ya here on the farm!" It was a phrase echoed thousands of times across the poverty stricken country. The word school wore an air of privilege for the wealthy or accomplished.

In a black dress down to her ankles and a homemade white bonnet, Jean struggled filling the pot. Then, returning to the house, she and her mama slid it on a big hook over the fire. Then stoked it, dodging the sparks. "Yah! Gut!" Mama muttered. "Now scoop out some water and put it over there." Her wrinkled hand with swollen knuckles pointed to a corner in the room.

Jean struggled, hauling the big corn sack to the pot. Earlier, the men scraped it off the cob with a pocketknife. Now, the ladies added the kernels to the boiling water. Palaz or corn meal, some folks called it mush, covered with gravy was a family favorite.

A limited supply of beans, potatoes, and carrots were stored in the shed. Even though the food supply was adequate, they never took anything for granted. Living in a communistic country brought many uncertainties.

Hot water, a pinch of salt, some crushed oats, and they had oatmeal for breakfast. Fresh eggs came from two healthy chickens in a cage out back. Every winter Orville's grandma moaned. "Just keep Millie healthy. It's our only source for milk."

Every week a horse drawn wagon rolled down a dirt road filled with flour sacks. It looked like enough to feed an entire army. The government must've thought everybody could live off the white powdery stuff forever.

Grandma baked bread in another corner of the fireplace. With a few ingredient changes she added cinnamon rolls, donuts, and pie to the menu. Everybody's mouth watered just thinking about the aroma of fresh baked apple pie.

The men were strong. Like a chain gang with a rake and hoe over their shoulder, they marched the mile to the fields every day. Baked beneath a hot sun, they struggled breaking up the hard ground.

Meanwhile, back home Elizabeth, the youngest, stayed busy ironing clothes. On a snug fit towel over a table, a hot piece of iron with a dresser handle taken from the fire, smoothly slid over the cloth. Back and forth Lizzie went constantly replacing the iron with another hot one. It was an exhausting job, yet she never uttered a complaint.

Following a good hot meal, the folks gathered around the fireplace for some good old fashion chitchat and fun. Occasionally a local newspaper provided topics for conversation.

In a battered sport coat John loved to demonstrate his disappearing egg trick. First, he put an egg into a cloth pocket mama sewed together. Following some fast moves it vanished before everybody's eyes. Now the pocket was empty. And they all laughed when they saw it reappear under his arm.

The hours slipped away guessing where the bean was. Taking turns, three coffee cups were manipulated before their very eyes. "Wipe the grin off your face Jean." Lizzie lifted the cups. More laughs echoed throughout the room when she came up empty the second time around.

Common jokes often filled the evening with laughter. An old favorite was the disappearance of farmer Dan. Legend has it that one day Dan was out milking his cows when suddenly a loud noise came from the barn. Quickly, as they all gathered to see the sight, Dan was nowhere to be found. Word has it that with a bruised utter, Molly gave him one swift kick that sent him into outer space. Only a big hole in the side of the barn remains to this day.

Small talk squeezed its way into all the humor. Harsh working conditions and freedom were frequent topics of conversation.

To brighten the mood Uncle Joe played his banjo. Without any formal lessons, the flat notes were melodious to a deft ear. Singing, clapping hands, and dancing around the room with a partner was good medicine for weary hearts.

Often, oblivious to their surroundings, Pa's mind would drift off into another world. Grinning, he mumbled. "Yep! Sure is a nice house."

"Whatta ya mean, Pa?"

"Oh nothing Joe. Just thinkin' 'bout the time we built this place. For the life of me I never thought it would get done."

"Oh?" Jean questioned, dropping her jaw and rounding her lips.

"Yep! Did it with an ax. None of those fancy tools like those folks in the city have. Just an ax, hammer, a few nails, and this here saw. Busy. Hard work." His voice started to waver. "Chiseling away. All day long and late into the night we worked. Finally a house." Suddenly the room got quiet.

People in Charos belonged to close knit families. There was no place to go. Big tanks and soldiers monitored the streets. Walks weren't pleasant. Fear was a way of life. Government approval was necessary just to visit a friend in the next town.

However, things never stayed the same. Pa died, thus reducing help on the farm. Eventually Uncle John left the country with Orville's Aunt Jean for better opportunities abroad. Left behind, Uncle Joe and Lizzie struggled with Mama to edge out a living from the land.

One day while Lizzie was hutched over a bucket of water peeling potatoes, she heard Mama moaning in the other room. "You all right, Mama?"

"Oh honey." A weak voice replied. "I'm so sick. I don't think I can go much further."

Quickly Lizzie wheeled around and rushed into the other room. Then, stooping, she cupped her mother's head in her hands when Joe walked into the house.

"Wow! Mama! It's cold outside. I wouldn't send my dog out there if I had one." Joe groaned, removing a thick knitted scarf, hat, and coat, before flopping into a chair near the fire.

Winter has arrived in Charos. Homes were buried in snow that covered the landscape. Occasionally a horse drawn carriage weaved its way through the hills. While people huddled around a fireplace, thick black rings of smoke spit out of chimney tops.

"Joe! Mama's not well!" Lizzie shouted, hoping to draw his attention. After repeating her cry several times, finally the snores dissipated following one more last desperate plead. "Joe! Do ya here me? Come here! Please! I'm in the bedroom with Mama!"

With a drooping chin, choking on his saliva, he stirred. "Ah! Ah! Ah! Whose there? Whatta ya want?" He muttered, sitting up to clear his throat.

"Come here this minute! Hurry!"

Without hesitating he rushed into the other room.

"Shhh!" She motioned, placing her finger over her lips.

"It's OK." Mama whispered. "Just need to rest. Get some rest." Struggling for the right words, she drifted off. Sleep came easy to the woman who toiled a lifetime caring for her family.

"Come with me." Lizzie led Joe back into the other room. Then, near a blazing fire, she stirred a pot of chicken soup for Mama.

"Times are changin', Lizzie …and not all for the good. Charos, like all of Rumania is now under Russian rule. Yet it remains poor."

"Yeah! Well what else is new around here, Joe?" Lizzie mocked. "Let's just go out and create a new government." Chuckling. "I'm sorry. I'm listening."

"Since I married Sarah …"

"Yeah! Ya got that right." Lizzie interrupted.

"We settled down …right here in Charos …"

"Yeah. A local church gal …as if you could leave Charos if ya wanted to." Lizzie continued to mock most of the conversation.

"Mama's having a seesaw battle with her illness …Better that Sarah and I stay behind and care for her."

"Stay behind? Where am I goin'?" Lizzie looked frightened.

"I think it's time for you to leave the country."

"Oh?" Surprised, the thought never crossed her mind.

So one day at nineteen, Lizzie was buried in a hay wagon. While people worked in the fields, Joe and cousin Mike drove the wagon into the next town. It was a long trip. No potty stops. Not much to eat. Lying still. Bumpy roads. Aching muscles. It was a ride to test a person's patience and endurance.

Weaving through the tall corn stalks, a huge locomotive puffed thick black smoke into the sky. Then after rounding a sharp curve, old number ninety-nine came into view before a group of weary folks trembling with fear.

After gradually coming to a halt, people rushed to board the train. Worried faces, uncertain about their future, hugging bundles of all their worldly possessions close to their chest, squeezed through the narrow doors.

Lizzie wore a long black coat resting on her shoulders. Joe thought it best that she travel light with only a few dollars and a couple of sandwiches in her pocket. Fate will take care of the rest.

The train conductor in a black tattered suit, white shirt and tie, paraded down the isles of three passenger cars. Staring, with an evil eye, diminished the hopes and dreams of the new passengers. "OK! Show me your passports." A cold and tactless demeanor just added more coals to the fire.

Lizzie was nervous when he approached her. "Ma'am!"

Staring at the floor with folded arms, she tried to ignore him.

"Ma'am! I'm speakin' to ya!" He shouted, while getting angry. "Show me your passport. No one leaves this town without government approval."

Quickly, in overalls and a straw hat Joe intervened. "Sorry Sir. She lost it. The soldier at the last corner said she could get a new one in the next town."

Pondering the thought, looking at the innocent face of a girl wrapped in a scarf knotted at her chin, he was convinced.

So, following a big hug as tears welled up in her eyes, Joe took off faster than the speed of light.

As friends and family waved from the platform, slowly the big wheels started to turn. The engine huffed and puffed, spitting out rings of black smoke through a tall stack into the air. Picking up speed, the little station left behind got smaller and smaller until it disappeared out of sight.

Traveling along cliffs on mountainsides, through dark tunnels, on bridges over streams and rivers, and through marshy forests, old number ninety-nine chucked along. To an owl perched high up in a tree, or a deer scrambling across the tracks, it looked like a streak of light.

Europe. Rumania. Hungry. Austria. Germany. Belgium. Familiar towns were soon only memories of hopes and dreams. Bucharest, Budapest, Linz, Munich, Bonn, and Brussels flashed through travelers' minds seeking freedom.

Without heat and other amenities on the train, Lizzie was cold and hungry. Fear often smothered her own hopes and dreams. Trusting in God, she believed all things were possible.

During many brief whistle stops Lizzie saw once prosperous towns now lie in ruins. Buildings were in flames, and people lay in the streets. Military tanks everywhere. The crackling sound of gunshots were heard in the mountains.

Leaving London, England, Lizzie experienced the turbulent waters of the high seas. Tossed about the waves, the ship's deck swayed to forty-five degree angles. Nauseated with frequent bouts of vomiting, kept her sick most of the time, and experiencing a real test of endurance.

Finally, a jubilant crowd saw the Statute of Liberty, a welcome sight. Smiles mixed with tears told them that a long troublesome journey was over.

In New York City, Lizzie raced off the ramp into the arms of Uncle John and Aunt Jean. There were hugs, kisses, and lots of chitchat to catch up on old times.

From New York to Cleveland, Pennsylvania to Chicago, Lizzie stayed busy doing odd jobs while living with family. Whole heartily she rolled up her sleeves to clean homes and do laundry in an old ringer-washing machine.

Later as a child, Orville never forgot his mother, Lizzie, stringing the long clothesline secured by big hooks across the backyard where they lived. And, the endless hours ironing shirts late into the night, folding them, and placing them either in boxes or dresser drawers. The Chinese must've had a knack for running a hand laundry business.

In Chicago Lizzie seized the moment to learn a trade. After browsing through a local newspaper, she answered an ad to making shirts at The Stitch It Shirt Factory. Gratified to have work, her only complaint was aching feet after operating the peddle on her sewing machine all day.

On the other hand Orville's dad was an American.

"Oh come on, Orville. Who ya tryin' to kid?" The coach interrupted. "Before the pilgrims landed everybody was from the Old Country."

"Yeah I know. But what I mean is my dad was born here."

"Oh?"

"Yes! He was born in a small coal-mining town, just outside of Birmingham, Alabama. Folks worked in the mines all day, and they suffered. Many of 'em got Black Lung disease and eventually died."

"I pity those people." Orville touched a soft spot in the tough skinned coach.

"Home for my dad was a small frame house. A light bulb hanging on a bare wire lit the room. It reminds me of Jackie Gleason in the Honey Mooners, an old TV show."

"Can't be all that bad? After all he didn't live in a cave." The coach grinned. "Things could've been a lot worse." His sarcastic mood returned.

"A big block of ice kept their food cold. I remember my Mama sayin' Pa always complained about having to empty the water pan underneath the box."

"Ice box?" The coach mocked. "Don't ever let people hear ya say ice box around here. We call 'em refrigerators."

"Baths were in the big round metal tub parked in the middle of the kitchen floor. Folks shared the water …lots of buckets of water …lots of trips to the well."

" …no privacy there …"

"Nope!"

"Wow! Can't imagine takin' a bath in somebody else's dirty water."

"When Pa became of age the country fell on hard times. The depression put lots of people outta work. To cope Pa got work at a steel factory just outside Chicago."

"Where? What factory?"

"Not sure. I think somewhere in Indiana."

"So where'd they meet, Orville?"

"Mama and Papa were church goin' people. They met singin' in the choir. Eventually they got married and not too long after Annie and me were born."

"Twins?" The coach interrupted with bulging eyes.

"Yep! They didn't want a common name so they called me Orville."

"Ha! Ha! Ha! Ha! I'll be damned. Here he is. We have some unknown kid playin' baseball in the major league."

TWENTY-FIVE

Chicago, Illinois. 1944. The windy city. People came from all over to get work. There was an old saying: "If you can't get work in Chicago, you can't get it anywhere."
Deeply involved in World War Two, with the end hopefully in sight, the boilers were working overtime putting out manufactured goods for the war. Chicago was no exception with its tall chimneystacks pouring out black smoke into the sky. And people were happy just to have a job.

On any given day a south sider out for a walk could ingest the delightful aroma of the stockyards. From all over northern Illinois trucks hauled pigs, hogs, and cattle to their final destination. Pending on which way the wind blew, occasionally people on the near north side could smell the same odor.

Cars backed up for miles, creating a traffic jam at a railroad crossing. Looking over the crossing gate, with red lights blinking in cadence to the sound of a tinkling bell, gawking eyes counted the freight cars as they went by. "Must be a hundred of 'em." A

232

little boy stretched his neck to see over the dashboard. A network of track carried freight cars to various industrial spurs throughout the city. Meanwhile, drivers got impatient as tempers flared and they blew their horns.

Four passenger stations dotted the city. A junior high class boarded the Illinois Central train at midnight at the same station that bares its name. After partying all night, they toured Springfield, Illinois the next day, looking at all the Abraham Lincoln sites, the envy of any American History fan.

Traveling southwest, people flocked to the Polk Street Station and boarded the Santa Fe Railroad. Riding high off the ground in a dome car, they saw the gorgeous sites of the Grand Canyon, Indian Reservations, cactus spread out on the desert, Adobe Huts, the Alamo, and more.

In the heart of downtown Chicago was the Union Station. Like all the other stations it was frequently packed with people. Long lines gathered at the ticket windows. Several rows of benches accommodated families, military personnel, an elderly couple, and other excited passengers eager to take a trip.

Traditionally twice each year, the Martins took Aunt Sophie to the B & O Station for her return trip to New Castle, Pennsylvania. Only a few people congregated in the huge depot on Sunday night waiting to board a train. Finally, the blaring sound startled everybody. "Attention please! Now boarding at gate number ten for New castle!"

Little Andy, Sophie's nephew, was in his second heaven at the train station. Walking toward the front of the train he stared at all the cars. Aunt Sophie always traveled coach. Standing next to the engineer, he stared at the track that laid out before them, while listening to the loud roar of two big engines. Later, he saw the conductor wave his flashlight as the train slowly started to move. It was so much fun watching other trains come and go on the different spurs.

At night, downtown Chicago lit up like a Christmas tree with all its neon lights. Decorating the tall buildings, a pedestrian didn't have to look up very far to see the Kemper, Kraft, or Chicago Tribune sign glowing beneath the stars.

In the less populated neighborhoods outside the Loop, (a popular name for the downtown area) were the traditional Ma and Pa stores: Klein's corner drug store, and Ulein's restaurant where a scoop of mash potatoes smothered in gravy were always a favorite. Adolph's butcher shop. Louie's grocery store. Michael's cleaners. There were so many small communities within a big city.

Chicago provided a variety of housing to its citizens. From the high rises for the well off, to an apartment in a building complex, to single dwellings for families, neighborhoods were formed where people bonded together.

And in a one-room apartment, a closet for a kitchen, and a bathroom down the hall shared with other tenants in the building, lived the Crocker Family. Surviving the Great Depression, and now in the midst of a war, they were happy in spite of the cramped living conditions in which they lived.

Leroy Crocker was proud of his family. Annie was the spitting image of her mother. Like father and son, he dreamed of one day taking Orville fishing. And he just couldn't say enough nice things about Lizzie. He worked hard and wanted the best for each one of them. However, things would change. Some for the better and some for the worse.

"She was sick. Very sick." Orville told the coach, back in the dugout during the game.

"Who?" The coach shouted, drawing the attention of all the other players, as he lost track of whom Orville was talking about for the moment.

"Annie, my sister. She had a big pain in her side."

"Oh?" The coach looked puzzled.

"They rushed her to the hospital. The doctor said it was her appendix. They had to come out."

"You gonna be all right?" Aunt Martha asked at the hospital.

"Yah!" Lizzie replied in her broken English accent. "The worst is over. She had the operation and is doin' OK. The doctors said she'd be comin' home in a few days."

"Wow! Three days in the hospital. Such a long time for a little girl." Martha always showed a lot of compassion during a crisis.

"Two years old." Lizzie shed a tear mixed with joy. "Too young to be sick like that."

"Now don't you go a cryin', Liz." Martha gave the tired little lady a big hug.

"Oh hush! I'll be all right. I don't want anybody fussin' over me. I've been carin' for myself all my life, and I ain't gonna stop now."

Annie came home wrapped in a blanket to a big celebration. Toys lined her corner of the room joined by a closet kitchen. The bathroom shared by the other tenants in the building was down the hall. Friends and relatives alike filled the room.

Again, the doorbell rang. "Hello Lizzie!" The double chin tall lady with curly hair never stopped talking from the moment she arrived.

"Come Sara. Let me get you some coffee." Aunt Lee led her toward the kitchen before she pulled away.

"Oh nonsense girl. I came to see my little girl."

"You mean Lizzie's girl don't ya?" Aunt Millie reprimanded.

Ignoring all the small talk, Sara daintily tiptoed over toward little Annie while wagging her behind.

In a huddle, the folks doled over her with lots of hugs and kisses.

Meanwhile, Orville got lost in the crowd. While seeking for some attention of his own, his mother slapped him on the bottom and sent him into the corner. It wasn't fair for a two-year-old boy.

"Lizzie! When did ya get here? How long have ya been in Chicago?" A friend greeted.

"Mike! Ya ought to have somebody look at that cheek of yours. When was the last time ya saw a doctor?" The little old lady asked, while staring at him.

"Pa kept the grass cut every Saturday ..."

"Grace bakes the best cakes ...makes ma mouth water just thinkin' about 'em."

"Annie and Orville are so big. It seems just like yesterday that they were still babies."

"She looks so happy over there. It's hard to believe she had that, that ..."

"Operation, Sally. The doctors said an operation."

Lots of small talk filled the room. And after being passed from one set of arms to another, filling her ears with sweet nothings, shc ran off to play.

The cups clicked saucers in unison after the adults sipped some coffee. "Nothin' taste better than a nice cup of freshly brewed coffee." Uncle Milt said, licking his lips. Summer or winter, these people loved their coffee blended with conversation.

It was time to catch up on old times. Annie's operation gave them a good reason to get together and they enjoyed every bit of it. Time passed quickly. No body wanted to leave.

Living in America was like a breath of fresh air or a cup of cold water in the desert. They were survivors of the 1929 depression and escaped war torn Europe. They self taught themselves the English language, had no formal education, and did mundane jobs just to earn a living. They were glad to be alive.

Meanwhile back in the dugout. "So what's the big deal, Orville?" The coach shook his head in disbelief.

"She was sick. Anybody …"

"Doesn't everybody get sick? Don't answer that. It's a part of life."

"She's my sister. Only two years old. Anybody …"

"These guys get sick." Again he pointed to the bench. "Sometimes they don't feel like playing ball. But they hang in there and play even if they don't feel like it." The tough skinned coach didn't have a soft spot anywhere in his body.

"I said coach, before ya interrupted me that anybody can have setbacks."

"Setbacks?" The coach continued to mock.

"Yes setbacks!" Orville remained firm. "Didn't you ever have a setback?"

"Don't ask me. I don't like questions. I'll ask the questions."

The past brought back memories that made the present unforgettable to the Crocker family. A simple celebration for little Annie was such an occasion. However, as pleasant as things appeared, the future brought many more interesting challenges.

TWENTY-SIX

Illness strikes the Crocker family again. After getting through one major hurdle, they suddenly encountered another that will change their life completely.

"I don't care about your family, Orville. All I wanna know is how ya got here." The coach shook his head while staring at the ground. "Ya just don't look like the professional baseball player type. I've never seen ya before ya parked yourself with all these other guys on the bench, and I don't know how ya got here."

"And it bother's ya, coach. Doesn't it?"

"No! I don't get bent out of shape for nothin'. All I wanna know is who are ya and how'd ya get here."

"The boss wanted another player, and here I am." Orville did his best to explain the situation that brought him to the team. However, the coach's stubbornness did not allow him to hear what Orville was saying.

"Boss!" The coach shouted. "Who in the world is the boss? Sounds like some kind of an office job."

"I mean the manager, coach." Through the years Orville gained a lot of street smarts and developed a tough attitude. "The general manager, Sir! The one who does the hiring?"

"Ha! Ha! Ha! And why did he pick you?"

"He needed a hitter. Someone who could hit the ball, coach."

"Ha! Ha! Ha!" More laughs. The coach tapped his knee before placing his foot up on the dugout apron. "And you can hit?" His eyes stared at Orville from head to toe with a puzzled look on his face.

"I'm tryin' to tell ya coach how I got here. Isn't that what ya wanted to know?"

"I thought I already told ya, I ask the questions." A moment of silence gave both of them a chance to think. "Oh never mind. Go ahead. Continue with your story."

"Just about the time my sister came home from the hospital my Pa got sick. At first no one thought much about it."

"Probably just a bad cold," Mama said.

"Eat right, get a good night's rest, and go to work. Common sense ruled the day. It was Mama's way of caring for the sick."

"Sounds good to me, Orville. I don't think there is any real cure for the common cold." The coach agreed with Orville's mom. At last, there is one thing that the coach and Orville agreed on.

"But it didn't go away. The pain got worse. Eventually Pa spent more time at home than at work. A series of test revealed liver cancer.

"The treatment was comfort and time. Medication offered temporary relief. A hospital bed was stuffed into our tiny apartment. Rotating between hospital stays the dates grew closer till he was permanently hospitalized. Mama's trust in God helped her to endure along with much encouragement from friends and relatives."

In his final days his spirit was high and support strong. With rising medical bills, Leroy was admitted to the Cook County Hospital in Chicago.

One day a heavyset man, wearing a black suit and carrying a Bible, stepped into the elevator. Calling out numbers the operator stretched her arm to open the door. "Second floor watch your step please." And the floors rolled by till they came to number five.

Passing beds in an eight-bed ward, Pastor Bob approached Leroy near the window. Outside the sun shined bright beneath a clear blue sky. Trees rustled in a mild breeze. Surely, it was a nice day to be outside.

Sitting up, Leroy glanced at the morning newspaper spread across his lunch table. Watching his eyes roll across each line, thoughts of peace surged through his mind. No fears. Even though it was often difficult to understand, God has a better way.

"Mornin' Leroy!" The Reverend greeted while shaking his hand.

"Oh hi Pastor. What brings you up here? Thought you might have better things to do."

"Always humble. That's my Pa. Never thought of himself as a center of attention."

"Yeah! I can see some of that in ya, Orville. I suppose I should give ya some credit for being here. Maybe ya can hit a ball. Maybe further than I think ya can. But ya sure don't look like the baseball player type to me." Like the defense attorney in a court case, the coach was full of doubts. And he wasted no time trying to undermine his opponent.

"Just happen to be passing by, Leroy." The Pastor winked while tapping him on the shoulder.

"What's new at the church?"

"Not much, Leroy. I wanted to stop by and see how you're doing."

"Doin' fine, Reverend, under the circumstances." Despite more frequent bouts of pain, Leroy forced a smile.

Following more small talk the Reverend concluded his visit quoting John 3:16 ...and He loves you so much that he died for you and me ...remember that."

"Yep!" A faint voice replied.

The Pastor knew Leroy very well. As a long time member of the church, his heart was in the right place. There was no point talking about it anymore.

"Just remember, Leroy. Everything works out for our good according to Romans 8:28."

"Yep!" Again the faint voice replied as his eyes slowly closed taking him into another world briefly.

"Take care brother." The Pastor whispered before leaving

the room.

Leroy received many visitors. "Till I got sick, I didn't realize I had so many friends."

Aunt Millie never missed a day at the hospital. Come rain or shine, as long as there were streetcars, the eighty-year old granny was always there. Proudly, wearing her angle high dress and black-laced shoes, she marched toward Leroy's bed.

"Mornin' Millie! What ya got in the bag?"

Ignoring him, she placed a brown paper bag on his lunch table.

"Why should I ask, Aunt Millie? Ya always got somethin' to bring me."

"Oh hush, Leroy! Here! Drink this!" She demanded, handing him a chocolate milk shake, his favorite.

"Another shake Millie?"

"Just drink it. It builds ..."

"Yeah! I know. It builds strong bones and teeth. I should drink three glasses of milk every day."

"Yes! Now drink." Like a busy body mother hen, she sniffed the aroma of clean pajamas and towels before placing them in the drawer. Then she put a toothbrush, paste, and hairbrush on the lunch table, and encouraged him to freshen up for the day.

Uncle George, a fellow janitor, always found time to make frequent visits to the hospital. Emptying garbage cans, filling coal bins, and cleaning hallways was hard work. "It don't get done if I ain't thar," he said, when people complained about never seeing him around.

"Did ya get that new conveyor belt, George?"

"Yep! After replacing it twice I finally got the right one from Cook's Hardware."

"Don't hurt your back. Leave fillin' the coal bin to those young guys."

"Don't worry, Leroy. Ya know how hard it is gettin' those guys to work."

"Yeah! I know! Like pulling teeth."

"Yah-ah-ah-ah!" George agreed without using a lot of jargon.

"How's Uncle Cliff's leg? Did he see a doctor yet? Should've never walked up those steps. I told him months ago to fix that step."

Shop talk. In spite of Leroy's illness, the topic of discussion was always business. Even though George meant well, experiencing hard times himself, he never took anything for granted.

Charles and Allison were long time members of the adult Sunday school class. Frequently, following church services, they would coffee clutch with the Crocker's, to catch up on the latest gossip. Now, like family, they stood by Leroy.

"The class wanted you to have these flowers, Leroy." After sniffing the aroma, Allison placed them by his bed.

"Make sure they get lots of water, Allison."

"Of course, Charles. Do you think I'd let 'em go without water? Never mind. Don't answer that." After giving him a mean look, she turned around and faced Leroy. "How are you feeling lately?"

"Fine, Allison. Just fine." The slow soft voice replied, concealing his true feelings. "I'm as good as can be expected under the circumstances."

Padding his hand. "You take care, Leroy. Hang in there. We're all prayin' for ya."

Leroy smiled.

"You betcha! You'll be on your feet in no time." Charles nodded. "Yes Sir! It won't be long and we'll be back at the lake fishing." He smiled with the thought of both Leroy and himself fishing to their heart's content. "I can see 'em biting now: Perch! Walleye! Bass! Wow!"

"The flowers are lovely." Leroy mumbled, while slowly turning his head to look at them.

"From Betsy's garden, Leroy." Proudly with thumbs up, Allison grinned.

In between all the chitchat that filled each day were moments of silence. Daily, getting weaker, Leroy struggled to stay awake and be polite.

"Caught between caring for the two of us my mom remained strong. Tough. She never displayed a sign of weakness."

"Maybe that's where you get that stubborn streak in you, Orville. Sometimes I think you're a tough cookie to crack." The coach conceded a moment of weakness, not common to his tough demeanor.

"Maybe so, coach. I learned to live with a lot of things the hard way."

"Oh?"

"Yes! Let me get back to my story, coach."

"Sure! I'm listening. Go ahead. I've got nothin' better to do." More sarcasm flowed from his lips.

"My dad didn't get better." A tear rolled down Orville's cheek as he took a deep breath. "It was only a matter of time and I think everybody knew it."

"How are the kids, Lizzie?"

"Just fine, Leroy. They're just fine. They're looking for their daddy to come home."

"Good! Though I doubt if it will ever happen. Getting weak Lizzie. My strength is leaving me. Day by day I'm getting weaker. Can't hold up much longer."

"Nonsense, Leroy! You're gonna get well." Lovingly, she cuddled his hand in hers while kissing his fingers.

Gotta get well. I gotta take care of ma kids."

They continued to talk. The words flowed slow and methodical. They got softer and softer until no more. Slowly his eyes closed. Silence filled the room. Lizzie shed a tear while struggling to smile.

In the years that followed Lizzie was bound and determined to care for her two children. From an old ringer washing machine and a clothesline in the backyard she opened up a laundry business. Late at night she pressed shirts over a hot ironing board.

Eventually she became a seamstress. On a pedal sewing machine she hemmed skirts, made dresses, and patched holes. Orville can still remember the patterns spread out on the kitchen table. "Ouch!" She pricked her finger while sewing a button on some pants.

"Later she started cleaning other apartments in the building we lived in. Reluctantly, Ann and I tagged along with a coloring book, some dolls and cars. How boring. I'd rather be outside playing with my friends. And for a while all things were well."

"So ya grew up without a dad. And who was left to teach ya, Boy? Ya must've had a tough life." The coach pondered the thought of role models.

TWENTY-SEVEN

Three streetcars stalled on a track at Webster Avenue. Block just one streetcar and before long they're backed up for miles. The waiting game began. And angry drivers sounded their horns.

A perplexed driver at the front of the line rolled down his window to speak to the officer, waving his arm, disillusioned by all the commotion. "Officer! What's going on here? Where are all these people goin'?"

Stumped, the officer tipped his hat forward so he could scratch the back of his head. "All of a sudden. Outta nowhere they came. Lots of people blocked the intersection. Don't know where they're goin'. I'm having trouble controlling the traffic."

The cars crossing Webster Avenue on Clark Street started to back up. Soon there were more traffic jams at other intersections as well, that drew people's attention.

A siren echoed throughout the neighborhood. The red flashing dome light reflected off the surrounding buildings. Dodging the other cars and pedestrians, the black police car with a gold star on the door, weaved through the traffic at high speed.

At the corner of Clark Street and Webster Avenue, the traffic light methodically changed colors on designated intervals. Red. Yellow. Green. Over and over again it repeated the process. But it didn't matter as all vehicles came to a sudden halt while people rushed to the park to satisfy their own curiosity.

It was Chicago in 1948. A large crowd gathered to watch. Curious eyes scanned the scene in awe. The near-north-side community was spellbound.

"But what does all this have to do with you becoming a baseball player?" The coach asked, back in the dugout, interrupting Orville's trend of thought.

"Ya asked me how I got here coach. Didn't ya?"

"Well yeah!"

"So I'm tellin' ya! OK?"

"Well OK! Go on. Tell me some more." The coach was caught off guard for the moment.

"For a while things went well. Mama worked hard. My sister and I stayed outta trouble until we encountered another setback."

"Oh?"

"Yep!"

"Now what?"

"I'm getting to it, coach."

The coach nodded his head.

"Nothing could go wrong with me. I was the teacher's pet in kindergarten. I was a straight A student in first grade. That is until one Sunday afternoon."

"Don't tell me you too? I thought you were unshakeable. Nothing could go wrong with Or-Or-Or-Orville Hodge." The coach joked with a silly grin on his face.

"Mama said we were getting ready for church. But I didn't wanna go to church. Instead, I snuck outta the house, went to the park, but never got there. People rushed passed our front window aroused by a lot of curiosity."

"Where they goin', Uncle John?"

"Don't know, Martha." He put down his newspaper.

"Sure looks like a lot of people." Lizzie grasp a drinking glass to dry in a towel while staring out the window.

"I wonder where they're all going."

Probably just in a hurry to get somewhere, Linda."

"Probably to the zoo." Ann stood between the older folks, hugging her doll near the window.

"Maybe I'd better go have a look."

"Nonsense, John." Martha insisted before looking at cousin Al. "You go son. See what's going on."

"But don't dilly-dally around too long. We gotta get ready for church." Lizzie's one-track mind let nothing stand in her way.

The big red fire engine raced through the neighborhood. "Stay out of my way!" The driver shouted. Speeding through intersections, people stared in awe.

Down the street at Lincoln Park West Blvd and Webster Avenue the crowd gathered. Cars backed up for miles in all directions.

In the center of the intersection a red light reflected off the trees and buildings from a police car. Two officers kept the curious seekers back, while a local doctor and neighbor cared for Orville, laying in front of a green Studebaker in a coma. He mumbled incoherently and cried. There were no signs of bleeding.

"Better let him lie still till the professionals get here." Dr. Smith remained calm.

Slowly the big red fire engine weaved through the crowd. Then, wrapped in a blanket, a fireman carefully placed him inside the cab of engine number eighty-eight. Without hesitating, Bob wheeled her around and rushed toward the hospital.

Down a long corridor, Dr. Silverman led a group of doctors in green scrubs to Orville's room. Well recognized as a Neurologist, Lizzie requested his consult.

"Doctor! Is surgery a possibility?" The resident asked, eager to handle his first big case. Thoughts of all the options quickly raced through his mind.

"Good question, Doctor, Doctor, Doctor?"

"Dr. Monroe." The young red head with a flattop hair cut like George Goebel, a famous entertainer, was very inquisitive.

"Ah yes, Dr. Monroe." Dr. Silverman acknowledged, looking over his dark rim glasses on the tip pf his nose. "Gotta see the Boy first. I'm not sure what I'll find. Right now it's impossible to know what I'll do next."

"Doctor! Any bleeding? Any lacerations? Sutures required?"

"None, Dr. Masters." The doctor strained to read his nametag. "According to his chart everything appears to be internal."

"That means pressure on the brain. Perhaps lots of pressure." Dr. Logan interjected, raising his eyebrows. "Can't begin to imagine brain complications."

"Yep!" Dr. Silverman nodded.

"What about fractures?" Dr. Jordan asked. "Probably needs an orthopedic man."

"Don't know yet. Lots of tests have been done. Lab work. X-rays. The works. But we gotta be careful. Don't wanna move him just yet too much."

"Any response?" Is he alert?"

"Nope. Not so far."

"Doesn't talk?"

"Coma boys." Dr. Silverman reminded them. "He's been in a coma for three days. Just lies there and weeps incoherently. For now all we can do is wait and observe."

"Any other injuries?"

"That's what we're gonna find out."

Orville's room was filled with toys. Plastic horses, cowboys, and Indians. Coloring books. Cars. Trucks. Yoyos. Story books. There were lots of toys for a six year old.

An entire wall was decorated with get-well wishes. There were poems with flowers and birds on Hallmark cards, and pictures of Charlie Brown cartoons. Norman Rockwell pictures accompanied with serious jargon expressing the best intent for a speedy recovery.

Friends and relatives from everywhere beckoned Orville's room. They were a close-knit family. And there he lay oblivious to his surroundings.

"Martha, how are ya? The Boy …"

"…he looks so innocent …how did it happen?"

"How's Lizzie taking it? She works so hard …"

"Is he in any pain?"

"When I heard about it I couldn't believe my ears." A lady

said, cupping her chin in a pair of wrinkled hands.

And the condolences continued to flow throughout the room.

Weaving her way through the crowd, a nurse sought Lizzie's attention. "Doctor Shyrock wishes to see you." Holding her hand, she led Lizzie into an office down the hall.

"Please have a seat, Lizzie." The warm passionate man has been the family physician for many years.

"How's my Boy doin', doctor?"

"Not good." After removing his glasses, sitting back in his cushioned armchair, he launched into the most serious presentation he ever gave in his entire life.

"Oh?" A tired lady with many years of hard work didn't show her age.

"We've done all we can do, Mrs. Hodge." A tear trickled down her cheek while listening to him talk.

"So now what, doctor?"

"Wait and observe. We wait." The doctor tried to be consoling with every word. Nothing came easy for the moment.

"In other words do nothing. Is he going to die?"

"I don't know yet. I've been in touch with a lot of people. Meanwhile we wait and see. Keep him comfortable."

And so the days passed. Two weeks in a coma. Orville had a large lump over his right ear. The possibility of surgery becoming a reality drew closer each day. He required a private nurse around the clock.

No signs of healing had the doctors concerned. "Perhaps there was some swelling on the brain. Perhaps he may have some perception disorders." Dr. Steinberg looked worried. "Gotta rule out that possibility."

The day was tense. A decision was made. "If we don't see any signs of improvement tomorrow, we operate." Dr. Amador mentioned to a group of specialists, draped in white coats with stethoscopes peeking out of their pockets, pointing to a diagram.

Outside the hospital window the day was bright and sunny beneath a clear blue sky. Trees rustled in a mild breeze. The temperature already reached into the upper 70"s. However, inside, all was dark and gloomy.

"Want some coffee, Lizzie?"

"No thanks, John …had lots of coffee already …,feel water logged."

"It'll be all right, Lizzie. Everything is in God's hand. He will provide." Aunt Martha taped her on the shoulder, while sitting on the arm of the big chair.

"Lizzie! Have one of my cinnamon rolls. Another cup of coffee and a roll will help settle your nerves." Madeline Frederick, adopted granny and longtime friend, makes the best cinnamon rolls.

"Mrs. Larson, go home! You've been here all night. Please! Go home and get some rest."

The sound of footsteps in the hospital corridor perked everybody's attention. Dr. Amador, in surgical scrubs, led a group of doctors into room thirty-eight. The conversation wasn't about baseball or the weather.

Huddled around Orville's bed with the other doctors, Dr. Amador shined a flashlight in his eyes, listened to his heart, and measured the circumference of his head. Then, after leaving the room, he muttered to Dr. Burns. "Cancel the surgery!"

Orville spent his entire summer vacation, two and a half months, in the hospital. He had to learn how to walk all over again. "People said I experienced a miracle the day I went home from the hospital."

Orville was a straight A student. There wasn't anything he couldn't do. He was the teacher's pet. However, since his accident things were different. School offered the greatest challenges, especially second grade.

"Good morning class." Miss Baker greeted as she walked over to her desk. The heavyset lady with a double chin in a black dress and two inch laced shoes looked like somebody out of The Walton's, a popular TV show.

"Good morning Miss Baker." The class returned the greeting with their knees together and hands folded on their desk.

"Today, we are going to learn about addition and subtraction. Now take out your little brown envelopes. Please notice class, that you each have several little pieces of green and red paper. You should have about a dozen of each color."

This is where the problem began. Orville laid out ten green squares and stared at them. It was senseless. He felt stupid.

"What's wrong Orville?"

Nervously, he looked up at Miss Baker. "I don't know." Silence followed for the moment. "I didn't know what to say. I waited for her to say something to me."

"Remember what I told the class, Orville?"

Previously, she instructed them to put ten pieces of paper on their desk and then take three of them away. "How many do you have left, class?" Confused. Orville couldn't comprehend what she was talking about.

On another occasion Miss Baker asked the class to put three pieces of paper on their desk and then add two more. "Now class, what do you see?" Again Orville felt stupid. His mind couldn't process simple addition and subtraction.

Throughout his childhood, he struggled. He was a slow learner. Although he advanced with his peers it took him longer to catch on.

Meanwhile, back home Lizzie continued to work hard to earn a living. Short on sleep there just weren't enough hours in the day to get everything done. Money worries. More bills. "Sometimes I wonder where the next dollar is comin' from." She often complained to herself.

TWENTY-EIGHT

The excitement on the field at River Front Stadium continued. Fans sat on the edge of their seats in a tie game, Cubs 3 Redlegs 3 in the bottom of the ninth with two on and two out. And while oblivious to the entire action-taking place, the coach remained engrossed in a conversation with the newcomer on the bench.

"So Boy, you're a kraut. Your folks are from the Old Country. There is no silver spoon in your mouth." Scratching his chin. "But I'm still wondering how ya got here."

"I'm not a kraut! And my Mama's from Rumania. Not all my folks came from the Old Country. I don't know where my Pa's folks came from."

"OK, Boy! Don't get riled. Sorry."

"Ya make me mad coach, with all that Boy stuff."

"Sorry Boy. Whoops! I mean sorry. It's just that ya look so young compared to all the other guys here. No offense. I just don't think ya fit in as a professional league baseball type."

Orville heard it before and probably will hear it again. But he didn't want to admit it. Sometimes he felt like a book being judged by its cover. It wasn't fair. Is anything in this world fair? Sometimes Orville didn't think so. However, as his skin got tougher, he learned to reluctantly accept it.

"Yep coach! Just let me show ya I can play ball."

The coach chuckled. "Yeah! You'll get your turn. Ya got here some way. I'm not always sure how, but you'll get your turn."

"Just give me a chance." Orville pleaded. "All I ask for is a chance."

The coach nodded his head with a grin. "So you're livin' in Chicago. Then what?"

"My Uncles were all carpenters by trade. But the Depression made jobs scarce. To cope, a series of events got them into janitor work.

"It was hard work. None of that pushing a button stuff, sit back and watch a machine do all the work. Instead, lots of manual labor. Ya know what I mean? Roll up your sleeves kind of stuff, grab a shovel, and get out there and work. I heard the word work a lot till I was sick of hearing it. Work! Work! Work! Workin' hard takin' care of buildings. And let me tell ya again. It was hard work. I can still feel the sweat rolling down my face just thinkin' 'bout it."

"Where'd all those Uncles come from?"

"Huh?"

"Ya said your mom had a couple of brothers, Joe and John."

"Yeah? So?"

"So where'd all those other guys come from?"

"Relatives coach. Don't ya have any relatives?"

"Don't get smart with me! I hate people who think they know it all." The coach felt his own ego starting to rise. Wearing the Redleg uniform and being a coach gave him a feeling of superiority. He didn't like being challenged by a newcomer.

"Yes Sir, coach!" Quickly Orville was brought back into the real world. "Perhaps it was a stroke of luck that got me here in the first place." The Boy pondered the thought.

"Yeah! Go on! Relatives you say."

"The Old Country coach. Just like my mom, they all came from the Old Country. At different times of course. Depending on the circumstances. War. Government. Working conditions. Ya know what I mean?"

"Yep!"

"They scattered across America in bunches. Some of them stayed in New York. Some went to Cleveland, while others went to New Castle, Pennsylvania. Some of them went to Chicago."

"Yep! I'm listening." The coach nodded his approval, understanding for the moment what Orville was saying.

"But they all fell on hard times. The government, employment, and all that kind of stuff."

"Yeah, yeah, yeah. I know all that. Tell me more about here."

"My Uncles needed work. They couldn't speak any English and had no job skills, so they took anything they could get. They developed a grateful attitude for everything they had. Just to be alive in a free country was enough. Work hard and play by the rules was their motto."

"So they all were Uncle John's."

"Yeah! You could say that. They were like my Uncle John and all became hard working janitors."

"Why? Is that all they had in the Old Country? I can just imagine janitors all over the place. Ha! Ha! Ha! Ha!" Orville didn't appreciate his sarcastic laugh.

"They did what nobody else wanted to do, janitor work."

"What's so bad about that? Doesn't look hard to me."

"Why do ya doubt what I say? Do I have to prove it to ya?" Orville was getting angry and about to lose his patient.

"I'm just askin', Boy! Just askin' ya a simple question. Ya don't have to get all worked up." The coach braced himself for another argument.

"Back in those days …"

"Just keepin' the heat goin' and all that kind of stuff looks easy to me."

"Let me finish, coach." Orville didn't appreciate the interruption. The coach was starting to invade his territory with stuff he knew better than anybody else. Nobody was going to make a fool out of Orville when it comes to janitor work.

"Sorry! Ya didn't have to get mad."

"In those days with a shovel in hand, morning and night, they filled coals bins. Lots of back breaking work. They climbed stairwells with a heavy garbage can on their back. Went garbage pickin' separating paper from metal cans and bottles."

"No Sir, Boy. Whoops! I mean Orville. Doesn't sound very pleasant to me either. So they earned a living working as janitor's for apartment buildings in different towns and cities."

"Yep! They learned to take advantage of every opportunity that came their way to stay alive."

"Then what, Orville? Ya ended up in Chicago. Then what? The coach listened intensely while staring directly at Orville.

"During the Depression Uncle John ended up doin' janitor work too."

"Orville! Go with your cousins and bring down the garbage while I stay here and fill the coal bin. It wasn't much fun for a six year old. I can still picture my Uncle saying that over and over again.

"I watched cousin Al grab a big cardboard drum with a strap fastened at both ends and flip it up over his shoulder. Then, leaning forward, he struggled carrying it up five flights of stairs. Once he reached the top landing, we moved down the different landings filling the drum with garbage. At the bottom, again we struggled getting back to the furnace room, where we separated paper from all the metal cans and glass. Eventually, a scavenger service picked up the drums filled with empty bottles and cans. Sweat poured down our faces and drenched our backs in those days, and there were many of them."

"Ha! Ha! Ha! Ha! Your Uncle had the little kid working." A cynical laugh penetrated Orville's nerves. The coach loved it when circumstances always put him above the other guy.

"But I was only six years old and my cousin three years older than I."

"So!"

"I was always being hassled. There wasn't a day that went by when I wasn't being accused of not being able to do anything right."

"All the time?"

"Not exactly coach. But most of the time."

"Back in the coal pile, Uncle John lowered his shovel close to the ground and pushed it along, filling its mouth with another heap of coal. Then, bracing his legs while bent over with puckered lips, he quickly lifted the shovel, carried it several feet, and flung it up high over his head into the mouth of the coal bin. An hour later, with a tired body, the bin was filled. Without automatic thermostats to control the flow, he did this two or three times a day during the winter months.

"But that's not all. In the summertime it was time to manicure the lawns. Walking the mile every week he cut the grass, trimmed hedges with aching shoulders, and climbed tall ladders to put up window screens."

"So what's the big deal? Everybody has to work." The coach raised his eyebrows with a puzzled look and scratched his head.

"Work. That's right, coach. Lots of hard work."

"Hard work?"

"Yep! They all worked up a good sweat. No big machines or motors to do the work for them. They had nothing but a manual lawnmower. Imagine pushin' one of those around all day, coach."

He gave a silly grin and stared at the floor in the dugout. For the moment he was stuck for just the right word to say. "Yeah. I never thought it would be that hard."

"Yep. Those choppers trimming the hedge were just oversize scissors."

"Scissors?" The coach questioned, shouting.

"Yep! And with aching muscles to get the job done."

"OK! Big deal. The Uncles are all janitors. Good hard working janitors." The two baseball players finally agreed on something.

"My Uncle John and Aunt Martha often took rides on Sunday afternoons just to break the monotony. The stories they told us were endless and often drove me crazy just thinking about them."

"Doll (a nickname for Martha). Doll. Where's the picnic basket?" Uncle John searched the room.

"Over there." She pointed to the kitchen table. "Full of food and where you can always find it."

"Skip the sarcasm, Doll." His angry mood never made taking a trip into the country very pleasant. "I'll put it in the car." In an alley next to the building, John opened the back end of his Plymouth Station Wagon, and placed the basket next to the soda chest and blankets.

After one last look to make sure the house doors were locked, they got cozy in the car. Then, John turned on the ignition key while applying his foot lightly to the gas pedal. After struggling to start, with a little more gas the engine started to purr like a kitten. Carefully, after backing out of the alley, it wasn't long before they were on the open road traveling toward Indiana.

Away from the big city, and the pressures of work, John and Martha started to relax. Opening the car windows, they leisurely inhaled a breath of fresh air. Soon smiles expressed feelings of contentment.

"Where are we, John?"

"Comin' up to Dyer, Indiana, Doll."

"Good. It look's like it won't be long to Maggie's Ice Cream Parlor."

"I suppose ya wanna stop."

"Of course. Don't we always?"

Maggie's was a favorite-going meeting place. Folks from all over stopped in at the little shop to have some ice cream. The man behind the counter in a white-shirt, rolled up sleeves, and apron, loved to dip his scoop into the ice cream bucket. One two three scoops, with smiles and bulging eyes the folks could taste the chocolate, strawberry, and vanilla flavor just looking at it melting on a cone.

The travelers loved to talk while browsing through the shop. As the older folks got caught up on the latest gossip, the kids stared at toys on a shelf behind a glass window. Boys, with bulging eyes about to pop out of their socket, pictured themselves playing with a rubber ball or plastic car. The girls wanted a coloring book or doll. Mothers would never hear the end of it till they purchased a toy for each one of them. "Finally, we can get back on the road." One mother thought, after putting some change back into her purse.

The old Plymouth coughed and sputtered and wanted to die till John gave her more gas. Then, after squeezing out of a close-knit parking place between two other cars, they were back out on the open road again.

"Look John, at all the beans." Like the spokes on a wheel spinning, the rows quickly passed by. Straight rows. Rich black dirt between them. For miles the bean fields spread reaching out to touch the sky.

Rounding a corner they soon entered corn country. There were tall stalks of corn soon to be harvested and sent off to market. "Corn on the cob. The thought of melted butter makes my mouth water, John."

"Yah. You must be thinkin' of food, Doll."

"Oh John!" Martha took a deep breath of fresh country air. "I just picture it on my dining room table."

"Good for you, Doll. You just keep dreaming." Lending half an ear to her comments, John kept driving with his mind in another world. "Pee-U! What's that?" Suddenly, startled back into a world of reality, he wrinkled up his nose.

"Must be cows, John. Must be cows up ahead on a cow farm."

"Doubt it! Smells more like hogs! Pigs! Mud! It's enough to take my breath away."

"Pigs?"

"Yes pigs, Doll. Look! There they are over there." He pointed to a pen with a couple dozen hogs, dirty, rolling around in some mud, and chewing on some mush from a trough.

After leaving the farms behind, the fresh air brought a sigh of relief. Beneath a clear blue sky the sun shined brightly warming the earth below. Trees rustled in a mild breeze, while birds flew about searching for food or twigs to build a nest.

"I sure miss the country, Doll. Ever since I left home years ago I thought I'd never return. Out here, away from the big city, it's like heaven on earth. Maybe a good place to retire some day.

"Watching the yellow markers dividing the highway, the broken lines quickly went by. No traffic lights. Cars became scarce the further away we got from the big city. There was nothing in our way. Easily, we got up to one hundred miles per hour." John loved to dream.

"Slow down dear." Martha muttered, tapping his hand. Often on these trips, she'd be forced to raise her eyebrows and take a deep breath, watching the telephone poles go by faster than a person could blink their eye.

Eventually the four lanes narrowed down to two and soon

they found themselves on small country roads burrowing through the woods. Occasionally an open lot displayed a home with a long drive way. Soon more homes appeared closer together dotting the dirt roads.

As they rode along the mailboxes quickly went by with some red flags up while others had them in the down position. The names on each box intrigued both Uncle John and Aunt Martha: Johnson. Burns. Applegate. The list was endless with a story to tell behind each one. Lots of fond memories put them in another world for the moment.

"Where we goin', John?"

"Up ahead, Doll. Don't ya remember that place we always gathered at with the family for a picnic?"

"You mean that place across from Mrs. Grosses house?"

"Yep! That's the place." John chuckled. "I'm always amazed, Doll, at how much ya remember."

The mailboxes continued to pass. Peterson. Brady. Carter. Following a rusty old box hanging on for dear life to a post, their station wagon turned right, and slowly rolled over some loose boards above a creek. Then, climbing up a long hill, finally they reached the top overlooking a field covered with weeds knee high.

"It's for sale, John!" Martha looked surprised, staring at the sign. "No more picnics. What'll we do? Where will we go? Do the folks know about this?"

"Now hold on, Doll. Don't get excited."

"Excited! You'd be excited too, if …"

"Don't raise your voice at me, Doll." John interrupted.

"But it's our happy hunting ground. Now it's all gone."

"No! It's not all gone."

"Hah?"

"No ma'am! Heinz, on the next farm over yonder told me that old man Kruger wants to sell."

"Yes indeed coach, and sell he did." Orville continued to tell his story, while leaning on a bat in the dugout.

"And is that how ya wound up on the farm?"

"Yeah! You could say that. But it's a never ending story."

It was a big day when Schlotz's tractor moved in. First, the land was cleared and the big scoop began digging. After lifting the huge bucket up high into the air, it swung around and tipped it, thus emptying the dirt into a dump truck. There wasn't much for all the Uncles to do until the hole was dug.

To accommodate the men in the weeks ahead, a shed was built down a beaten path not too far from where they worked. Studs, large sheets of wood, and some tarpaper made a nice shelter from the weather and a good place to sleep. The bathroom was an outhouse that everybody detested. A hand pump provided their only source of water. A campfire kept them all warm on chilly nights. They learned to live in the rough and like it.

"Jon! Hand me some nails. My apron is empty." John shouted down a row of men working.

"Yeah! As if I supply nails for every one." Han's replied, pounding a nail into a board while manipulating a toothpick in his mouth.

Down the line, around the square in the big hole, the Uncles, all hard working men, kept busy setting up the cement trough that would eventually be the foundation for a new house.

"More nails!" Other men echoed, as if a chain reaction started chanting, demanding more nails to fill their aprons.

Han's turned to look at the man working next to him. "You take my place while I go and get some more nails." Then, putting his hammer down, he climbed over the man and walked toward a tall ladder leaning against the ground at the other end of the row. After pausing for a moment, he stared at Jack. "What are ya doing?"

"We just got finished staining some boards."

"So! Do somethin' else! Go to work!" Han's hated procrastinators.

"My arm hurts. I've been pounding all morning. My arm hurts."

"I don't care. There's work to be done."

"But Uncle Han's. I can't."

"Do ya want your mother to kiss it and make it better?" Lots of sarcasm flowed among the men and boys. Chuckling, Han's shook his head and grinned, before climbing the ladder.

Close to another trough the loud motor turned the barrel that was mixing cement. On two wheels and a peg firmly planted on the ground, Schlotz's mixer blended sand and water that would eventually form the floor and baseline of the house.

Soon the cement blocks were up, completing the walls to the basement. More studs created a frame for the main floor before more cement blocks and a flat roof completed construction on the house.

"Hey! Over here!" Uncle Andy shouted, motioning to the driver in Beard's Lumber truck to back it up close to a clearing of land.

"OK, boys! Get your muscles ready." Uncle John led the way. As always, the big leader in the family ever since older brother Joe was left behind in the Old Country; he never shied away from responsibility.

One by one the men lined up near the truck to get some boards. With sun baked backs and shoulders, they carried them to the building site. Soon the boards stood next to some sawhorses and a power saw.

"Turn on the saw." Uncle Sam demanded. Immediately two other Uncles lifted a board and placed it over two sawhorses. Then, the third Uncle took a pencil from his left ear, marked the wood accordingly, and proceeded to place the spinning teeth of the saw against it. Not long thereafter, a stack of desired lengths were ready to be securely placed on the frame of the new house. "Let the building begin!" Uncle Dan shouted.

Like in the movie The Witness, all the Uncles teamed up to make a frame. It was a proud day looking at that frame and the boards nailed in place to complete the barn next to a silo in the movie. Likewise, all the Uncles grinned from one ear to the other, looking at the fruits of their labor.

"Good job!" Uncle John padded one of the Uncles on the back.

"Yah! The good Lord is with us." Another Uncle expressed gratitude from his own heart. And soon with a cup of hot coffee in hand from a grill over a fire, chatter started to echo throughout the countryside.

The celebration wasn't too far off. Birthdays, weddings, and deaths were always big events for friends and relatives to gather.

Aunts. Uncles. Cousins. Sisters. Brothers. There were lots of people that gathered for the house-warming occasion. It was a time for fun and relaxation.

As soon as everybody arrived, the kids quickly got into a game of tag. Patsy started them off. The big Oak tree was the safe spot and only one person could touch it at a time. When Johnny touched it, Sue got off. Through the garden, weaving through the apple orchard, and around the house, Patsy chased Kenny. After Ken caught his breath he chased Mike, stretching his arms as far as his muscles would allow, hoping to tag him. Laughing, talking, and telling jokes, they all had fun.

Later, they played hide-go-seek; Nancy and Connie tossed a rope around while Betty jumped over it to the rhythm of a song. A couple guys walked down to the Creek to catch frogs. There was so much to do in the country.

Meanwhile, back at the house, Uncle John started a charcoal stove. The newspaper, stuffed between a bed of coal in the V-shaped container, ignited after being lit by a match. Fanning the flames, soon he had white-hot coals cooking the pork chops. Orville preferred hot dogs, but no one ever listened to him. "You need good nourishing food in your stomach." Mama scolded.

Tired and hungry they all gathered on lawn chairs and blankets to pray before filling their plates. On a picnic bench was the traditional potato salad along with fresh sweet corn. Everybody was anxious to sink their teeth into the kernels smothered with hot melted butter and covered with salt. Several people took two or three cobs. There was lots of food to go around. Lemonade and ice tea were served from an ice-cold chest.

On a full stomach, they gathered in a circle to chat. Everybody enjoyed a good laugh, and the kids knew when they were being talked about, when they spoke in German.

So two hours south of Chicago, they gathered on a one hundred acre farm in Cedar Lane, Indiana. With a barn and a house in place, the Uncles started farming. Besides a small garden with a variety of vegetables to feed the folks, the money crop was corn. Twenty-five dairy cows and a few dozen chickens also kept the folks busy as well. Like a dream come true out of a fairy tale, they could live happily on the farm forever.

But not all was well back home. Hard times eventually led Uncle John and Aunt Martha to farming full time, and thus leaving the janitor work behind. With grateful hearts, all the Uncles pitched in, rolled up their sleeves and went to work.

Orville's mom wasn't doing very well either. Burning a candle on both ends along with single parenting and work, took its toll on her physically. And, with a declining income, often left her wondering where the next meal was coming from.

When Mrs. Gross died, Uncle John came to the rescue. The gentle elderly lady who resided in Cedar Lane for many years, now willed her property to the farm, and Uncle John gave it to Orville's mom.

"So we packed our bags, left the big city, and moved to the country. I suppose it's true, behind every cloud is a silver lining. And, even though we never changed our name, we assumed the name Hodge as a part of the blended family."

TWENTY-NINE

Suddenly everything came alive. Seats rumbled. Cheers out numbered boos. The kids stood on their seats. More hot dogs were gulped down in the midst of all the excitement along with some ice-cold soda or beer. The fans were on there feet, applauding one of there all time greats. And the approval rate just shot up to an all time high.

"All right, Gus! It's about time!" The man with the potbelly mumbled, while manipulating a cigar in his mouth.

"He should've come to bat long time ago, Marty."

"Ya can't take him outta the line-up."

"Hah?"

"Ya can't shuffle the line-up around just to put in one of your favorite player's."

"Hah?"

"Never mind, Gus. It's no use talkin' to ya. Ya can't hear anyway." After a long pause and feeling frustrated. "When ya gona get a hearing aide?"

"Hah? Can't hear what your sayin' over all this noise."

Down a couple of rows. "Ice-cold soda! Soda here! Get your ice-cold soda!"

"Mom! Can we have some?"

"Ya already had two. I suppose ya want another hot dog too."

"Please!"

"Yeah mom! I want some soda too."

"Me too."

"Now see what ya started, Billy?"

Soon three boys and a girl were sipping soda. Even mom conceded and got one for herself as well. The tinkling-burning feeling going down their throat added to all the excitement.

As a standing ovation continued, the fans wouldn't let up. More hands clapping. More cheers. They loved to hear themselves talk.

"One hit! All we need is one more hit!"

"What'd he do last time at bat, Amos?"

"Struck out!"

"But he never strikes out twice!"

"I hope not!" After a brief pause. "At least not now!"

"If anybody can do it he can." Jean's soft sweet voice could hardly be heard over the crowd.

"I never saw so many people get so excited before in all my life."

"Home run! Home run! Home run!"

"Relax Oscar! It's only a game." Laurie couldn't care less. "It's only a game!" Thoughts raced through her mind.

"If he just meets the ball ..." Art motioned with his arm how the ball would travel just over the shortstop's head into short left field. There were a lot of armchair ball players at the park.

"Show 'em your stuff!"

"Don't be afraid to hit the ball!"

"Swing at something good. None of that stuff outside the plate!"

"Hello baseball fans! Jack Quinland here, along with Lou Boudreau on WGN radio! Well ya hear the fans. A standing ovation. If anybody can get the job done, it's this guy."

"That's right Jack. Timing could not be better. Let's see what the skipper is going to do."

"That leads to some interesting questions Lou. Will he let him hit? Walk? Or hope for a wild pitch that will advance the runners?"

"A lot depends Jack, on the position of the outfielders."

"Oh?"

"Yeah! I'm not quite sure just how the Cub manager wants to play this one."

"Get 'em out is all I can think of."

"Well sure. Of course." Pause. "But I'm sure he'll play the outfield short. Hoping to force at third or second base. It would be risky to focus on home plate. Especially since there's only two men on. It would take more than a force to get 'em out."

"Tag!"

"That's right Jack. And he could miss the tag."

The fans remained confident that the end was in sight. "This is the man that can do it." Molly, a middle age lady who attended all Redleg home games boasted to a friend sitting next to her. Surely, she is a diehard baseball fan.

"Ladies and gentlemen!" A loud voice blared over the PA system throughout River Front Stadium.

Suddenly the cheers ceased, even though everybody remained standing. It was so quiet that people could hear a pin drop.

"Now batting! Number five! Johnny Bench!"

And the cheers resumed. Four, five, ten minutes passed before they finally settled down.

"I walked out of the dugout, swinging a couple of bats, toward home plate, with lots of thoughts racing through my mind."

To stay loose, Kenny Holtzman pitched to Randy, on his knees, behind the plate. For nothing better to do, the umpire leaned forward, and watched the ball sail over the diamond from the catcher's shoulder.

"After getting a sign from the first base coach, I stepped into the batter's box. I couldn't see the ball. He must be manipulating the stitches to a comfortable position in his hand from behind his back. Finally, from out of nowhere, I saw it sailing toward me." The thoughts continued to race through Johnny's mind.

The ball made a loud thud sound when it landed in the catcher's glove. "Strike!" The ump gave the sign and the fans voiced their disapproval. Quickly, the right-hander stepped out of the box.

"To stay loose I took a couple more warm up swings before looking at the third base coach. The hold sign was on. As my eyes shifted to the first base coach, the hit and run sign was on. Help! I didn't know what to do."

Then the coach met Johnny half way between third and the plate. "He'll probably want ya to go after a bad pitch. Don't bite. Let it go by. It'll even up the count." He motioned with his hands.

"But coach!" Doubts raced through the man's mind, holding the bat.

"You havin' problems understandin' what I said?"

"No!"

"Then go to it." The coach tapped him on the butt, wheeled around, and headed back to the third base coaching box.

"But coach!"

After stopping in his tracks, he mumbled with his back facing the star-player. "Do I detect some reluctance in the tone of your voice?"

Soon the first base coach raced across the diamond to join them. A brief meeting off the third base line commenced.

"You say hold, and you say hit and run. What's a guy suppose to do?" Confused and puzzled, Johnny tried to maintain his composure.

Once the two coaches got their signals straightened out, play resumed. As they both stood stoically in their perspective boxes, number five choked up on his bat and stared at the ball, now hidden in the web of Kenny's glove.

He leaned forward and shook his head several times. Finally, after getting the sign he wanted from Randy behind the plate, he went into an abbreviated wind-up and delivered another stinging fastball.

"I saw it sailing toward me. My fingers were twitching. I gestured to swing ..."

Amy sat on the edge of her seat when the ball sailed by the batter. "Ball one!" The umpire shouted, while putting his hands together behind his back. The fans cheered. And Amy let her eyes roll across her scorecard to the ninth inning. Then, she followed the rows down to where her eyes met the name Johnny Bench. Next to a mark for a strike she drew a circle. "Now the count is evened up." The thought stayed with her when she focused her attention back on the man in the red and white jerseys.

After the next pitch, a number two lead pencil quickly marked the square on a scorecard with a strike. "Ball!" Surprised, a fan looked up at the big electronic scoreboard to confirm the call. Sure enough, It was a ball. "It looked like a ball heading straight for the plate from where I was sitting." Frankie flipped over his pencil, erased the mark, and after flipping it over again, scribbled the correct one.

Patiently, the next fan waited for the call. Everybody heard the loud thud sound in the catcher's glove. Silence. And a pencil placed ball three in the little square on the scorecard.

The feelings throughout River Front Stadium were mixed. Cheers equalized all the boos. They watched in awe. Fears of a less desirable outcome started to surface.

As Amy sipped on her soda after taking a bite out of her hot dog, she heard the fans moan. A called strike two and a full count brought everybody back to the edge of their seats.

The fans were anxious. Feelings were upbeat. Mixed with shouting voices and rumbled seats, they started chanting: "Hit! Hit! Hit! We wanna hit!"

To compensate the tension, Johnny briefly stepped out of the batter's box and looked down at first base. When he returned to the box, the runners took a short lead off their base.

After an abbreviated wind-up, the ball arched its way toward the plate. As Randy braced himself for the catch, all he saw was a piece of wood sending it into left field. The fans were on their feet again following it into the corner.

Billy Williams hustled to get it. After rebounding off the wall, it rolled out into the field. The fielder bare handed it and wasted no time throwing the ball toward the plate. Faster than the speed of light it sailed into Randy's glove, who kept both of his knees firmly planted on the base.

Meanwhile, Pete Rose, who already rounded third, slide on his rump halfway down the line. Then, after scrambling to get back on his feet, he raced and dove for the third base bag.

Back on his feet, Randy took a couple of steps forward while looking at first base. But it was no use. Lee May already stood safely on second. So he threw to Ron, hoping to tag the leading run, and end this inning once and for all.

When Pete's hands landed on the ground after his famous nosedive, he was three inches short of the bag. No doubt about it. And, as Ron brought his glove close to the ground for the tag, the third out was about to send this game into extra innings.

But wait. After the third base umpire gave the out sign, he spread his arms indicating the safe sign. Surely, the fans were spellbound, watching in awe.

"But where's the ball?" Fans asked, looking puzzled and confused.

The ball slipped out of Ron's glove and rolled over the foul line back out on the field. So let the arguments begin. The entire Cub bench left the dugout.

THIRTY

Five thousand people, like one big happy family, lived in Cedar Lane, Indiana. Mingled among the farms were homes scattered throughout the community. A tall chimney stack, spitting out thick black smoke into the sky, reminded the folks of new business' coming to town along with better opportunities in the future for everybody. "America. A good place to live." Gladis reminisced smiling, while rocking in her chair on the front porch and knitting a sweater. "Hush! I wish those kids would go play somewhere else. All that noise. I can't hear myself think. Not to mention I'm trying to count all the stitches on my knitting needle."

Adolph's Meat market was another favorite meeting place. Located in the heart of town, the folks gathered there frequently to purchase fresh meat and get caught up on the latest gossip. And, like a good neighbor, there was a lot to talk about.

"Mornin', Sara!"

"Well hello, Gertrude."

"I didn't know you shop here."

"For heaven's sake." Sara smiled and motioned, flipping her hand. "Well of course. Been shoppin' here for years."

"Number ten! The voice shouted beneath a handlebar mustache on a man with a long nose, wearing a white hat with a United Way pin.

"Did ya here 'bout Betty?" Sara whispered in Gertrude's ear.

"No! What 'bout Betty?" Gertrude looked surprised.

"Number ten! Is there a number ten here?"

"How's she doin'?" Gertrude's curiosity was aroused. Unfortunately, rumors spread like wild fire in Cedar Lane.

"Number ten! Last call for number ten." The man in the white shirt, wearing a long white apron dragging on the floor with a bib, placed his hands firmly on his waist and stuck out his chest. The wait was about to end when he started to read off the next number.

"Oh yes! Excuse me Gertrude. Here I am, number ten." Sara stretched her short body, extending her arm over the tall counter, handing Adolph her tag marked with the number ten in big numbers.

"What'd ya gonna have today, Sara?"

"Half a pound of ground beef, and six pork chops, please. Make them lean."

"Comin right up. Will there be anything else?" Adolph slide the big glass door back, and took out some meat with his big scoop.

People. People doing things with other people. That's what Cedar Lane was all about. Throughout the community the folks enjoyed each other's company.

Down the road, a mile or two over the hill, on the right side of the street, stood an old hanger, which is now The Sky's The Limit airplane repair company. A little over a hundred people proudly went to work each day repairing DC-3's for future military use.

There was nothing unusual about all the cars that decorated the parking lot. All makes, shapes, sizes, and colors took folks from home to work every day. From toil and hardship to living in America where freedom prevailed, their smiling faces engaged in lots of conversation that told the whole story.

A long line of workers filed into the cinder brick building with the curved roof. Wearing a path to the dressing room, they hung up their jackets, placed a lunch pal on the floor in their locker, put on an apron, and went to work.

"Ya still wearin' the same overalls, Ralph?" Harry moaned, while pressing the trigger on his air gun, removing a bolt from the engine on the left wing.

"What's it to ya? My miss's keeps patchin' 'em up. Says as long as the material is good, keep wearin' 'em."

"No offense pal." Harry suddenly got apologetic. "It's just I see ya in 'em all the time. Why, even the label on your hip pocket is gone."

"Who cares? Besides, I don't see ya wearin' your Sunday goin' suit to work." Ralph defended his pride, while carrying a box full of bolts over to the ladder. "Don't worry 'bout my overalls. Just get up that there ladder and fasten these here bolts. The boss will be comin' by and think we ain't workin'."

"Last week I went fishin'."

"Still have that boat of yours?"

"Never got rid of it, Ralph. Yes Sir! With that little three horse power Johnson motor, takes me all over the lake."

"Ha! Ha! Ha!" Ralph laughed. "Did ya get caught in the Lilly patch again like ya did last year?"

"Nope! But I remember all that seaweed messin' up my motor." Harry paused long enough to regroup his thoughts. "Caught some good size Bass though." Chuckling while holding up both hands. "You should a seen 'em."

Camouflaged in some trees that dotted the community stood Portage Elementary School. Looking up at the tall windows that surrounded the two story red brick building, decorated with third grader crayon drawings, everything appeared peaceful and quiet until the people's eyes focused on the playground. It was recess time, a fifteen-minute break that allowed the children to get out of the classroom for some fresh air and fun.

In her short, blue plaid dress and pigtails, Mary chased Lu-Anne in the schoolyard in a game of tag. Weaving through a softball baseball game at one corner of the lot, she nearly tripped over second base during the chase. Billy ran out of the baseline to avoid a head on coalition. "Hey! Watch where you're goin', Mary.

We're tryin' to play ball over here." Roger shouted, racing in from centerfield.

"Oh be quiet, Roger. I'll be outta your way in a second." Mary stuck her nose up while racing to the opposite corner of the schoolyard. Immediately, the boys started chasing her before returning to their own baseball game.

"Now where is LuAnne?" Mary mumbled. "There are so many people here. I'll never find her." Then, noticing a yellow blouse and a red handkerchief waving in a mild breeze from another gal's pocket, she saw her friends. Janet, Sandra, and Margo waved their hand, daring her to chase them and get tagged.

All the children cramped into the small schoolyard to play. From tossing a pink rubber ball around, to shooting hoops into a basket, to laughing and telling jokes, they all had fun. And when the bell rang, reluctantly, they all went back to their classrooms. "Time flies when we're having fun." Tony's thoughts remained in the schoolyard as he walked back into the building.

Many homes surrounded Portage Elementary School. Small wood frame houses, the pride and joy of a hard worker, mixed with some brick bungalows, spelled out a way of life that made a person proud to be an American. And just around the corner from Mulberry Drive, a couple of blocks down the street, the Martins were having a party.

Cars filled the driveway while the overflow parked on the street. The big low price three, as they came to be known: Chevrolets, Fords, and Plymouths, lined the curb. "It's enough to make a person sick." Roy moaned, peeking through the blinds of his front window from across the street. "Makes ma eyes score just thinkin' 'bout it." Reluctantly, the old man limped back to his favorite rocker in the living room.

When the doorbell rang, Jeanie rushed to answer it. "Hello Polly! Welcome! Come on in! I'm glad you could come." Quickly, she took a warm dish out of her hand. "Let me take that and put it in the kitchen." Pausing for a moment, she looked at Polly's husband. "Hi Paul. How are ya?" Without waiting for an answer, she smiled before walking toward the kitchen.

"Pardon me, Jeanie! Where should I put this?"

"On the stove. The Pork and Beans need to be heated up. It's nice that the Johnson's thought enough to bring 'em. Everybody likes Pork and Beans, Lisa."

Like a bunch of busy housewives, the ladies gathered in the kitchen to prepare all the goodies. One lady licked her fingers while another dried her hands on a towel. Wearing a white-laced apron over a black dress, Marilyn placed some homemade cookies next to a chocolate cake. Scattered already on a table were an assortment of pies, potato salad, hamburgers, and lots of ice-cold soda pop. It was enough food to feed a king.

"Who made the cake?"

"I don't know, but it looks delicious. Chocolate frosting over two layers, makes ma mouth water just looking at it."

"Oh hush, Mabel. Look at all the other cakes. Yellow cake. Marble. Fruitcake. And that Coconut cake over there."

"Don't forget that Carrot cake."

"And the pies. Good gracious. Butterscotch. Blueberry. And Banana."

"I hope Jeannie has some vanilla ice cream to go along with the Apple pie."

After taking a deep breath. "I don't think I'll have enough room for desert after I finish eating. There's enough food here to feed an army."

Outside, in the backyard, the men talked over a beer or some soda, while munching on some pretzels.

"Harry! Help me with this table." Struggling, they hauled a picnic table out of the garage and placed it close to the sidewalk that dissected the yard.

"Chuck! Don't just stand there. Put your drink down and help me with these chairs." A dozen folding chairs were placed around the table.

"Whatta ya want with these blankets, Nick?"

"Good ya asked, Kevin. Just put 'em on that bench for now. We'll probably use 'em later as the evening gets cool."

"Glad ya invited us over Nick. The lady of the house and me didn't have much doin' tonight. Probably just another boring evening at home."

"Well I'm glad you all could come. Ya know Pete, you and Stella are always welcome here."

"Me too, Nick."

"What'd, you too, George. How can you invite them to Nick's house when it's not your house?"

"I don't mean that. I'm just sayin' I'm glad to be invited too."

"Me too." Albert chimed in, raising a drink clasped in his hand.

"Me too ..."

Friday nights were time for the fights. The radio was a good reason to bring them all together. The small brown radio, attached to a long extension chord leading into the house, stood in the center of the table. Everybody got comfortable in their lawn chair and stared at the noise box, as if it were some great invention, ready to jump off the table and attack them.

"Turn it on, Ben. Let's get goin'. Don't wanna miss a thing."

"Hold your horses! I'm getting there." Lenny reached across the table to slide the cover up on its track to expose all the numbers and dials before turning the switch on.

As the noise settled down from all the fans in the arena, the announcer introduced the fighters. "In this corner, in black trunk's from ...The Raging Bull, Jake LaMotta." The crowd echoed a mixture of cheers and boos. "And in this corner, in white trunk's from ...Sugar Ray Robinson." More cheers and boos with the fans jumping up and down in their seats.

"Ladies and gentlemen! Welcome to the middleweight Friday night fights. To the hundreds of you gathered here in Madison Square gardens, we have an exciting one for you tonight. It's one you folks out there in radio land won't wanna miss either." Following more cheers and chatter from a bunch of excited fans, the bell sounded, signaling for Round One to begin.

"OK! After touching each other's gloves the fighters hustled back to their own corner. Then, Sugar Ray aggressively approached The Bull and raised his gloves to protect his stomach and his face while pacing back and forth on each foot." The fans cheered. "Quickly Sugar Ray lands a punch to his stomach. The Bull rebounds with a punch of his own, but Sugar Ray duck's." More cheers from the fans.

"Another left punch by Sugar Ray.

"The Bull rebounds with a hard punch that hits Sugar

Ray's chin.

"Sugar Ray waste no time pinning The Bull in the corner. Finally, the referee separates them when their arms lock. More punches and the bell sounds. Round One is over."

By the third Round the action picks up. Both fighters become more aggressive. More punches. Quicker movements around the ring. Then, the bell sounds and it's over.

Following a pep talk from the coach, a cool sponge wipe across the face, and some mouthwash, they are back in the center of the ring swinging at each other again. The Bull tried some possum tactics to lure his opponent into his corner. After he willing absorbed some punches while remaining relentless, he then let loose with his own ferocious counterattacks. And the fans cheered, enjoying every minute of it.

But Sugar Ray remained on the offensive. The master puncher kept hitting hard while avoiding punches from his opponent. Then, he let The Bull have it with a sharp left hook that sent him to the mat. Motioning with his arm, the referee started counting: "One, two, three …"

"Thatta boy, Ray! Let 'em have it!" George shouted, while re-adjusting his position on the bench near the table.

"Who ya rooting for? I thought ya wanted The Bull to win."

"I did, but …"

"Yeah!" Harry interrupted. Before long all the guys budded into the conversation challenging George.

"Hey!" Chuck shouted, above all the commotion, hoping to get someone's attention. "Where's Beverly?"

"Ah, be quiet." Ben motioned with his hand. "She's probably out with Angie or some of her friends. Who cares anyway? Let's get back to the boxing match."

"She's out with Gordie. Friends and family gather here every Friday and she's out with that guy again."

"Don't be so sarcastic, Nick."

Often they took long walks on the beach just for some peace and quiet to break away from family tradition. The high school sweethearts loved each other's company. Holding hands, they strolled through the lake ankle deep in their bare feet.

The short blonde, with the Doris Day hairstyle in a navy blue dress, was attractive to all the guys. Thin ankles. Smooth skin and nice sun tan. With all the boys to choose from, she picked Gordie.

"It's so nice out here, I wish we could stay all night."

"Me too, Beverly." The tall boy with the crew cut and freckled face held her hand.

"Don't squeeze, Gordie. Just be more gentle."

"Sorry, Bev. By the way, are your folks still mad at your goin' out with me?"

"Wasn't it a good movie? I like the way she stood her ground with that man." Beverly smiled, staring up at the sky.

"Yep!"

"It was a shame when those other guys gave her a hard time. When they tried to corner her in the parking lot."

"Yep! A good movie."

"Gordie!" Beverly stopped in her tracks to turn around and look up at the six-footer. "You're not even listening to me. What are ya thinking about?"

"Nothing much, Beverly."

"Look at me! Hold me! Put your arms around me. I wanna be hugged." Attempting to overcome a shy streak, he gently hugged her.

"Thank you."

Choking up for the right words to say. "You're, you're, and you're so nice to hold."

"Kiss me, Gordie!"

"Huh?"

"Kiss me you fool!"

"Ahhh!"

"Please!"

"OK!" Gordie soon developed a bad case of the nerves. After looking around to make sure that no one else was looking at them, with eyes ready to pop out of his head, he lifted her up on her tip-toes, and bowed his head to touch her lips.

"Thank you."

As they continued to walk along the beach they engaged in more small talk. "Do ya ever wonder what's on the moon?"

"Nope! Can't say that I ever thought 'bout it." Gordie said, feeling stupid while shrugging his shoulders.

Dreaming. "I have." Smiling while staring up at the sky. "It's so romantic."

Stepping out of the water, they sat on a big log and dried off their feet. Then, as they slowly, clumsily, walked through the thick sand up the knoll toward the car, Beverly suddenly fell into Gordie's arms.

Surprised. "What's wrong? Why'd ya do that?"

"I don't know, but my foot hurts."

"Oh, it'll be all right. Think nothin' of it."

"It's not going away, Gordie. It hurts. I can't walk on it."

Using Gordie as a crutch, she hopped back to the car. Later, reluctantly, her parents drove her to the local hospital for some X-rays.

Gordie sat in the ER waiting room, looking at some magazines. Slowly, he turned the pages while allowing his mind to wander. "I just know the guy sitting next to me doesn't like me."

"Relax pal." Nick tapped his knee. "Everything's gona be all right."

Everybody in the room looked up when the door opened. Slowly, a man wearing a white coat with a stethoscope dangling around his neck stepped forward, holding a clipboard. "Mr. Martin!" Patiently, he waited for a response, rolling his eyes over all the curious faces in the waiting room.

"Here doctor! Here I am doctor. Over here." Nick stood up and waved his hand. After pausing momentarily, the doctor walked up to him and shook his hand. "Mr. Martin?"

"Yes, doctor!"

"I'm doctor Shoemaker. Come with me." The doctor led Nick through that same door, down a narrow corridor, and into a small office cluttered with papers.

Meanwhile, the waiting room was stuffy. Gordie took a deep breath, but it had no affect on his nerves. "I need some fresh air. I don't feel good. Get me outta here." Finally, he walked over to a drinking fountain to get some water before leaving the room.

Outside the ER waiting room, he raced down a stairwell at the end of the hall toward the cafeteria. Then, at a vending machine, he put a couple of quarters into the slot and waited for a Coke to drop down into a tray. After flipping the tab, he quickly gulped down the ice-cold liquid, and allowed it to burn his throat all the way down. Then he walked toward another elevator at the other end of the hall.

The light inside the elevator lit up the glass door as it came down to floor level. Then, slowly the door opened. "Ground floor, everybody out." Mark, the elevator operator, watched the people step out of a crowded space. Once it was empty, Gordie, along with a couple doctors stepped into the rectangular box. After Mark closed the door, he turned the handle and the elevator started moving upward toward the next floor in the hospital. "Floor please."

"One." Dr. Samson replied.

"Three."

"Four." Gordie thought he'd go along for the ride. Then walk down the stairs and return to the ER.

On the second floor a volunteer boarded the elevator pushing a small cart with some snacks. "Hi Mark. One, please."

"Sorry, Peggy. We're goin' up."

"That's OK. I'll go along for the ride."

On the fifth floor three nurses and a surgeon, dressed in green scrubs, boarded the elevator. Then. Mark reversed the lever and it started to descend passing the numbers that labeled each floor.

As the light lit up the glass door when it passed each floor, the elevator remained filled with people. With standing room only, and bumping shoulders, soon the cramped quarters started to echo the chatter of whispers.

"Who is that boy, Marge?" A nurse asked, cupping her hands close to Eleanor's ear.

"I don't know."

"Is that Mark, our favorite elevator operator?" Another nurse was curious.

"Why is he wearing a hearing aid?" Dr. Jordan looked puzzled.

"I don't know."

"I suppose he wears it in his right ear so we wouldn't notice it."

"How long has he had it?"

Ignoring the wise old saying that says curiosity killed the cat; eyes bulged as the chatter continued. "I hope he doesn't hear us."

"Oh nonsense, Cindy. There's no way he could hear us."

Chuckling. "Isn't that why he's wearing that hearing aid to begin with? Look at him. Smiling. That little thing tucked nicely in his ear. A wire wrapped around his ear and hugging his neck as it disappears in his collar."

"Oh hush! His mother never told me that he was hard of hearing."

"She probably has a hard time accepting his disability."

"Poor boy!"

"Ground floor. Main floor. Everybody out." A long arm stretched to reach the handle. Then, pulling it down, the glass door slid open and everybody got out.

Finally, the boy wearing beige pants with an accompanying dark brown suit coat, eagerly got back to his real interest. Descending to the basement, he placed his hand on his inside pocket to turn up the volume on his transistor radio.

"Hello baseball fans! And here we are in the ninth inning. The Cincinnati Redlegs and the Chicago Cubs. A seesaw battle tied. Surely a pitcher's dual. Folks stay tuned. You're listening to WGN radio and Cubs baseball out of Cincinnati."

"Gee whiz! I sure hope I didn't miss anything." Mark quickly got fully engaged back into the play-by-play action.

"So here we are baseball fans. Once again the bases are loaded. And!!! There are two out. Whatta they gona do? But wait! I see some commotion in the dugout. One coach just picked up a couple of baseball bats out of the rake, and threw them against the back wall. Another coach started shouting some obscenities. The manager is pacing back and forth in the dugout, while scratching his head. Meanwhile, no one is swinging a bat in the batter's circle on deck.

"What's up boss?" The batting coach kept his distance from a hot-tempered manager.

"How should I know?" The manager gestured, raising both of his hands with palms up.

"Hey! Let's go! Get a batter out here! We don't have all day!" The first base umpire stared at the Redleg bench with a mean look on his face.

"Hold your horses, ump." The coach tried to remain calm before looking at the manager. "Whose left?"

"I've got a couple of pitcher's sitting over there. That other guy sitting at the end of the bench has a sprained hand."

"But wait! What about?"

"Orville! No way. He couldn't hit the south side of a barn at a time like this." The manager shook his head. "He doesn't have the experience."

"Yeah coach! Orville!"

"No way." Again the Redleg boss tried to convince himself that there was a better way.

"Yeah! Orville!" Several guys started to get on the boss. "We don't have any other choice. The worse we could do is go into extra innings."

"Yeah! And lose our pants for sure."

"C'mon boss!"

"Ya really think it would work?"

"Hey look! Ya got this guy cause ya needed a good hitter. All season long he put 'em outta the ballpark during practice sessions. Now's his chance." A teammate was almost on his knees pleading with the coaches. "Please tell him to do it. Please!"

Meanwhile, the fans started to grow restless. Soon they were chanting. "We wanna hit! We wanna hit! We ..."

"Hey! Get a batter out here!" Again the umpire approached the dugout. "Let's go or I will penalize you with a fine!"

The Redleg manager paused momentarily to ponder the thought before scanning the bench. Then, reluctantly he listened to the other coaches. "Hey Orville! Get out there and bat!" So he stepped out of the dugout swinging a bat. "Hey Boy! Remember what I taught ya in training."

Thoughts started to race through Orville's mind. "Inside I felt nervous. All season long I was a bench warmer. Now, with my first big chance to play ball, I felt a cold sweat starting to chill my back. My mind told me I didn't want to be here. Turn back a little voice whispered in my ear. But my heart said keep going."

"Ladies and gentlemen! Attention please!" The voice of the announcer in the ballpark echoed loud and clear over the PA system. "Not listed on your scorecard is number eighty-eight now batting, Orville Hodge!"

As the fans cheered, they displayed mixed emotions. "Huh?" A man chewing a cigar with a potbelly asked, raising his eyebrows. "Who is this guy?"

Down a couple rows of seats another fan spilled her soda when she heard the announcement. Shocked. "I never saw him before."

"Must be some leftover no other team wanted." The man looked angry while eating some peanuts. "I don't think the manager has a brain in his head right now."

"Me neither." The man's wife agreed even though she had no real interest in a baseball game. The fans were honored by her presence only to please her husband.

"The Unknown Baseball Player. That's what he is. Some Unknown." Reluctantly, a group sitting behind home plate in the upper deck formed their own opinion. "Hey gang! I got an idea. Let's forget all the negatives for the moment, and rally behind this guy."

"I agree with Ralph." Molly stood up.

"Focus on the positive, Ralph. That's what ya always try to do when we get-to-gether."

"What ya thinkin', Jim?" Betsy asked, with curious eyes. "You got a better idea?"

"Sure."

Soon the band played some upbeat music to excite the fans, while another group of people started chanting: "Orville! Orville! Go Orville! Or …" And as he continued to walk toward the batter's box he received a standing ovation.

Standing just outside the batter's box all kinds of thoughts raced through his mind. Kenny stayed loose on the mound watching the ball sail across home plate after several warm up pitches. A crackling sound penetrated Orville's eardrums every time the ball landed in Randy's glove, thus sending goose bumps down his spine.

"Play ball!" The ump motioned with his arms.

So Orville stepped into the batter's box and took a couple of warm up swings while keeping his eye on the ball. "From my playing days back on the farm, I remember some one saying don't worry about the color of the pitcher's eyes, or how he combs his hair. Just keep your eyes on the ball. I'll never forget that.

"The thought of all these fans watching me didn't make me feel any better. I think I heard someone say thousands of 'em. Just the thought of it makes me wanna run away. Then, I remember my mama always sayin': Stand up! Be firm! Be a man! Don't be a quitter.

"Folks often told me to lighten up. Don't be so serious. Standing here in the batter's box I started to tense up, thinking if I let up and relax, I might lose my power of concentration completely. The serious look on my face displayed my true feelings."

The ball sailed toward the plate. Twitching his fingers, jerking his bat, Orville was anxious to hit it. Quickly, dipping just off the edge of the plate, he decided to let it go by. "Ball!" The ump shouted, giving the sign. The fans cheered.

A high pitch sailed under his chin. Randy stretched extending his arm to catch it. Then a low pitch to the far side of the plate tempted Orville to swing his bat. "Ball!" The ump shouted. "3 and 0." The fans cheered. "One more ball and the game is over. Hang in there, Orville. Show 'em your stuff." An excited fan stood on his seat to get a better look at all the action.

Kenny circled the mound while rubbing the ball in his bare hands. Then, back on the mound, he manipulated the stitches on the ball in his pitching hand, being careful to keep it hidden behind his back. Finally, bringing his hands together at his chest, he kicked his right leg up high into the air before delivering the next pitch. Sailing toward the plate, Orville watched it dissect the plate, waist high. After hearing a loud thud sound as a fastball landed in Randy's glove, Orville stepped out of the batter's box. "Strike!" The ump shouted, giving the sign, cocking his arm. The fans booed.

"Hey! What'd ya doin', Orville?" The first base coach shouted, cupping his hands close to his mouth. "Look at me! Get the sign! Ya gotta swing some time."

"His sarcasm didn't help me feel any better." Orville's mind continued to race with many thoughts. "Some times I wish he weren't there, staring at me. It gives me the jitters."

On the next pitch the ball curved off its given path half way between home plate and the mound. Watching the ball sailing toward him, Orville acted quickly. Without a second thought he arched his back to avoid it from hitting his arm. "Surely it's a ball and will force the third base runner home with the winning run." Orville was dreaming. But instead the ball hit his bat and sailed high into the air. Descending, it landed in the second row of seats, just inches away from Ron Santo, the third baseman's glove. "Full count!" The ump shouted. "Ball 3, strike 2." The fans booed.

Orville fouled off several more pitches. A ground ball rolled passed third base into foul territory. Billy Williams dove for a fly ball in the left field corner. Another pitch destined for the bleachers and a home run missed fair territory by inches. It became a cat and mouse game between the batter and the pitcher. Orville's only thought was to protect the plate. The fans echoed a mixture of cheers and boos. The tension mounded. Anxiously, they sat on the edge of their seats.

"I stepped out of the batter's box and called time. The ump raised his arm to give the signal honoring my request. More thoughts raced through my mind. I didn't wanna be here. But mama's comments made me change my mind. Just do it, she'd say. Say you'll do it and you will. Whatever it is, just do it and you will. Sounds like some old fashion home spun theory. But it works. So I stepped back into the batter's box. Soon a cool breeze started to wipe against a cold sweat on my back. I was nervous. My stomach was in knots. After taking a couple more warm up swings, I tried to persevere.

"When the next pitch left Kenny's hand, it sailed very fast toward me. So fast, I wasn't sure my timing would allow me to connect with the ball. As it approached the plate, I closed my eyes and swung viciously. I heard the wood connect with the ball, but wasn't sure where it went."

The fans stood up and cheered while watching, as Orville toss his bat aside, and started to trot down the base line toward first. Meanwhile, the ball continued to sail high into the air toward center field.

"I didn't wanna look. When I opened my eyes, all I saw was the first base coach encouraging me to run."

The fans continued to cheer. Seats rumbled. The band played. Fireworks exploded behind the big scoreboard.

"I didn't see any of the other guys running in front of me. The bases were empty. So I ran."

The cheers grew louder. No body could here themselves think. The fans went ballistic. They were ecstatic.

"As I rounded second base, I saw the third base coach smiling. When I approached the bag he shook my hand and padded my rum as I rounded third for the home stretch. Then I knew we won the game. Tears started to roll down my cheeks when I saw all the guys. A greeting party waited to welcome me home. The Redleg dugout was empty. I did it. I earned my membership. I was part of the team. My hard work finally paid off."

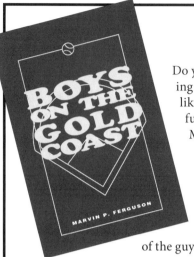

Do you enjoy watching, listen to, and telling stories about baseball? Some people like to mimic their favorite players. It's fun to picture yourself as Babe Ruth, Mickey Mantle, Ernie banks…

BOYS ON THE GOLD COAST is that kind of story. Exciting action puts you right on the playing field, feeling the beat of every pitch, seeing the ball sail high into the air, or watching one of the guys sliding head first into home plate.

However, grumpy old parents forget what it's like to be young and foolish. They say, "Don't waste your time playing ball. Instead, work! Corner lots are for parked cars, not baseball."

But Mr. Peterson, "Pop", comes to the rescue. Working together, they embark on an uphill battle to put together a boys' baseball team.

And it's fun to dream. Through the eyes of one of these boys, throwing his tennis ball against the garage wall, he becomes a major league baseball player.

Order Boys On The Gold Coast By Marvin P. Ferguson
Price: $10.95
Shipping and handling: $2.50

Reply form:

Name_____

Address _____

City _____ State _____ Zip _____

Send above Reply Form with payment ($13.45 for each copy) to :
Parker Publishing
P.O. Box 65
Island Lake, Illinois 60042-0065